The Venezuelan Revolution –
a Marxist perspective

Alan Woods

Third edition

The Venezuelan Revolution – a Marxist perspective
By Alan Woods

First published by Wellred May 2005
Second edition September 2005
Third edition January 2006
Introduction by Rob Sewell
Copyright © Wellred Publications

UK distribution: Wellred Books, PO Box 50525
London E14 6WG, England
Tel: +44 (0) 207 515 7675
Email: appeal@socialist.net

USA distribution: Wellred Books, PO Box 1331
Fargo, ND, 58103, USA. wellredusa.com

Wellred on-line bookshop sales: wellred.marxist.com

Typeset by Wellred
Printed by intypelibra, London, England

British Library Cataloguing in Publication Data
A catalogue record for this book is available from the British Library

ISBN: 1 9000 0721 5

Cover design by Espe Espigares

CONTENTS

Chronology

February 1989 Caracazo uprising and massacre under President Carlos Andres Perez after years of IMF austerity measures

Feb 4 1992 Lt. Col. Hugo Chavez leads failed coup against Perez and is imprisoned.

1994 Chavez freed from prison.

Dec 6 1998 Chavez elected President on anti-poverty, anti-corruption platform. Holds referendums approving new Bolivarian Constitution, revamps courts and congress.

July 2000 Chavez convincingly wins six-year term as President.

Nov 2001 Decrees 49 economic laws, ranging from oil to agriculture, using enabling law passed by pro-Chavez legislature

Dec 10 The corrupt Venezuelan Workers' Confederation (CTV) and Fedecamaras (Venezuelan Chamber of Commerce) stage lockout

Feb 25 2002 Chávez appoints new directors to PDVSA, the state oil company

April 9 CTV and Fedecamaras declare lockout to cause maximum disruption; plans to organise a coup against Chávez

April 11 Opposition and Chávez supporters organise demonstrations. 13 die in clashes and 100 wounded. Opposition media campaign blames Chávez supporters and urges his removal. Rightwing military chiefs backed by Washington stage a coup against Chávez.

April 12 Pedro Carmona, a wealthy businessman, is installed as President. Chávez refuses to reign and is taken to a secret location. National Assembly dissolved.

April 13 The masses take to the streets and coup collapses ignominiously.

August 11 The Supreme Court acquits four senior military officers who led the coup.

Dec 2002 - January 2003 Bosses' lockout to destablise the country, but defeated by workers' opposition.

August 2003 New democratic trade union federation (UNT) formed.

August 15 2004 Chávez wins national referendum on his Presidency; the Opposition are in disarray.

October 31 Bolivarian candidates win federal and local elections.

Jan 2005 Venepal, the paper company, is nationalised.

Jan 31 Chávez announces the need to transcend capitalism and build socialism.

July 18 All closed businesses to be reopened under workers' control.

July 27 Opinion poll gives Chavez 71.8% approval.

August 10 Chávez's supporters win 80% of city and district council seats.

Introduction

This book is a collection of articles by Alan Woods, which traces the history of the Venezuelan Revolution through all its most important stages right up to the present. The author has been a consistent champion of the Venezuelan Revolution since its inception. He helped to initiate the Hands Off Venezuela Campaign, which has been spectacularly successful and is now active in more than thirty countries. He is well known in Venezuela, which he has visited on several occasions and spoken to big meetings of Bolivarians, and given interviews on radio and television. He has also held personal discussions with President Chávez, which are recounted in this book.

It is worth pointing out that the author took a firm stand in support of the Venezuelan Revolution at a time when practically the whole of the Left took no interest in it and even denied that there was a revolution at all. Several of the articles reproduced here are aimed at combating sectarian prejudices towards the Venezuelan Revolution. Only very recently, after President Chávez has publicly come out in favour of socialism has there been a marked interest in Venezuela in the European Left, which still remains absolutely confused concerning its character and perspectives. However, as these articles will show, Alan has always pointed out that the only way forward for the Bolivarian Revolution is socialism:

"Right from the beginning we have pointed out that the Venezuelan Revolution has begun, but it is not finished, and it cannot be finished until the power of the Venezuelan oligarchy is broken", he writes. "This means the expropriation of the land, banks and big industry under workers' control and management. It means the arming of the people. It means the setting up of action committees linked up on a local, regional and national basis. It means that the working class must organise independently and strive to place itself at the head of the nation. And it means that the Marxist tendency must strive to win over the majority of the revolutionary movement."

There can be no doubt that Latin America is currently in the vanguard of world revolution, and within the Latin American continent, Venezuela is in the front line of this revolutionary process. It would be no exaggeration to say that Venezuela is now the key to the international situation and the developing world revolution. It therefore follows that the class-conscious workers and youth in Britain and elsewhere must follow the events in Venezuela very closely and assist the revolution with every means possible.

This book by Alan Woods is essential reading for all those who want to understand what is happening in Venezuela today. But this is no mere description of events. It is a powerful Marxist analysis of the Venezuelan Revolution, its weaknesses and strengths, its contradictions and unique characteristics. The book was not written with the wisdom of hindsight. Every chapter, beginning with the coup of April 2002, was written as the events were unfolding, and traces the course of the revolution through all its vicissitudes.

These articles, which were published in our website *Marxist.com*, appeared almost simultaneously on the Spanish language website of *El Militante*. We know that they had a big effect within Venezuela itself. They struck a responsive chord in the revolutionary activists and many Bolivarians were keen to read and study them. They were immediately downloaded from the internet and printed out, pinned to notice boards and circulated by hand amongst the Bolivarian Circles and trade unions. This shows the degree to which our analysis corresponded closely to the living experience and aspirations of the masses.

It was the impact of Alan Woods' articles that enabled us to come into contact with the most advanced and class-conscious elements within the Bolivarian movement. It demonstrated the possibility of establishing a dialogue between the Marxists and the Bolivarian activists and this has borne fruit with the creation of the Revolutionary Marxist Current, which is growing stronger every day. The secret of its success lies in its ability to link the immediate tasks of the national democratic revolution with the question of workers' power. The article "Theses on revolution and counter-revolution in Venezuela" skilfully outlines a transitional programme, which acts as a bridge from the immediate day-to-day tasks to those of the socialist revolution.

The book is being published at a decisive moment. Events within Venezuela are unfolding with lightning speed. The coming to power of Hugo Chávez in 1998 opened the floodgates for social change. It marked the beginning of the Venezuelan Revolution as the masses poured onto the stage of history determined to put an end to the rule of the oligarchy. But, as Alan Woods has consistently argued, under present day conditions it is impossible to achieve these goals without a radical break with the bourgeoisie. This analysis has been shown to be correct. Over the past five years, the demands of the Bolivarian Revolution – in essence the demands of the national-democratic revolution – of national independence, land reform and increased democracy, have repeatedly come up against the constraints of capitalism and the ferocious resistance of the bourgeoisie, backed by US imperialism.

The Venezuelan Revolution, having scored a series of important victories, now stands at the crossroads. To succeed it cannot stand still. It has aroused the burning hatred of world imperialism and its local agents, the corrupt oligarchy, who are hell bent on its destruction. They can never be reconciled to the existence of the revolution, which acts alongside Cuba as a beacon to the masses throughout Latin America. That explains their continued attempts to overthrow the regime of Hugo Chávez, which is now being expressed in the efforts of the so-called anti-terrorist George Bush to organise a terrorist assassination of the President.

The frenzied hatred of the imperialists is no accident. The recent sharp turn to the left within Venezuela, represented by the nationalisations of Venepal and CNV and Hugo Chávez's speeches in favour of socialism, expresses the forward march of the revolution. "I am convinced, and I think that this conviction will be for the rest of my life, that the path to a new, better and possible world, is not capitalism, the path is socialism, that is the path: socialism, socialism", stated Chávez recently. This represents a decisive change in Hugo Chávez, who in the past tried to work within the confines of capitalism. Of course, the task now is to translate these words into deeds.

President Chávez has on several occasions made favourable references to Trotsky's theory of Permanent Revolution. This states that the tasks of the national-democratic revolution can only be achieved by the working class and oppressed masses coming to power and proceeding in an uninterrupted (hence "permanent") manner to the socialist tasks. The revolution begins in one country but in order to succeed has to spread beyond its borders.

This idea expresses an objective necessity. In essence, this is the idea of Simon Bolivar, the great 19th century leader of the national democratic revolution against the Spaniards. Bolivar stood for the creation of a single democratic republic of Latin America and the Caribbean. But after his death, his ideals were betrayed by the bourgeoisie which divided the living body of Latin America into a series of national states. For 200 years the bourgeoisie of Latin America have shown their compete inability to solve a single one of the national democratic tasks.

The counter-revolutionary role of the bourgeoisie was already understood by Marx and Engels, who originally coined the term "Permanent Revolution":

"… it is our interest and our task to make the revolution permanent, until all more or less possessing classes have been forced out of their position of dominance, until the proletariat has conquered state power, and the association of proletarians, not only in one country but in all the dominant countries of the world, has advanced so far that competition among the proletarians of these countries has ceased and that at least the decisive productive forces are concentrated in the hands of the proletarians. For us the issue cannot be the alteration of private property but only its annihilation, not the smoothing over of class antagonisms but the abolition of classes, not the improvement of existing society but the foundation of a new one." (Karl Marx, *Address to the Central Committee to the Communist League*, March 1850).

Nowadays the vision of Bolivar retains all its force and validity. But it cannot be realised by the so-called national bourgeoisie, which, as Lenin explained many times, is capable of playing only the most reactionary role. This has been amply demonstrated by the attitude of the Venezuelan bourgeoisie to the Chávez government. The perspective of Bolivar therefore remains an objective necessity, but in the context of the 21st century it can only be realized through the creation of a democratic Socialist Federation of Latin America, as a stepping-stone to a World Federation of Socialist States.

In the period of more than a decade since the collapse of Stalinism there has been an unprecedented worldwide ideological offensive against Marxism and socialism. We are informed that history has ended, that the only system possible is the capitalist system, and that revolution is off the agenda. The experience of Venezuela shows that this is false. The Venezuelan Revolution is a fact. And it is equally a fact that through its own experience it is coming to the same conclusions that were pointed out by the Marxists – and specifically by Alan Woods – in advance: that only by expropriating the landlords and capitalists and moving towards socialism can the Venezuelan Revolution succeed.

The victory of a socialist revolution in Venezuela would shake the capitalist world to its very foundations. It would spread like wildfire throughout Latin America, where there is not a single stable bourgeois regime from one end of the continent to the other. A victorious socialist revolution in Venezuela would change the world. On the other hand, the defeat of the revolution at the hands of the oligarchy and its paymasters in Washington would deal a heavy blow against the movement of the masses everywhere. All conscious workers and militant youth therefore have a duty to defend the Venezuelan Revolution with every means at their disposal. A careful study of this book will be of immense assistance in helping the vanguard to understand the Venezuelan Revolution, the better to defend it and help it to triumph.

Rob Sewell, London, updated 12th August 2005

Chapter One

Revolution and counter-revolution in Venezuela

London, April 14th, 2002

Dramatic events are unfolding in Venezuela. On Saturday April 13th, less than 36 hours after a group of right-wing businessmen and army generals had assumed control, the coup collapsed in a welter of confusion. Shortly after 10 pm, interim President Pedro Carmona Estanga resigned and was reportedly under arrest. Vice President Diosdado Cabello was sworn in as president by National Assembly President William Lara after Carmona was forced to reinstate the assembly's elected members and other public officials he fired on April 12th.

Finally, amidst scenes of wild rejoicing, Hugo Chávez, having been flown by military helicopter to the Miraflores Presidential Palace, was reinstated as President of Venezuela.

The counter-revolution in Venezuela was spearheaded by the recent anti-Chávez strikes in the Venezuelan oil industry. These were counter-revolutionary strikes – the equivalent of the lorry-owners' strike that was organised by the CIA against the Allende government in Chile. These strikes were organised by the management of the Venezuelan oil industry (PDVSA) in alliance with the right-wing trade union bureaucrats of the CTV. That the movement towards reaction was headed by oil interests was no accident. The PDVSA managers wanted to end the restrictions on oil production and return to their previous position as the single largest oil supplier to the United States.

The coup itself flowed from the events of April 11th, when a demonstration said to be 350,000-strong was organised against the Chávez government. Since the media in Venezuela are virulently anti-Chávez, this figure is almost certainly exaggerated. Press agency reports put the real number at no more than 50,000. Government security forces and pro-Chávez militia were alleged to have fired into a crowd of unarmed anti-Chávez protesters, killing 15 and wounding 157 people. The right wing used this as an excuse to demand the resignation of President Hugo Chávez. But in fact, later reports have indicated that most of those killed were *pro-*

Chávez demonstrators who were apparently shot by snipers on rooftops. The whole thing was a manifest provocation.

The class interests behind the coup were obvious. The head of the counter-revolutionary government was a wealthy businessman, Pedro Carmona – the chief of the bosses' association. His first action was to rescind Chávez's so-called anti-investment laws – that is, all those laws intended to defend Venezuela's interests and raise the living standards of the masses. The corrupt and rotten Venezuelan bourgeoisie is incapable of playing a progressive role. Its plans would signify putting the country and its considerable oil wealth firmly in the grasp of US imperialism. The PDVSA managers had already drawn up a plan for restoring and expanding production that could bring Venezuela 300,000 barrels per day above its OPEC quota.

Role of US imperialism

The coup was headed by the Venezuelan bourgeoisie and their cronies in the armed forces (FAN). But the hand that pulled the strings was clearly in Washington. This plan was born and bred in the United States. The Bush administration, delighted at the thought of Chávez in handcuffs, was preparing to take over the Venezuelan oil industry through the back door, allowing "aid" to go to the new Caracas government – in the form of oil investment. This is part of the broader strategy of US imperialism after September 11th to intervene aggressively everywhere.

The US's interest in Venezuela is partly economic. There is talk in America of an economic recovery. But this is still weak and unstable. Demand in North America is picking up, but in Europe this is happening to a far lesser degree and Japan remains in deep trouble. In such a situation, the oil markets are necessarily volatile. And any serious disruption in oil production at this stage would have the most serious consequences for the world economy. What is required for a serious recovery is not only an increase in demand (which can have an episodic character) but an increase in profitability. Profit margins still remain depressed. An increase in the price of any one of the factors of production would depress profit margins still further, sending the world economy into an even steeper fall than before. In this sense, the convulsions in the Middle East hang like a threatening storm cloud over the economic scenario.

The Israeli-Palestinian issue is stirring up the whole region in a most alarming manner (Hezbollah, Syria, Jordan and Egypt are all getting involved). Things are getting complicated! And then there is the price of oil... This has fluctuated violently, reacting to OPEC's supply curtailments, threats of war, increasing violence in the Middle East and political instability in Venezuela itself. The chaos in the Middle East seems to have forced Washington to postpone its plans for an attack on Iraq. It appears that last weekend's summit between the US President and British Prime Minister Tony Blair in Crawford, Texas, did not yield very positive results. Even such a great enthusiast for wars as Tony Blair was compelled to warn Bush in private that it is sometimes better to look before one leaps. But postponement does not mean abandonment. Sooner or later the American boot will descend on Iraq.

Bush is determined to press ahead with his plans for military aggression against Iraq, but is uncomfortably aware that the general chaos in the Middle East (underlined by the failure of the Powell mission to force an Israeli withdrawal from Palestine) can lead to a catastrophic drop in oil production that would lead to spiralling prices and destroy any prospect of an economic recovery. The USA is in urgent need of a guaranteed oil supplier that is conveniently several thousand miles away from the Middle East.

The imperialists are attempting to keep oil prices low. There are rumours that Russian producers, following Putin's line of collaborating with US imperialism, are scheming to steal Iraq's market share before the end of Baghdad's 30-day oil export embargo, called earlier this week to protest Israel's recent occupation of Palestinian territories in the West Bank. In this worldwide drama, Venezuela is a key actor. The policies of Hugo Chávez were threatening the interests of the big oil companies and causing increased concern in Washington.

With growing instability in the Middle East – where Iraq has just cut its oil production – it was in the interest of the USA to undermine OPEC cohesion. Before the inauguration of Chávez in February 1999, Venezuela was OPEC's biggest oil-production quota-evader. As recently as December 1999, Venezuela was exceeding its production quota by a million barrels. But the new government, in its attempt to stand up to US imperialism, transformed Venezuela into OPEC's most enthusiastic quota-enforcer. During his presidency Chávez led the charge for numerous production cuts and toured the world last year to press for cuts in oil production, which met with a certain success. This inevitably brought Venezuela into conflict with the big oil companies and US imperialism.

But there is a wider dimension to the activities of US imperialism in Venezuela, which far transcends the question of economics. The US military is actively involved in a dirty war against the FARC and ELN guerrillas in neighbouring Colombia. It is well known that Chávez maintained friendly relations with the Colombian guerrillas. That alone would be sufficient reason for the CIA to want to depose him.

But the main reason was none of these. The main thing was that the radicalisation of the masses in Venezuela threatened to spread to other countries in Latin America, which is now in the throes of a deep economic and social crisis. By removing Chávez from power, US imperialism hoped to tighten its grip on Latin

America. It would be a lesson to the masses in other countries. And in addition, the installation of a more friendly and pliable government in Caracas would lead to an increase in Venezuelan oil production, thus bringing more stability to oil prices. In short, a very sound business proposition! All that was required was a little coup...

How the counter-revolution defended "democracy"

Predictably, the right-wing coup was greeted by scarcely concealed satisfaction by the bourgeoisie internationally. These hypocrites described the events of April 11th as a "return to democracy" in Venezuela! This was the line taken by the Madrid daily paper *El País*. However, the same paper was compelled subsequently to print eyewitness reports stating that there were many cases of brutality and violence by the counter-revolutionary forces. Chávez supporters were forced to go into hiding as the armed forces moved to arrest them. Prisoners were taken to army barracks where they were beaten and tortured. Such are the methods of the bourgeois "democrats" in Venezuela!

Venezuelan Army commander General Efrain Vasquez Velasco – the principal leader of the military rebellion – attempted to prevent any movement against the new government by implementing an aggressive "disarmament plan". The new regime immediately launched searches of private property and vehicles in an attempt to seize all unregistered weapons and arrest Chávez supporters. He ordered the army to "identify, disarm and dismantle" the civilian militias organised as Bolivarian Circles.

A witch-hunt was initiated against all supporters, pro-Chávez members of parliament and officials of the legally elected government. Vasquez Velasco confirmed that military and civilian police were conducting a national search for former vice president Cabello and Libertador Municipality Mayor Freddy Bernal, on the grounds that Cabello was the chief organiser and financier of the armed Bolivarian Circles, and that Bernal was supposed to have commanded sharpshooters who shot at the anti-Chávez protesters from rooftops in downtown Caracas on April 11th.

The victorious reactionaries set about systematically demolishing all the progressive decrees of the deposed government, which had been elected by an overwhelming majority. They sought absolute powers for themselves – an unelected gang of conspirators – while cancelling 49 decrees of the democratically elected government, suspending and arresting elected members of the National Assembly, plus 20 judges (so much for the independence of the judiciary!), 12 governors and all pro-Chávez mayors. All these activities earned them the applause of the western "democracies" as "steps towards the restoration of democracy" in Venezuela! George Orwell could have written a very good novel about this.

From all the reports, the counter-revolutionaries were over-confident. They were convinced that there was little or no danger that the supporters of Chávez could launch a successful counter-strike to regain control of the government. At worst, they anticipated isolated outbreaks of violence in Caracas and other urban areas, which they could easily control. They also feared that pro-Chávez elements in rural regions could try to link up with Colombian guerrillas operating inside Venezuelan territory.

But these gentlemen reckoned without the Venezuelan masses. Despite the fact that Chávez had not carried the revolution out to the end, and the crisis in Venezuela had begun to have adverse effects, the masses instinctively realised the threat posed by the counter-revolution. Having recovered from their initial shock, they poured onto the streets of Caracas and other cities, sweeping all before them.

The collapse of the coup

The role of the masses was decisive in defeating the counter-revolution. Faced with the spontaneous uprising of the masses, the attempts to impose a dictatorship immediately ran into the sands. Without the support of the armed forces, the bourgeoisie could not establish a dictatorship. But the reaction of the masses rapidly aggravated the splits within the army. This was not supposed to happen! It seems that Carmona's short-lived interim presidency unravelled because the bourgeois counter-revolutionaries – doubtless under the pressure of the CIA – tried to go too far too fast, opening up a rift between them and a section of the generals who, quite correctly, feared civil war.

The leaders of the coup began to split and argue among themselves. From this moment, the coup was doomed. Stratfor reports on the events that led to its collapse:

"The economic and political measures Carmona announced at his April 12th inauguration – including the National Assembly's dissolution and the dismissal of the Supreme Court judges and other key government officials – were not what had been agreed upon by the political, civic and military factions that built a centre-right coalition to back Carmona and were reaching out to the moderate centre-left.

"The right-wing coup-within-a-coup was engineered by a group of military officials who are protégés of retired Gen. Ruben Rojas, in partnership with ultra-conservative businessmen and politicians – some of whom belong to the extremely conservative Catholic Opus Dei organisation. The Carmona government's defence minister, Rear Adm. Hector Ramirez Perez, is a long-time protégé of Rojas, while Carmona's choice for foreign minister, Jose Rodriguez Iturbe, belongs to Opus Dei."

In other words, the reactionaries overreached themselves. When Carmona announced the National Assembly's dissolution, the civilian-military coalition supporting Carmona's interim government collapsed immediately, while the balance of forces swung back in Chávez's favour. With the growth of protests on the streets, Carmona's civilian and labour support evaporated, and the FAN also split into at least three distinct groups now struggling for power inside the military.

Realising that the situation was escaping from his hands, Vasquez Velasco – in a nationally televised address – conditioned his continued support for Carmona to the immediate reinstatement of the National Assembly. Carmona immediately complied. However, reinstated National Assembly President Lara hastily deposed Carmona and swore in Vice President Cabello as acting president, pending Chávez's return to the presidential palace. The rebellion collapsed like a house of cards. And the army was split wide open.

Splits at the top

It is clear that Chávez still has considerable support, not only among the masses, but also in the army. General Baduel declared himself in rebellion against the Carmona government even before it was sworn in April 12th. Having command of 2,000 elite paratroopers and a large arsenal of weapons and munitions, this was no small threat! Division Gen. Julio Garcia Montoya, permanent secretary of the National Security and Defence Council, also declared himself in rebellion and made his opposition to the interim government known through a telephone interview with Cuban television that was then broadcast back to Venezuela.

Stratfor continues: "One group is led by Army commander Gen. Efrain Vasquez Velasco, who emerged in April 11-12th as the leader of a centre-right faction of career officers who oppose Chávez's attempts to politicise the FAN and shift the country away from capitalist democracy. Vasquez Velasco's group negotiated the agreement with civic and political opposition leaders that installed Carmona as a consensus interim president.

"A second group consists of ultra-conservative officers in all four branches of the FAN. Some of these officers are long-time protégés of Rojas, and others – including some Opus Dei members – hail from the Christian Democrat Copei party, which long has been dominated by former President Rafael Caldera (who also is Rojas's father-in-law). Stratfor's sources report this group planned to launch a coup against Chávez on February 27th, but aborted the scheme under strong pressure from centrist colleagues inside the FAN and from the Bush administration in Washington.

"The third group consists of pro-Chávez officers – including Gen. Raul Baduel, who commands the 42nd Parachutists Brigade based at Maracay in Aragua state. This is Chávez's former unit, and Baduel is one of his closest friends and political allies in the army, sources say."

Alexis de Toqueville pointed out long ago that revolution begins on the top. The latest reports show clearly that the ruling class in Venezuela is split. And this split extends to the tops of the state and the armed forces. This, as Lenin explained, is the first condition for a revolution. The failed attempt at counter-revolution will have exacerbated these contradictions and splits in the ruling class, and created the most favourable conditions for a complete social overturn. The reactionaries have been forced onto the defensive, and for a time will be paralysed and unable to act. A courageous word from the top would be sufficient to deprive the reaction of its social base and permit even a peaceful transfer of power to the working people.

There are moments in history that are decisive. It is a question of "either...or". The counter-revolution has thrown down the gauntlet. Their first attempt has failed. But it will not be the last! The bourgeoisie and its supporters in the military are determined to get rid of Chávez by one means or another. Their resolve will be stiffened by Washington, which has many reasons for wanting to overthrow the Chávez regime.

Marx pointed out that the revolution needs the whip of counter-revolution. The present situation is reminiscent of the *tancazo* in Chile – the abortive first attempt to overthrow the Allende government – which was defeated by the movement of the masses. There is no doubt whatsoever that if Salvador Allende had taken advantage of that moment to appeal to the masses to act, the revolution would have easily succeeded. But when the opportunity was thrown away, the counter-revolutionaries in the armed forces (let us recall that Pinochet was supposed to be a loyal "democrat") regrouped and prepared a bloody coup a few months later. This is a very serious warning to the workers of Venezuela!

The role of Chávez

After the events of April 11-13th, the situation is completely unstable. Nothing has been resolved. The situation resembles in many respects that which existed in Cuba in 1960. It is not generally realised that when Castro first came to power, he did not intend to nationalise the means of production. His programme was a programme of democratic reforms that did not go beyond the limits of the capitalist system. In fact, his publicly declared model was... the USA.

However, on a capitalist basis there is no way forward for countries like Cuba and Venezuela. Castro's attempt to carry through reforms to improve the conditions of the Cuban people immediately brought him into conflict with US imperialism and the big US monopolies that controlled the Cuban economies. In order to defend the gains of the revolution, Castro was compelled to nationalise the property of US imperialism and eliminate capitalism in Cuba.

Although the Cuban Revolution did not follow the classical model of the October Revolution, and the workers never held power through the rule of democratically elected soviets, nevertheless Castro had the support of the masses and the expropriation of landlordism and capitalism in Cuba represented a blow to imperialism and a big step forward. The US imperialists burned their fingers badly in Cuba. Their attempt to destroy the revolution by relying on counter-revolutionary forces armed and financed by the CIA ended in a humiliating defeat at the Bay of Pigs.

There is no doubt that Washington feared that Chávez might go down the same road as Castro, whom he is known to admire. However, the drama is not yet played out. Venezuela is still in deep economic crisis; the gulf between the classes is profound. There is a growing polarisation between left and right. The immediate crisis has resulted in a setback for the counter-revolution. However, the conflict is far from over. The balance of forces that shifted so decisively back toward Chávez on April 13th can swing the other way equally rapidly. He will be under the remorseless pressure of US imperialism. The bourgeoisie, with the active support and encouragement of the CIA, will intensify its campaign of sabotage and disruption.

The real Bolivarian Revolution

It is not even certain that Chávez has sufficient support in the National Assembly to retain the presidency. According to an informal count in the assembly and the FAN, roughly 75 percent of the assembly's members oppose allowing Chávez to continue as president. The former Interior and Justice Minister Luis Miquilena, who commands a sizeable block of moderate votes inside the dominant pro-Chávez Fifth Republic Movement (MVR), will be a key powerbroker in any effort to end Chávez's presidency by legal and constitutional means. The position of Chávez is therefore extremely precarious. If he does not do what the capitalists and imperialists demand, he can be deposed by the National Assembly itself.

Chávez is no doubt an honest man who wants to act in the interests of his country and his people. His intentions are good. But in politics as in life, intentions are never enough. The problem is that Chávez is not a Marxist, and is inclined to be inconsistent. That can be fatal in a situation where the balance of forces is so unstable. If Chávez were a Marxist, he would appeal to the masses over the heads of the National Assembly. The establishment of action committees in every factory, oil refinery, and army barracks is the only way to defend the revolution and disarm the counter-revolutionary forces. The working class must be armed to defend itself against the danger of another coup. Only decisive action can prevent a new crisis in which the counter-revolution will assume an even more violent and murderous character.

The position of the army is a crucial factor. The reactionaries in the barracks have suffered a serious setback. But they will already be regrouping, with the active assistance of the US embassy. The next 24 to 48 hours could be decisive. If firm action is not taken to defeat and disarm the counter-revolution, civil war could erupt, with fighting between military units that support or oppose Chávez. If the working class acts with sufficient energy, the rank and file of the army can quickly be won over to the side of the revolution. The best of the officers will follow them, isolating the reactionary elements in the general staff. The revolution can still succeed with minimum violence and loss of life. But if the revolution hesitates, it is lost. The way will be prepared for terrible bloodshed, ending in a brutal military dictatorship later on.

Above all, it is necessary to smash the resistance of the bosses and their cronies. For the immediate expropriation of the property of the imperialists and the Venezuelan bourgeois! The only way to remove the danger of counter-revolution is to eliminate its basis of support – by expropriating the capitalist class. An emergency decree to this effect must be put to the National Assembly. If the counter-revolutionaries in the National Assembly attempt to block it, then the only way forward is to dissolve the Assembly and rule through the elected popular committees.

Workers of Venezuela! Everything depends on you now. By your actions, you have defeated the counter-revolution. But your victory is not secure. A terrible danger hangs over your heads and that of your families and loved ones. Remember what happened in Chile! Do not trust those who tell you that all is resolved, that the situation must calm down, that democracy is now safe in the hands of the National Assembly! Unless and until the power of the capitalists – those local office boys of US imperialism – is overthrown, the conquests you have made will never be safe.

Rely only on your own strength and unity! Build action committees to defend the revolution and defeat the reaction! Extend them and link them up, on a local, regional and national basis. Once the power of the working people is organised, no power on earth can resist it. The stage will be prepared for the final, inevitable showdown between the working people and the forces of reaction.

You face a powerful enemy in US imperialism. But in reality, this enemy is a colossus with feet of clay. You have powerful allies in the millions of exploited and oppressed people of Latin America. These people are finding their feet and their voice – in Argentina, Peru, Ecuador, Colombia – in one country after another, the workers, peasants and unemployed are beginning to fight back. These are the mass reserves of the Venezuelan Revolution!

Long ago, Leon Trotsky spoke of the Permanent Revolution. This is the only way forward for countries like Venezuela. The facts must be faced. The bourgeoisie cannot play a progressive role in Venezuela. Only under the rule of the working class can you even begin to solve the problems. On the basis of a socialist planned economy, under the democratic control and administration of the workers themselves, immense progress can be made. But the revolution in isolation could not last for long. Either it spreads to other countries, or it would be destroyed sooner or later. Internationalism is therefore a matter of life and death for the Venezuelan Revolution.

Hugo Chávez has spoken of the Bolivarian revolution. When Simon Bolivar raised the banner of revolt against Spanish imperialism, he had in mind a war of national liberation that would unite all the peoples of Latin America. But this dream was betrayed by the so-called national bourgeoisie that organised the Balkanisation of Latin America. This is the true cause of the enslavement and oppression of a mighty continent.

The only way to defeat US imperialism is by uniting the revolution in Venezuela with the struggles that are taking place in all Latin America. Everywhere, the capitalist system is in crisis. It offers the people nothing but poverty, misery and unemployment. It subjugates whole nations to the control of US imperialism and the dictatorship of Capital, turning the words "democracy" and "sovereignty" into meaningless phrases. All that is required is one victory and the rotten and bankrupt capitalist regimes would collapse everywhere. The road would be open for the realisation of Bolivar's dream in the only form possible – as the Socialist United States of Latin America.

Last December the Argentinean working class showed the way. The Venezuelan working class is now in the front line of the Latin American revolution. All eyes are now fixed on Venezuela. The stakes are very high. A decisive victory in Venezuela would transform the whole situation. But victory is by no means guaranteed.

It is necessary to draw serious conclusions from the events of the last three days. It is not possible to make half a revolution. It is not possible to improve the conditions of the masses and leave the rotten and reactionary bourgeoisie in control of the means of production. The land, the banks and industries must be taken out of their hands. The economic power must be in the hands of the people. That is the first condition for victory. Without that, no progress is possible.

What is required is a conscious and audacious Marxist tendency, which would participate in the Movement for the Fifth Republic (MVR) and give it the necessary revolutionary perspective, programme and strategy. The elements for such a tendency already exist. Everything now depends upon the speed with which they can organise, mobilise the working class, and lead it on the path to victory. The victory of the Venezuelan Revolution would light a fire that would set all Latin America ablaze.

Chapter Two

Venezuela: The revolution at the point of no return

London, September 4th, 2002

The revolution in Venezuela has reached the point of no return. In two stormy days in April, the bourgeoisie attempted a coup d'état against the reformist government of Hugo Chávez. Although it was backed by big business, right-wing trade union leaders and the US embassy, the coup failed. In just 36 hours the whole thing was over.

The first attempt at counter-revolution was defeated by a spontaneous uprising of the masses. This was a real inspiration to the workers and youth of the whole world. With no party, no leadership, no programme and no clear idea of where they were going, ordinary men and women from the poorest districts of Caracas simply rose up and began to take their destinies into their own hands.

The quality of leadership is a key element in revolution as in war. Moreover, it is just as important to the counter-revolutionary forces as it is to the working class. Having taken power into their hands, the coalition of businessmen, political adventurers and disaffected army officers immediately began to quarrel and split over what to do. When faced with a serious challenge by the masses, they collapsed like a pack of cards.

The collapse of the coup created extraordinarily favourable conditions for dealing a decisive blow against the counter-revolution and going onto the offensive. There can be absolutely no doubt that if Chávez had wanted to, capitalism in Venezuela could have been overthrown last April. Moreover, at that time, this could have been achieved relatively painlessly, without a civil war.

Unfortunately, Chávez let the opportunity slip. Instead of calling on the masses to take decisive action, he temporised and attempted to conciliate the counter-revolutionaries. This was a fatal mistake. As a result, the balance of forces is now less favourable than it was. The reactionaries are moving more cautiously, but they are once again going onto the offensive, making use of the judicial apparatus.

On August 11th, Venezuela's Supreme Court voted to acquit four senior military officers of charges that they led a coup against President Hugo Chávez in April. The acquittal vote was the third time in three weeks that a majority of the high court refused to indict the officers; two previous writs of indictment also were rejected. This indicates a new and dangerous stage in the conflict.

The Supreme Court's decision was a blow to Chávez. It is clear from this that the reaction is regrouping and organising its support at the tops of the state apparatus. The move by the Supreme Court prepares the ground for the future indictment and impeachment of Chávez, charges which would in turn prepare the ground for a "legal" coup.

Everybody knows that Chávez was the victim of a civil-military coup in which he could have been assassinated. But by voting to acquit the officers, the Supreme Court has cast doubt on the legitimacy of the government. This indicates that Chávez has lost control of the highest level of Venezuela's judicial system. The legal establishment, reflecting the pressure of the bourgeoisie and imperialism, has in practice taken the side of the *golpistas* against the democratically elected government.

The vote has opened a legal door for Chávez's political opponents to step up their strategy of seeking his impeachment and removal from the presidency on corruption or other criminal charges. This would then prepare the ground for a coup d'état. This deadlock can only be solved by an open struggle between the classes. No amount of manoeuvring at the top or constitutional ballet dancing can resolve the contradiction. It can only be solved on the streets and in the factories and army barracks. The revolution is in danger! A bold lead is needed.

The manoeuvres of the Supreme Court are clearly only the tip of the iceberg. The question of power would be posed point-blank. The question is a very simple one: *Who is master of the house? Who rules?* What are the options? Chávez could invoke his constitutional powers to convene a new constitutional assembly. This would in practice abolish the National Assembly, Supreme Court and other government institutions. Such an action would immediately bring matters to a climax. This he is seeking to avoid. But sooner or later an open clash is unavoidable. The only question is whether it will take place under conditions more favourable to the revolutionary forces or those of the counter-revolution.

Chávez's MVR party still has a small majority in the National Assembly, but cracks are opening up in the government itself. In any case, the final solution will not be determined by parliamentary arithmetic but by the struggle of living forces. If he attempts to circumvent this situation by convening a new constitutional assembly, this will bring him into headlong confrontation with the forces of reaction nationally and internationally. What forces can Chávez count upon in this struggle? Only the workers, the peasants and the rank and file of the armed forces.

The president claims he has the full support of the people and the military in confronting the Supreme Court and other enemies of his Bolivarian Revolution. These claims will now be put to the test.

Counter-revolution prepares

Ever since the events of last April the forces of counter-revolution have been regrouping and organising for a new offensive. A former political ally of Chávez's, the ex-Interior and Justice Minister Luis Miquilena, recently launched a new political organisation called the Solidarity Party as a rallying point for the forces of reaction. Miquilena is calling for a constitutional amendment to shorten the president's term in office and urged Venezuelans to "take and hold the streets" in order to compel the Supreme Court and National Assembly to get rid of Chávez "legally and constitutionally". Miquilena's new organisation is conspiring with the opposition Democratic Action party to launch a series of street protests, government work slowdowns and strikes in September to force Chávez's resignation.

The attempts by Chávez to avoid a showdown are misguided. Social tensions in Venezuela are rapidly approaching breaking point, a fact reflected in constant demonstrations and counter-demonstrations. Alarmed at the escalation of violence, Chávez has been appealing to the workers to disarm, while reports from the middle-class suburbs reveal that the enemies of the government are arming to the teeth. However, Chávez's speeches have evidently not prevented the workers from beginning to arm themselves. Hundreds of FAL 7.62mm assault rifles disappeared from military and National Guard arsenals after two failed military coups in February and November 1992, and most have never been recovered.

Unfortunately, in the absence of a firm revolutionary leadership with a coherent strategy and plan of action, the energies of the masses can be dissipated in a series of isolated and uncoordinated clashes, and even acts of individual terrorism. According to Union Radio on August 2nd armed civilians loyal to the President opened fire against Metropolitan Police (PM) officials on Sucre Avenue in western Caracas. The snipers were also said to have fired at a PM helicopter from rooftops of a poor neighbourhood during a second day of violent street disturbances by hundreds of Chávez supporters after the Supreme Court's decisions.

The snipers were later said to be members of a group called the Tupamaros based in the urban poor. But the Tupamaro leaders have denied the accusation and said they would only act as part of a larger national popular movement to defend the revolution. So this may be a provocation. Let us hope that this is true. The methods of "urban guerrillaism" have proved disastrous in Argentina and Uruguay in the past. The way to defeat the reaction was shown in April, when the coup was smashed *by the movement of the masses*.

It would be tragic if the colossal revolutionary potential of the working class and the youth were to be sidetracked down the path of so-called urban guerrillaism. What is required is not sniping and isolated shoot-outs with the army and police – the kind of incidents that can be used by the counter-revolutionaries to discredit the mass movement and justify repression, but serious preparations for an armed insurrection. What is required is not "urban guerrillaism" (that is, individual terrorism) but *an uprising of the masses, led by the working class, on a national scale*.

Mood can change

The balance of forces is still favourable to the revolution. But that will not last forever. In such a situation, the mood of different classes can change very quickly. Time is not on the side of the revolution but of its enemies. Already precious time has been lost. After the collapse of the coup, the forces of reaction were demoralised and disoriented. They have probably still not recovered from the blow. Recently, violent anti-Chávez protests erupted in the wealthy areas of Caracas near the Miraflores presidential palace and the Supreme Court building. But they were backed by just a few hundred supporters. This suggests that the middle class has not got much of a stomach for a serious fight at the present time.

However, this situation will not last. Even now the picture is uneven and shows contradictory processes. In the past few days National Guardsmen used tear gas on pro-Chávez protesters. In the past they have gassed anti-Chávez protesters on many occasions. But this seems to have been the first time they have turned against supporters of the government. This small but significant detail suggests that the work of the counter-revolutionaries in the army and police is continuing and getting results. Taken together with the Supreme Court ruling, it is a serious warning.

However, Chávez must have understood that the risk of being impeached and forced from power is increasing with every day that passes. The next coup will not be as peaceful as the last one. He may therefore decide that he has no alternative but to convene a new constitutional assembly. However, such a move can only succeed if he mobilizes the only forces that can be relied upon to fight and defeat the counter-revolution. His only hope is to appeal to the masses of workers, peasants and soldiers over the heads of the bureaucrats and reactionary officers.

The economic crisis is now the most serious threat to Chávez, who promised to improve living standards. Failure to deliver is undermining his base of support. The masses cannot survive on a diet of revolutionary speeches alone. If nothing is done to solve their most urgent problems, disillusionment and apathy will set in. The forces of reaction will seize the advantage and pass over to the offensive once more. The danger is very real. Recent polls show that Chávez still retains the support of between 25 percent and 30 percent of Venezuela's adult population. However, this is well down in comparison with the popularity that Chávez enjoyed after the defeat of the coup. Two-thirds of the population now see unemployment, inflation and personal insecurity as the three most important problems.

The world recession means that it is not likely that oil prices will recover sufficiently to give the Chávez government the fiscal resources to boost the economy. The only way open to it on a capitalist basis would be to increase the money supply by devaluing its currency or printing more *bolivars*. Either of these policies would cause an explosion of inflation that would erode the living standards of the masses and deepen the economic crisis, preparing the way for an even steeper fall in production and higher unemployment later on.

The economic crisis is deepening. The fiscal deficit is now estimated at more than 8 percent of GDP. To cover this, Finance Minister Tobias Nobrega recently announced that the government would increase oil output by about 400,000 barrels per day. Some sources predict that the economy will contract between 5 percent and 6 percent this year. Inflation is set to rise by anything between 25 and 40 percent in 2002, eating into already low living standards. The currency has depreciated rapidly, and more than 15 percent of the workforce is unemployed, according to some estimates.

There has been a flight of capital, with over $80 billion deposited outside the country. At the same time, according to the latest UN Human Development Index, 23 percent of Venezuelans are living on less than one dollar a day, and 20 percent are chronically malnourished. Venezuelan economist Gustavo Garcia has warned that real income per capita might drop by 7 percent this year. This would mean that the average Venezuelan's annual income, measured in constant terms, will have fallen to 1961 levels by the end of this year. (See Stratfor, 25th July 2002)

The point of no return

The Venezuelan Revolution has reached the point of no return. Only a general mobilization of the working class and the peasantry can save it. Organised in democratically elected revolutionary committees, they must be prepared to take the power into their own hands. The masses must be armed and prepared to smash the reaction wherever it raises its head. This is the only real guarantee of success.

In a way, this process has already started. The masses of the revolution's supporters are getting organised in the neighbourhoods, the factories and even in the barracks. We have seen the emergence of committee organisations up and down the country and these are getting coordinated at local, regional and national level.

There are the Bolivarian Committees, the Popular Revolutionary Assembly in Zulia, the Popular Coordination in Caracas, and amongst the workers the Class Struggle Democratic Trade Union Bloc. The latter demands trial and punishment for the coup organisers, the nationalisation of the media under workers' control, a sliding scale of wages and prices and a thorough nationalisation of the oil industry amongst other measures. It was originally set up in the industrial state of Carabobo and has the support of the union organisations at the Ford, Mavesa, Firestone, Goodyear, General Motors plants amongst others and the regional textile, electricity and other unions. The Bloc is now spreading to other regions. A similar organisation is present in the state of Aregua amongst textile, metal, beer, food and paper workers and at Iberia and Pepsi-Cola factories. In all these organisations there is a critical attitude towards the official organisation of the Bolivarian movement – the Fifth Republic Movement, MVR – many of whose leaders are accused of playing a disorganising and sabotaging role. The committees want the movement to go further. They even asked for a meeting with Chávez to discuss with him the criticisms they have of the official organisations of the movement and to push him to the left. A national meeting of popular organisations is scheduled to take place this month.

The tops of the army are coming under the pressure from the Venezuelan bourgeoisie and imperialism. The events of last April already showed that Chávez's control over the armed forces is tenuous. But it also showed that a section of the armed forces – probably the majority – are not yet willing to go down the road of counter-revolution. This is true even of a section of the officers, but much more so among the non-commissioned officers and the rank and file. Decisive action is needed to unite the revolutionary elements in the armed forces and isolate the reactionaries. Committees of soldiers and revolutionary officers must be formed in every barracks to disarm and arrest the counter-revolutionary elements.

The focal point of the counter-revolution is to be found in the boards of directors of the banks and big companies. Unless the power of the bourgeoisie is broken once and for all, Venezuela will never be free from the threat of counter-revolution. Expropriate the capitalists, bankers and landowners! Nationalise the banks and big companies under democratic workers' control and management! That is the only way to safeguard the Venezuelan Revolution and carry it forward.

However, the victory of the revolution in Venezuela would not be the end of the matter. Revolutionary Venezuela would confront international opposition from the first day. Using its stooges in the Organisation of American States, Washington would attempt to organise a campaign of sabotage, blockades and even direct military intervention against the revolution. We saw this in Cuba in the past, *but we also saw that the counter-revolution can be defeated.*

The only way to safeguard the Venezuelan Revolution is by adopting a resolute policy of proletarian internationalism. The revolution must not be confined to Venezuela, but must spread to other countries of Latin America, and ultimately to the USA itself. Faced with revolutions throughout Latin America, the USA would not be able to intervene. On the contrary, it would be faced with revolutionary movements at home.

The Venezuelan Revolution cannot stop half way. Hugo Chávez started the process, but only the workers and peasants can finish it by taking power into their own hands. The Bolivarian Revolution, if it is not to be reduced to an empty phrase, must mean the socialist revolution in Venezuela. And the working people of Venezuela must inscribe on their banner the aim of *the Socialist United States of Latin America*. That is the only perspective that can guarantee the final victory.

Chapter Three

The Venezuelan
Revolution in danger

Buenos Aires, December 6th, 2002.

*In Defence of Marxism received a letter from a Venezuelan Marxist comment-
ing on an article we published by Emilia Lucena. The following are extracts from
the letter relating to the present situation, with comments by Alan Woods:*
"Dear comrades, (...) In my opinion our country is passing through a pre-rev-
olutionary situation. In reality the working class and the people now have almost
all that is necessary, except a revolutionary leadership, which at this historic
moment in the history of capitalism, is *absolutely necessary* in order to overthrow
the capitalist regime. On the other hand, since April 13th, there has been a continuous development of organs of popular power, with thousands of Bolivarian
Circles, land committees, popular assemblies, class currents, all sorts of political
movements, etc. Nevertheless, this process also reveals the inexperience of the
popular movement, showing serious organisational weaknesses within it and,
what is even more serious, a great lack of coordination between its component
parts.

Another important factor to take into account is the dead weight of the mes-
sianistic leadership of Chávez. (...) This dramatically shows up the lack of a revolutionary party and, at the same time poses the urgent need for the mass movement to create a *popular action front*, to articulate the popular and working class
organisations, and to discuss a plan of action against the coup conspirators, and
out of such a front, to begin to work towards the construction of the party, a task
which is still only in its early stages. Another element that must be borne in mind
is that the organised workers' movement is not yet the vanguard of the process.
There are unions and class currents that have developed over the last year but they
do not yet represent the workers movement as a whole.

Here too one feels the lack of a revolutionary party. The hub of the mobilisation against the conspirators is still the popular organisations, that is, the
Bolivarian Circles and committees in the poor areas of the main cities, and also

the rural organisations and semi-urban communities (i.e., the shanty towns) but the workers' movement as such is not the vanguard of the struggle. (...)

As far as the present situation is concerned, I can tell you that the strike was a failure. At the moment, it has only affected 16 percent of the labour force. Nevertheless, the conspirators have concentrated on the oil industry (PDVSA) where they have caused some problems without having succeeded in paralysing the whole industry.

In Caracas, above all in the commercial sector in the East of the city, the stoppage was significant, however, in the poor areas the majority of shops were open, and even the banks were open with only a few exceptions. In the interior of the country the defeat of the strike was even clearer and more striking. For instance, in the prairie country of Apure and in Guayana, where the basic industries are concentrated (iron, steel, aluminium, electricity), the industries in Fedecamaras did not support the strike.

Since yesterday, in an action that reflects desperation but also the pressure of the most right wing section of the Coordinadora Democratica, Carlos Ortega called for an active strike, which was translated into violent acts in some cities, especially Caracas. This means that they are trying to create a situation of chaos on the streets in order to provoke eventually a military coup, combining this with an attempt to sabotage the workings of the PDVSA.

On the military plane, we believe that they do not have the strength to carry out a coup, or they would have already done so. As for taking over the factories, this has not taken place. The reports in Aporrea concerning Pepsi Cola have not been confirmed. Although the article appears to me to be correct in general terms, the final proposals, although correct, are of a propagandist character at the present time. We must bring them down to earth and adapt them to the specific situation in which the process now finds itself.

In this sense we are proposing another April 13th. We are calling for an emergency conference of workers and popular organisations to discuss the formation of a people's action front, with a plan of action and an economic plan and a social alternative, while at the same time calling for a mass mobilization next Saturday. In this way we think we can give a more concrete character to some of the points you raise in the article.

With revolutionary greetings,

M."

Comments by Alan Woods:

I received this interesting letter from Venezuela just as I had finished my [last] article. Written by an active participant in the struggle it merits the closest examination. It is quite obvious that comments written from a distance of thousands of miles can never do full justice to the events under consideration. Of necessity they have a somewhat abstract and general character. In order to make things more concrete it is absolutely necessary to obtain correspondence from the front line.

The letter of which we reproduce the most relevant parts allows us to see the process more clearly as it unfolds. These lines contain the fresh breezes of the revolution in a way that the reports in bourgeois newspapers could never do.

The most important thing that emerges from this report is that the forces of the revolution remain intact, and that the counter-revolution yet again seems to have failed. If this is confirmed, it means that the revolution is faced with an extraordinarily favourable situation. The generalisation of popular committees, which the author of the letter describes, is the most important factor in the situation. The proposal to call an emergency conference of the committees is absolutely correct and fully in accord with what is proposed at the end of the present article – that is, the need to link up the committees on a local, regional and national scale. This is absolutely the most crucial need of the moment.

A programme of action is needed. Yes! And who shall decide upon such a programme but the working people themselves in such a democratically convened conference? The Venezuelan Marxists will actively participate and propose our programme – the programme of socialism, of workers' power. We will fight to win the majority for these proposals. The people will be more receptive now than at any other time. Events will have educated them to understand who the enemy is and how to fight it.

Marx once said that ideas become a material force when they grip the minds of the masses. The combination of the experience of the masses and the patient work of the Marxists, the work of organisation, agitation and propaganda, must sooner or later bring fruitful results.

Naturally, as the Marxist wing of the revolutionary movement, our ideas will appear somewhat abstract and difficult at first, but life teaches, and the masses are learning from one blow after another.

Yes, it is true that at this stage the organised working class is not in the vanguard, and this constitutes a weakness of the movement. We will base ourselves on the most advanced and revolutionary elements, especially the youth, in the committees. They will push the whole movement forward. Sooner or later these ideas will penetrate the organised working class, although they are now lagging behind.

Incidentally, it is not the first time we have seen this. In the Russian Revolution the trade unions also tended to consist of the more conservative sections of the class, and many of them remained under the control of the Mensheviks even after October. Some of them (banks and railways) even adopted a counter-revolutionary position.

Nevertheless, while continuing to base ourselves on the most revolutionary elements, and concentrating on strengthening and extending the committees of action, we should by no means ignore the unions and leave them to the mercy of the scoundrels and counter-revolutionaries, but wage a struggle inside the unions to turn them into genuine organs of proletarian struggle, to purge them of corrupt and reactionary leaders and place them at the service of the revolution.

Finally, the author of the letter is 1,000 times correct to point to the question of the party and the leadership as the key to the whole situation. If the reaction has been once more defeated by the movement of the masses, this is a great victory. But it is by no means the end of the story and we would make a serious mistake if we imagined that the danger had gone away. I therefore see no need to change either the title of the present article or its basic content. The Venezuelan Revolution remains in danger, and will remain in danger until the working people finally decide to take the power into their hands.

I offer this point of view in all humility as a contribution to the discussion that is taking place in the Venezuelan revolutionary movement. I have every confidence that the workers, peasants and poor people of Venezuela will find the correct path, overcome all obstacles and triumph.

The Venezuelan Revolution in danger

The news from Caracas has an increasingly alarming character, as the forces of the counter-revolution step up the campaign to overthrow the legally elected government of Hugo Chávez. Yesterday the navy seized a government oil tanker pirated by a rebel crew, and Chávez vowed his military would stop sabotage of Venezuela's oil industry.

By its actions the counter-revolution is attempting to strangle the Venezuelan economy and plunge the country into chaos. Those behind the new attempted coup know that the oil industry is the country's life-blood. The so-called general strike (in reality a bosses' lockout with the connivance of right wing trade union leaders) virtually halted the loading of oil tankers, forcing Venezuela to free buyers and sellers from fulfilling oil contracts. Oil exports are critical to Venezuela's economy, accounting for 75 percent of total exports and half of government income. This is a matter of life and death for the fifth biggest oil producer in the world. After four days of organised disruption, oil exports ceased because 23 tankers were unable to load cargo, according to officials.

Behind the present chaos is the hand of Washington. Venezuela is a major oil supplier to the United States. Not satisfied with his plans for invading and occupying Iraq with the intention of grabbing its oil, Bush wants to seize the oil of Venezuela also. However, the immediate effect of these events has been to increase the price of oil on world markets. Crude oil and refined products futures at the New York Mercantile Exchange rose on Thursday partly because of events in Venezuela. The price of oil for January delivery rose 58 cents to $27.29 a barrel.

The counter-revolutionaries are demanding an immediate vote on Chávez's presidency, which they blame hypocritically for the economic and political turmoil that they themselves have been provoking. Quite correctly Chávez refused to give in to this blackmail. He has accused the leaders of the opposition of seeking to privatise the Petroleos de Venezuela S.A., the state-owned oil monopoly, known as PDVSA. "Assaulting PDVSA is like assaulting the heart of Venezuela," Chávez said in a nationally broadcast speech. "Nobody stops Venezuela."

The actions of the opposition are a direct threat to the Venezuelan Revolution. The bankers and wealthy businessmen want to put the clock back, to overthrow a democratically elected government by gangster tactics, to liquidate all the social reforms of the past few years, to sell off the country's valuable assets to the crooks and speculators and to place their boot on the throat of the working class and the poor once more. In this they have the firm support of US imperialism, which is interfering in the most blatant manner in the internal affairs of the country.

There is no longer any room for doubts or vacillations. The revolution is in danger! There are only two possibilities before it: either to advance boldly, to mobilise every ounce of strength to crush the counter-revolution, or else go down to defeat. *No middle road is possible.*

The great mistake that has been made so far is to imagine that the revolution could stop half way. It is extremely dangerous to think that it is possible to disarm the enemy by adopting a conciliatory policy. This is like trying to persuade a man-eating tiger to eat grass. Every attempt to conciliate has had precisely the opposite result to that envisaged. With every step back, the enemies of the revolution demand ten more. No further retreats or compromises are now possible. To entertain the slightest doubts on this would be to invite disaster.

Chávez denounced the attempt by a reactionary captain to seize the oil tanker Pilin Leon – named after a former Miss World – as "an act of piracy". This description is correct. Capt. Daniel Alfaro, a PDVSA employee, anchored his tanker filled with 280,000 barrels of oil off the western city of Maracaibo on Wednesday. Navy officials seized the ship Thursday and were talking with its crew, said Gen. Alberto Gutierrez, head of the army command in Zulia state. This sabotage on the high seas is being backed by the tugboat owners. Zulia Towing, the largest private tugboat company on Lake Maracaibo, pulled all 13 of its tugs from service to join the strike, a worker told the Associated Press on condition of anonymity. The company serves ships on both domestic and international routes, including oil tankers.

This is clear evidence of a nationwide conspiracy of private companies connected with the all-important oil industry to carry out a campaign of sabotage on a massive scale. The fact that the worker had to reveal the bosses' actions on condition of strict anonymity is sufficient to show who is really behind this so-called strike. Similarly, the nation's terminals stopped loading tankers on Wednesday. This is a serious threat. If a group of reactionary sea captains succeed in tying up the oil fleet, they can inflict major damage on the economy. According to press reports, at least five other tankers had anchored in protest and more were joining on Thursday. Decisive action is needed to stop this sabotage, but as of tonight (Thursday) the government had not yet arrested the tanker crew but was said to be looking for replacements.

Missed opportunity

This is the second attempt at a coup. Up to 50 people lost their lives during the last coup on April 11th. Dissident officers deposed Chávez the next day, but he was restored two days later after an interim government abolished the constitution, triggering a popular uprising. We consider that President Chávez made a serious mistake last April when he failed to take advantage of the favourable situation that existed after the failure of the coup to disarm and arrest the counter-revolutionaries and confiscate their property. This could, in our opinion, have been accomplished relatively painlessly at that time. However, the opportunity was missed. The result is the present counter-revolutionary uprising, which we predicted last September.

There is still time to take decisive action, but the situation will not wait forever. It is necessary to take immediate and firm action against the counter-revolution. Chávez has assured Venezuelans and international clients – he specifically mentioned the United States – that he would use the armed forces to keep the oil tankers afloat. He accused strike leaders of pursuing the same strategy they used to topple him in April: street confrontations, a general strike and an oil industry shutdown, all backed by Venezuela's news media. "Every time these sectors call a strike it's because they have a card up their sleeve, a hidden knife," he said.

This is absolutely correct, but it is necessary to pass quickly from words to decisive action. Denunciations alone will not stop the counter-revolution. It must be confronted with the revolutionary movement of the masses. They must be resisted on the streets, and the leaders placed under arrest. Counter-revolutionary factory managers and ship captains must be removed and the running of their factories, docks and ships be placed in the hands of committees of workers and engineers loyal to the cause of the revolution. Officers who refuse to take action against the enemies of the revolution must also be placed under arrest.

Such measures will of course be attacked in the yellow press as tyrannical and dictatorial. That is all rubbish. There is not a single self-styled democratic government in the whole world that would tolerate the deliberate sabotage of the economy for the purpose of the subversion of the legally elected president. Those so-called democrats like Bush and Blair would not hesitate to call in the army and use the full force of the law to protect the capitalist system if they felt it was threatened. Yet when a left wing government attempts to defend itself against an intolerable threat, actively backed and organised by a foreign power, it is supposed to be tyranny! Isn't this the most monstrous hypocrisy?

So far the army seems to have remained on the sidelines. The National Guard has been deployed in Caracas "to keep pro- and anti-Chávez rallies from clashing". The counter-revolutionary leader Carlos Fernandez, head of Venezuela's largest business federation, has accused the government of placing snipers inside an oil company building in Caracas to fire at opposition protesters. The purpose of this is quite clear: to prepare the ground for the use of violence by the counter-revolutionary forces.

Rumours are constantly being spread. Another "hero" of the counter-revolutionary mob, right wing union boss Manuel Cova, claimed secret police tried to raid his home early Thursday but were said to have been stopped by protesting neighbours. Using these alleged incidents as a pretext the reactionaries have announced more opposition demonstrations for Friday and throughout the weekend. Opposition marches have been staged in cities across the country, and several clashes occurred among demonstrators, Chávez supporters and police forces. In Caracas, pro- and anti-Chávez demonstrators are mobilizing. The tide of counter-revolution has once more been confronted with the resistance of the masses who have taken to the streets. The tendency towards civil war is increasing by the hour.

Onto the stage step so-called mediators – the Organisation of American States, the United Nations and the Atlanta, Georgia-based Carter Centre. The purpose of these is to try to ensure that the bourgeois counter-revolution succeeds as painlessly as possible. They act approximately like the "good neighbour" who intervenes when a gang of robbers are about to cut someone's throat, to ask the victim not to make so much noise as this will disturb the neighbourhood, but to reach a friendly "compromise" with the aggressor which will of course mean handing over all the money and in return (possibly) the saving of his life. The continuation of the lockout and the government's refusal to endorse early elections have, fortunately, derailed the peace talks sponsored by these good neighbours.

The international bourgeoisie are looking at these events with concern.

European Union and ambassadors from 22 OAS member governments issued statements backing OAS Secretary General Cesar Gaviria's efforts to restart negotiations. They would like to see the government in Caracas overthrown, but they are frightened of a repetition of the events of last April and fear that this time things can go a lot further.

No stable regimes

The neighbouring states of South America have good reason to be worried. At the present time there is not a single stable capitalist regime from Tierra del Fuego to the Rio Grande. In Buenos Aires, from where I write these lines, little children are dying of malnutrition in what used to be the tenth industrial nation on earth, a country with a rich agricultural potential that should be able to feed all the Americas and is now experiencing something like a famine.

Throughout this vast continent, with its colossal potential for the production of wealth, millions of men, women and children are suffering from poverty, unemployment and hunger. They are restless and discontented, and their discontent is slowly but surely turning into anger at their foreign and domestic oppressors. The election of Hugo Chávez was an expression of a burning desire for change. So was the election of Lula in Brazil and Gutierrez in Ecuador.

But a change of government is not enough. What is needed is a change of regime, a radical change in the social system. What is needed is to break once and for all the power of the oligarchies that dominate this continent and suck its blood. However, the oligarchy is used to wealth and power. It will not give up without a struggle. Power will not be handed over voluntarily. It must be taken from them.

The ruling elite will use every trick at its disposal. They are now mobilizing the middle class in Venezuela, and appealing to backward layers of the population who have been disenchanted by the lack of progress on the economic front. Nevertheless Chávez still has mass support. The middle class people on Maracaibo's boardwalk, dozens of people who blew whistles and banged pots and pans and flashed car headlights to support the Pilin Leon crew do not have the stomach or stamina for a serious fight. Determined mass action would disperse the rebels very quickly.

It is time to mobilise the full force of the revolutionary masses to inflict a decisive defeat on the counter-revolution. But this time the movement must not stop half way. It is necessary to destroy the social and economic base of the counter-revolution. This means expropriating the land, the banks and the big businesses, along with all the property of known counter-revolutionaries and that of the US imperialists.

Some will say that such measures will antagonise the United States and provide them with an excuse for intervening against Venezuela. But the United States is already intervening on the side of the counter-revolution in Venezuela, and has been doing so for a long time. Washington needs no excuses for such interventions, as the case of Iraq shows very clearly. It would be fatal to imagine that, by modifying our position, retreating and making concessions to please the US ambassador, that this will make George W Bush soften his stand. On the contrary! Weakness invites aggression. Such concessions will only encourage the imperialists and their local agents to make even more insolent demands.

It is true that by taking decisive measures to defend the gains of the revolution, it will be necessary to pass from defensive measures to an offensive programme of expropriation. But there is no other way. The Venezuelan bourgeoisie – that corrupt and degenerate fifth column that wants to sell the nation to imperialism at bargain basement prices – has gone over to the offensive. They have been consistent and implacable in defence of their class interests. The working class must be equally determined and courageous in defence of theirs. There can be no turning back, and no compromise is possible: either the revolution is carried through to the end, or it will perish.

For the imperialists and the bourgeoisie the crime of the revolution is not that it has done this or that, that it has behaved imprudently or used undiplomatic language. Its only crime is that it exists. The counter-revolution has only one aim – to destroy the revolution. Acting in legitimate self-defence, the aim of the revolutionary masses must be to destroy the counter-revolution. The petty bourgeois rabble is capable of making a lot of noise on the streets, but once confronted with a show of strength they will scatter like straw in the wind. This was shown in April, and it will be shown once again. The condition is that the masses show complete determination and that there are no more attempts at compromise.

The armed forces

In the equation of civil war – because that is what we see unfolding before our eyes – the conduct of the armed forces is decisive. In the tops of the army and police there are undoubtedly elements, open or hidden, who have been bought by the counter-revolution and the American embassy. There are others who are unsure which way to jump and are hesitating between the people and reaction. But for every open or covert counter-revolutionary there are ten, fifty and a hundred loyal soldiers of the revolution.

Nowhere have the consequences of a hesitant and inconsistent policy proved more negative than in the army. By failing to purge the tops of the army of reactionary elements in time, the conspirators have been allowed to continue their dirty work in the barracks. That such elements are present was clear from the coup last April. Since then they have been forced to be more circumspect, but many of them are still there.

Only a serious offensive of the masses can tilt the balance of forces within the army to the side of the revolution. Decisive action to smash the counter-revolution will paralyse the will of the reactionaries in the officer corps and encourage the rank and file soldiers and the officers who are on the side of the people.

The working class must put itself at the head of the nation. It must show a way out to the millions of unemployed, urban poor, the women and the youth, the landless peasants. It must establish stable organs of power in the form of elected committees. Form Committees for the Defence of the Revolution in every workplace, every neighbourhood, school, university, farm and army barracks. Link up the committees on a local, regional and national basis. Take the power into your own hands!

The threat of counter-revolution contains a deadly danger. Once in power the smiling mask of "democracy" will be cast aside to reveal the viciousness of the ruling class. The businessmen, bankers and landowners have had a terrible fright. They will want to take their revenge on the people, to make them pay for the years of "chaos" and "anarchy", to show them who is boss, to teach them a lesson they will never forget.

The masses must be armed against this danger. The only solution is the arming of the people and the formation of a people's militia under the control of the revolutionary committees. Let the militias patrol the neighbourhoods to protect them against counter-revolutionary terrorism and outbreaks of looting. Instead of looting the shops for food – acts of desperation that only push the small shopkeepers into the arms of reaction – let the local committees establish firm control over the transportation and distribution of food.

The price of food and other basic articles of consumption should be controlled by committees of workers, housewives and poor people to prevent speculation and cheating and ensure that everyone gets enough. Immediate steps must be taken to solve the housing problem by confiscating all empty and under-occupied properties, the second homes of the rich, etc.

The workers should immediately take over the factories and establish workers' control to restart production. Managers who have collaborated with the bosses' lockout should be confronted with a straight choice – help to get production moving again, or go to jail. Corrupt, inefficient and counterrevolutionary managers must be removed and replaced with honest people, engineering graduates and others prepared to serve the cause of the revolution.

In the countryside the power of the big landowners must be broken, the land nationalised and the peasants and agricultural workers encouraged to take over the big estates.

As soon as possible this situation should be regularised by an emergency decree nationalising the main enterprises, the land and the banks. A plan of production should be drawn up with the participation of all workers, scientists, technicians and so on, with the aim of mobilizing the full productive potential of the nation in the interests of the whole people, not for the enrichment of a handful of wealthy parasites.

It should be made clear that such measures are not directed against the middle class, the small shopkeepers and small businessmen, etc., whose property will not be touched. The enemy of the revolution is the oligarchy that is responsible for ruining the country and which robs and exploits the middle class as well as the working class. By nationalising the banks and installing a regime of planned economy, it will be possible to help small businesses by granting them cheap credit on easy terms. By nationalising transport and commerce, including the big supermarkets, it will be possible to eliminate the intermediaries who rob the small peasant while charging exorbitant prices to the consumer.

Shock waves

Such steps will cut the ground from under the feet of the counter-revolution and provide the Venezuelan revolution with an unshakable base of mass support. They will cause shock waves throughout Latin America that will reverberate in all the world.

For all the power of US imperialism, it would not be able to intervene directly. Not only does it have its hands tied with the projected invasion of Iraq, but it would be faced with mass opposition at home, beginning with the millions of Latino workers and the youth, which are already profoundly discontented.

Instead, US imperialism would try to get the neighbouring states to intervene. But this is also not a simple proposition! Colombia has a right wing pro-US government but is entangled in its own civil war. It would be difficult for Lula to justify intervention against Venezuela and such a step would cause an immediate crisis in Brazil.

In fact, so unstable is the situation that a socialist revolution in Venezuela would have an effect throughout Latin America like one domino falling after another. Far from contemplating a military intervention against the Venezuelan revolution, they would be facing the danger of revolution in their own back yard.

Does this seem so difficult? The alternative is a million times worse. Because the only alternative to this scenario is the defeat of the revolution and the victory of the counter-revolution in Venezuela. The consequences of such a defeat would be extremely serious not only for the people of Venezuela but for the whole of

Latin America.

The beginnings of a process of revolution in Venezuela aroused the hopes of millions of poor people throughout the continent. But the revolution halted half way, and this is not possible. One cannot make half a revolution; any more than one can be half born. A birth that halts half way ends in abortion, pain and death. It is time to cast aside all illusions. It is time to look reality in the face. It is time to carry out the Venezuelan Revolution to the end.

Above all, it is time for all those who stand for revolution and workers' power to unite in a single Marxist party that is able and willing to fight within the Bolivarian movement to put an end to all vacillations and to carry the struggle through to the end. The success of the revolution depends on the subjective factor, that is, on the revolutionary party and its leadership. Armed with the scientific ideas and programme of Marxism, no force on earth can defeat the working class.

❑ For the programme of workers democracy and proletarian internationalism!
❑ For a Marxist party!
❑ Forward to the victory of the Venezuelan Revolution!
❑ Forward to the Socialist United States of South America!

Chapter Four

Venezuela between
revolution and counter-revolution

Buenos Aires, December 10th, 2002.

The reports from Venezuela indicate a sharpening of the struggle between the contending forces.

On Friday a gunman killed three people and wounded 21 others at an anti-government rally in a plaza where rebel officers have held daily protests. This bloody incident bears all the hallmarks of a premeditated provocation. According to reports in *Clarin*, snipers mounted on motorbikes fired at a group which included dissident army officers. Police have arrested seven suspects, one of whom is Joao de Gouveira, a Portuguese national and a taxi driver by profession, who is said to have confessed to the shooting in Altamira Square.

We have no information about this Gouveira. It is impossible to say whether he is a professional provocateur or a deranged ultra-left or a terrorist manipulated by the CIA or some other state agency. This, however, is a secondary matter. The objective content of this action is that it is a provocation that is designed to discredit the revolution and provide support for the anti-government forces. In particular, it is intended to create an atmosphere of fear and panic that is conducive to the formation of a "Party of Order" among the army officers.

The revolutionary camp must be on its guard against provocateurs who have undoubtedly infiltrated themselves into the mass movement, with a view to causing disorder and panic. Their aim is to drag the mass movement into futile armed conflicts that can end with a large number of casualties. This is the main aim of the counter-revolutionaries. That is why the ideas of "foquism" and individual terrorism are so harmful to the movement. The groups that advocate such tactics are very easily infiltrated by the police and secret services and manipulated for sinister purposes. It is necessary to firmly oppose all adventurist tactics that put the whole movement at risk.

The way to defeat the counter-revolution is not through individual shoot-outs but through the actions of the masses themselves. And the masses are responding to the challenge magnificently! On Saturday about 100,000 Chávez followers poured onto the streets of Caracas in a human flood. This is the way to answer the enemy! By contrast, the number of counter-revolutionaries on the streets was much less. This is an indication that the willpower of the middle class is waning. That is quite typical of the petty bourgeois, which looks for quick successes and is easily discouraged when it meets resistance.

However, the struggle is by no means over yet. Troops ordered to seize the Pilin Leon, anchored off the coast, failed yesterday to retake the oil tanker which was seized by counter-revolutionaries because the crew said they would break maritime law to surrender control to unqualified officers. The aim of the reactionaries is perfectly clear: to cause the maximum chaos and disorder, to wreck the economy, to take the bread from the mouths of the people and thus create the conditions for a coup.

Having initially failed to bring things to a head by demonstrations, the attention of the reaction has shifted from the street to the state oil monopoly, PDVSA. Since the beginning of the present campaign of sabotage oil production has fallen 40 percent and key refineries are on the verge of closing. Since oil exports account for half of the government's revenue, this is a calamity for the country.

Hugo Chávez has ordered the army to increase its protection of oil sites and has warned that he may declare a state of emergency if the disruption continues to grow. He has also threatened to remove staff at refineries.

But the counter-revolutionaries are implacable. They understand that if this movement – the fourth this year – fails, they will find themselves in great difficulties. Behind the scenes the US embassy is urging them on. There is no shortage of dollars to finance these murky operations. Both sides understand that the outcome of the present test of strength will be decisive.

The counter-revolutionary forces do not feel strong enough to take power by themselves. The intention of the street demonstrations is not to stage a national uprising, but only to create panic and disorder in the hope that the reactionary elements in the tops of the army will be encouraged to carry out a *pronunciamiento*.

To the degree that the present situation is permitted to last, the possibilities of such a development will increase. The idea will gather force that "this cannot continue", "order must be restored". The risk of Bonapartist tendencies in the armed forces is very real.

Hugo Chávez has accused his enemies of sabotage and urged his people to "keep mobilised on the streets and in the countryside to defend the revolution once again". This is in fact the only way to save the revolution from imminent disaster. However, the mobilisation of the masses, by itself, is not enough. The movement requires not only courage and fighting spirit – it needs a clear goal, a programme and a strategy.

To do justice to the counter-revolutionaries, they have such a goal, and have consistently pursued it with skilful tactics, worked out by intelligent people who have no concern for constitutions, laws or any other scruples when it comes to defending their class interest. We should learn from our enemies, and show exactly the same qualities in fighting for the interests of our class.

The masses are responding with their customary energy and determination. There have been reports of factory occupations, including in the oil industry. This is the way forward!

Decisive action demanded

From all over the country messages and resolutions are pouring in from rank and file organisations of the Bolivarian movement demanding that the President take decisive action. In particular the people are enraged at the vile conduct of the press, the radio and the television. These powerful instruments in the hands of the capitalists are always used against the labour movement. At this moment they are being used by the counter-revolutionary forces in Venezuela to agitate against the legally elected government and in favour of a coup. The question is posed of occupation of the TV, radio and press offices in order to put an end to the manipulation of the news by the reactionaries.

In 1968 in France, the print workers obliged the millionaire press to submit to scrutiny by a workers' committee to ensure that the content of the newspapers was reasonably balanced. The papers had to publish the workers' point of view on the main questions of the day. This is probably the only time that the people of France could read the truth about the workers' struggle. The working people of Venezuela could do more than just follow this example.

Under the capitalist system the freedom of the press is an empty phrase. In all countries the media is owned and controlled by a handful of super rich tycoons who appoint and sack the editors according to their tastes. It is they who ultimately decide the political line of the media. A tiny group of powerful men, elected by nobody and responsible to nobody, is able to shape and mould public opinion, to make and break governments. And this is what they call "democracy"!

A workers' state would nationalise the mass media and provide free access to them to all political and social tendencies in proportion to their support in the population. In this way, the revolutionary committees would have television stations and daily papers, and could permit themselves the luxury of giving the wealthy press tycoons the democratic right to produce a small duplicated monthly which they could sell at the bus stops and market places.

When Chávez was elected four years ago, he promised a fundamental change in Venezuelan society. The people believed him. There is no doubt whatsoever of his personal honesty and his sincere desire to act in the interests of the mass of poor people, the workers and peasants. Important gains have been made, and these must be defended. But in the end, the real problem remained unsolved. The country's economy remained in the hands of a tiny oligarchy that has robbed and ruined the country. These wealthy and powerful men will never be reconciled to a free, just and equal Venezuela. As long as the land, the banks and the industries remain in their hands, no real lasting solution is possible.

What is required in Venezuela is a social revolution. The question is: who shall prevail? A handful of wealthy magnates backed by US imperialism, or the overwhelming majority of the people whose only crime is to seek a better life for themselves and their children? Those who talk grandiloquently about democracy conveniently overlook the fact that what they are advocating is that a tiny hand-ful of wealthy parasites should control the lives and destinies of the vast majori-ty of the people. That is not democracy. It is the dictatorship of Capital.

The economic sabotage has had a certain effect, provoking shortages in the shops and a wave of panic buying across Venezuela. As the conflict entered its second week, the National Guard has had to commandeer delivery trucks and force petrol stations to open. The shutdown has crippled the oil industry of the world's fifth-largest producer as wells, refineries, tanker ships, delivery centres and gas stations have stopped operating. The situation thus remains serious.

Outside Caracas, the National Guard seized at least three oil distribution cen-tres that had closed in the strike. The government hired civilians to drive tanker trucks – commandeered from their private owners – to petrol stations. The Energy Ministry said the private property would be returned to its owners "as soon as activities are normalised."

But here is the problem. There is no question of things ever being "nor-malised" in Venezuela until the fundamental contradiction is removed. What is necessary is to destroy the economic power of the capitalist class by expropriat-ing the commanding heights of the economy. This would make it impossible for the enemies of the revolution to conduct the kind of sabotage we are now wit-nessing.

More importantly, it would enable the people of Venezuela to mobilise the full productive potential of Venezuelan industry, agriculture and manpower to solve the burning problems of the masses.

For the present, the situation of unstable equilibrium continues. Egged on by Washington the reactionaries are even hardening their demands. Talks between the opposition and government were resumed Saturday night but appeared to make little progress. The opposition initially was seeking a referendum on Chávez's four-year-old government, but now it is demanding his immediate res-ignation.

The most serious aspect of the situation is the beginnings of what are clearly armed provocations, like the one that was staged last Friday. There is no doubt that this was intended to lead to even more serious clashes. Fortunately, so far this has not occurred. However, the need for some kind of defence force or militia is clearly posed.

The need for defence should be discussed in every committee and where possible arrangements should be made to set up defence groups to patrol the local areas and maintain order. The workers' districts must be protected against criminal elements and provocateurs who seek to disturb the peace and provoke conflicts. Specialised people with a knowledge of military affairs can be put in charge of these units. The purpose is not to cause violence, as some have suggested, but to minimise it and to deter aggressors.

The question of the army remains the central issue. The majority of the soldiers are on the side of the people. The closest contacts must be maintained between the barracks and the committees, and together they should keep a close watch on the movements and conduct of army officers whose loyalty is doubtful.

Progressive role

It is absolutely correct to place demands on the President and to press the leadership to act in a decisive manner. In the last analysis, Chávez himself is a personification of the aspirations of the masses, or, to be more correct, of the first confused aspirations of the masses that have been recently awoken to political life. In appealing to these aspirations and the striving for a better life for the poor and oppressed, Hugo Chávez undoubtedly played a progressive role.

But life moves on. The situation now is posed in darker colours. Venezuelan society is fractured and polarised to the left and right. The old vague slogans no longer have any value or use in this situation. What is needed is clarity and firmness. An ever-increasing number of people are beginning to see this and are loudly demanding a firmer hand and more decisive action in dealing with the enemies of the people. It is entirely correct and necessary to put pressure on the leadership to act. If they do so, the struggle can be won far more quickly and with fewer sacrifices.

But what is absolutely necessary is for the masses to continue to act from below, immediately to carry their demands into practice, without waiting for any lead from the top. This was how they won in April and this is how they can win now.

Unfortunately, Hugo Chávez has often displayed indecision in the face of events. Lacking a clear perspective, he finds himself under extreme pressures from left and right. He is being urged by so-called friends to behave with moderation, for fear of making things worse. With "friends" like these, one really needs no enemies! It is necessary to counteract these pressures by stepping up the pressure from below.

Undoubtedly, a great weight of responsibility rests on the shoulders of the President. As an old army man, all his instincts are against splitting the army. He does not want a civil war. But the fact is that the only way to prevent a civil war is by taking decisive action against the counter-revolution and arming the people. The Romans of old had a saying: "Si pacem vis, para bellum" – If you desire peace, prepare for war! It is the eternal dialectic of reformism and pacifism that they achieve precisely the opposite results to the ones intended. By arming and mobilising the masses against the danger of reaction, that danger becomes less, not more. By compromising and trying to avoid a fight, that is, by showing weakness in the face of reaction, the latter becomes more confident and more aggressive.

As for the army, it is already divided between the majority that is on the side of the people, and a minority of elements who have been bought by the counter-revolution. The only question is which of the two factions will emerge triumphant. Hugo Chávez should base himself on the masses and the soldiers who are with the masses in order to disarm and arrest the counter-revolutionary elements in the barracks. Do not trust those who pose as loyalists but who advocate a policy of conciliation with the enemy and complain about the masses "going too far"! Remember the fate of Salvador Allende, who trusted the "democratic" general Pinochet and refused to distribute arms to the masses who were willing to fight for the government.

Here and in other articles, we have advocated a definite line of action to save the Venezuelan Revolution and carry it forward. One may be in favour of these proposals or against them. But what happens at the end of the day will be decided by the masses themselves in the course of struggle. Their own experience will teach them which ideas are correct. The presence of a revolutionary Marxist party with a far-sighted leadership would enable them to find the right way in a shorter space of time. The marvellous resolutions from the local committees show that they are in the process of finding this way, and that in the committees there already exist elements that are fighting for a Marxist policy. Once the masses are convinced that this is the way in which to move, no force on earth can stop them.

Chapter Five

Encounters with Hugo Chávez

London, 29th April, 2004.

Last week, as readers of Marxist.com will already know, I visited Caracas to attend the Second International Gathering in Solidarity with the Venezuelan Revolution. It was held on the second anniversary of the defeat of the attempted counter-revolution of April 2002. In the course of one hectic week I spoke at several meetings, putting the Marxist case, mainly to audiences of workers and poor people – activists of the Bolivarian movement and the main protagonists of the Venezuelan Revolution. I attended the mass rally on 12th April and witnessed first-hand the revolutionary fervour that motivates the masses and enabled them to stop the counter-revolution in its tracks.

I also had the opportunity to meet and talk with the President of Venezuela's Bolivarian Republic, Hugo Chávez. As a writer and Marxist historian I am used to writing about men and women who have made history. But it is not every day that one has the opportunity to observe a protagonist of the historical process at close quarters, to ask questions and to form an impression, not from newspaper reports but from personal experience.

I should like to make a few things clear before proceeding to my subject. I approach the Venezuelan Revolution as a revolutionary, not as an external observer, and certainly not as a sycophant and a flatterer. Flattery is the enemy of revolutions because it is the enemy of truth, and revolutions need above all to know the truth. The phenomenon of "revolutionary tourism" I find profoundly abhorrent. It is particularly out of place in the case of Venezuela, because here the revolution finds itself in the greatest danger. Those who make stupid speeches that constantly assert the wonders of the Bolivarian Revolution, but conveniently ignore the dangers it still faces, are false friends of the revolution in whom no reliance can be placed.

A successful revolution always has many "friends". Those middle class elements who are attracted to power as flies to a honey pot, who are ready to sing the praises of the revolution as long as it remains in power, who do nothing useful to save it from its enemies, who weep a few crocodile tears when it is overthrown, and the next day pass onto the next item on Life's agenda – such "friends" are worth two a penny. A real friend is not someone who always tells you that you are right. A real friend is someone who is not afraid to look you straight in the eye and tell you that you are mistaken.

The best friends of the Venezuelan Revolution are the revolutionary Marxists. They are the people who will move heaven and earth to defend the Venezuelan Revolution against its enemies. At the same time, the true friends of the revolution – honest and loyal friends – will always speak their mind without fear. Where we consider that the right road is being taken, we will offer praise. Where we think mistakes are being made, we will give friendly but firm criticism. What other kind of behaviour should be expected of real revolutionaries and internationalists?

In speech after speech in Venezuela – including several televised interviews – I was asked my opinion about the Venezuelan Revolution, and answered in the following sense: "Your revolution is an inspiration to the workers of the whole world: you have accomplished miracles; the driving force of the revolution, however, is the working class and the masses, and that is the secret of its future success. However, the revolution has not been finished and will not be finished unless and until you destroy the economic power of the bankers and capitalists. In order to do this, the masses must be armed and organised in action committees, organised at all levels. The workers must have their own independent organisations and we must build the Marxist Revolutionary Tendency."

Democracy and the ruling class

Everywhere I spoke, these ideas were accepted with great enthusiasm. At no time was any pressure put on me to modify or change my ideas in any way. At every level, there was considerable interest in the ideas of Marxism. Contrary to the disgraceful lies and calumnies that are being disseminated everywhere (with a little help from the CIA), revolutionary Venezuela enjoys complete democracy. The bourgeois opposition, which is constantly conspiring against democracy, is allowed to put forward its ideas as freely as I was – more freely, in fact, since it owns the main television channels, which constantly pour out counter-revolutionary propaganda and even open appeals for a coup.

The arguments of the enemies of the revolution to the effect that Chávez is a dictator are ironic. Unlike the present occupant of the White House, who never won a majority and only enjoys the fruits of office because the election result was rigged, Hugo Chávez has won overwhelmingly in two elections and five other electoral processes have ratified his programme, all in the space of 6 years.

Chávez introduced a new constitution which is characterized by its extremely democratic character. Ironically, it is this new constitution that gives the people the right to hold a referendum to dismiss an unpopular government that is being utilised by the opposition to try to get rid of the Chávez government – though without success. Thus, both sides are appealing to the same laws and the same constitution.

In the beginning, the oligarchy did not know what to make of the Chávez government. They thought it would be like any other government. And in Venezuela, as in any other country where formal bourgeois democracy pertains, elected governments are a commodity like any other: they can be bought and sold – only the exact price needs to be decided. Hugo Chávez was an unknown quantity, but as a former army officer, surely he would soon see sense? For the ruling class, the speeches that politicians make in election campaigns are only the small change of politics – they are not to be taken seriously.

A British Conservative politician once said to a Socialist: "You can never win, because we will always buy your leaders." Following the same principle, the oligarchy tried to reach an agreement with the new government. They even wrote favourably about Hugo Chávez. Following the age-old guiding principle of Venezuelan politics, they thought that an amicable agreement could be reached on the following basis: "Look, this is a country with rich pickings: there is plenty for all of us. So there is really no need for an argument. Let us reach a gentlemen's agreement: you take so much and we will take the rest."

Unfortunately for the ruling class, not everyone is for sale. Even when the government passed a new constitution, the oligarchy did not despair. The new government passed a constitution that is the most democratic in Latin America, perhaps in the whole world. It gives rights to everyone, irrespective of race, colour or sex. Naturally, the oligarchy did not treat this seriously. After all, what is a constitution but a mere scrap of paper? The reasoning of the oligarchy was impeccable, and reflected the reality of all laws and constitutions in a formal bourgeois democracy. They are not really to be taken seriously. They are an adornment that is designed to draw a veil over the real situation that is the continuing domination of a wealthy minority over the majority.

Democracy, parliament, elections, free speech and free trade unions are seen by the ruling class as a necessary evil, which may be tolerated as long as they present no threat to the dictatorship of the banks and monopolies. But as soon as the mechanism of democracy is used by the masses to introduce a fundamental change in society, the attitude of the ruling class changes. They begin to shout about "dictatorship" even when the government has, as in Venezuela, been elected by the overwhelming majority. They use their economic muscle, their control over the economic life of the nation, their control of the mass media and the judiciary to harass, sabotage and undermine the democratically elected government – *that is to say, they resort to extra-parliamentary methods to overthrow the government.*

To imagine that laws and constitutions will save the government under such conditions is the height of naivety. The extra-parliamentary actions of the ruling class cannot be defeated by speeches in parliament and appeals to the constitution. It can only be defeated by the extra-parliamentary action of the masses. The experience of the Venezuelan Revolution confirms this affirmation one hundred percent. For it is one thing to approve a constitution that gives rights to the majority, and another thing to turn these rights into reality. In order to act in the interests of the majority it is necessary to confront the vested interests of the oligarchy. This cannot be done without an all-out struggle.

The coup of 11th April

As soon as the oligarchy realised that they could not reach an agreement with Chávez, that he could not be bought, they began to attack him. The elite began to organise and mobilize its forces. They used their control of the mass media to whip up the middle classes into a frenzy. They used the CIA to bribe corrupt trade union leaders to organise reactionary strikes, following the pattern of the lorry drivers' strike against the government of Salvador Allende in Chile. They staged an investment strike, shipping billions to bank accounts in Miami. They were preparing the ground for the counter-revolutionary coup of April 11th, 2002.

It goes without saying that all the threads in this conspiracy went back to Washington. Why does US imperialism hate Chávez? Why does it fear the Bolivarian Revolution? So far, Chávez has not expropriated the property of the big US companies in Venezuela. He has not halted the shipment of oil to the USA. He has not nationalised the property of the oligarchy.

In part, the hostility of Washington to Chávez is dictated by his fierce determination to resist the impositions of US imperialism. He was from the beginning one of the firmest advocates of maintaining a high price of oil – a policy that goes against the interests of US capitalism that is struggling to get out of recession and needs to keep oil prices low. In the past, Washington could rely on a pliable government in Caracas that would (for a suitable sum of money) adopt a policy more to its liking. The Venezuelan oil company PDVSA, though formally nationalised, was controlled by corrupt bureaucrats who ran PDVSA like any other capitalist enterprise and were more than friendly to the big US oil companies.

The real reason for the undying hatred of US imperialism to Chávez, however, must be sought elsewhere. At the present time there is not a single stable capitalist regime from Tierra del Fuego to the Rio Grande. A revolutionary wave is sweeping the entire Latin American continent. This fills the strategists of Capital in Washington with fear and foreboding. The eyes of the world are fixed on the Middle East, an area of vital economic and strategic importance to US imperialism. But Latin America is seen as the USA's backyard. Events in the South affect the USA in a very direct way.

Hugo Chávez's Bolivarian Revolution is a direct threat to US imperialism because of the example it gives to the oppressed masses in the rest of Latin America. It has roused the masses from their long winter sleep and impelled them to struggle. The revolution's list of practical achievements is impressive. It has carried out some serious reforms in the interest of the workers and the poor. One and a half million people have been taught to read and write and a total of 3 million people have been enrolled in education plans at different levels. Twelve million people, many of whom had never seen a doctor, have received medical attention from Cuban doctors who have been sent to live in the villages and shanty towns. Nearly two million hectares of land have been distributed to the peasants.

These are real gains. But the real gain of the revolution is more important and more intangible. It cannot be weighed, measured or counted, but it is decisive. The revolution has given the masses a sense of their own dignity as human beings, it has imparted a keen sense of justice, it has given them a new sense of their own power, it has given them a new confidence. It has given them hope for the future. From the standpoint of the ruling class and imperialism, this represents a mortal peril.

At present the correlation of class forces remains favourable for the revolution. Chávez's personal popularity is unchallenged. The polls give him 60 percent or more. In reality, his support is even greater if we consider which forces support him. Everything that is alive, creative and vibrant in Venezuela is with the revolution. On the other side stand the forces of reaction and conservatism – all that is degenerate, corrupt and rotten.

For the first time in the almost 200 years history of Venezuela the masses feel that the government is in the hands of people who wish to defend their interests. In the past the government was always an alien power standing against them. They do not want to see the return of the old corrupt parties.

A revolution, as Trotsky explains in the *History of the Russian Revolution*, is a situation where the masses begin to take their destiny into their own hands. This is certainly the case in Venezuela now. The awakening of the masses and their active participation in politics is the most decisive feature of the Venezuelan Revolution and the secret of its success.

Two years ago the spontaneous uprising of the masses defeated the counter-revolution. This is what served to accelerate the whole process. But two years later a new mood is developing in the masses. There is frustration and discontent. The aspirations of the masses have not been satisfied. They wish to go further. They want to confront and defeat the forces of the counter-revolution and are pressing forward.

But on the top there are other pressures from those who feel the Revolution has gone too far, those who fear the masses on the one hand and imperialism on the other. They want to apply the brakes. The two contradictory tendencies cannot coexist forever. One or the other will have to win. Upon the result of this internal struggle the future of the revolution will depend.

This central contradiction is reflected at all levels, in society, in the movement, in the government, in the Palace of Miraflores, and even in the President himself.

Chávez and the masses

For decades Venezuela was ruled by a corrupt and degenerate oligarchy. There was a two party system in which both parties represented the oligarchy. When Chávez founded the Bolivarian Movement, he sought to clean out the stinking Augean stables that were Venezuelan political life. This was a limited and very modest objective – but it met with the ferocious resistance of the ruling oligarchy and its servants.

Two years ago, on 11th April, the oligarchy, with the active support of Washington, attempted to overthrow Chávez through a coup d'état. He was arrested and hijacked. The plotters installed themselves in the palace of Miraflores. But within 48 hours they were overthrown by a spontaneous uprising of the masses. Units of the army loyal to Chávez went over to the masses, and the coup collapsed ignominiously on April 13th.

At the II International Gathering in Solidarity with the Venezuelan Revolution I estimate that there were about 150 foreign delegates, mostly from South and Central America. On the evening of April 13th we gathered on the tribune in central Caracas, just outside the palace of Miraflores to see the immense demonstration that commemorated the defeat of the coup.

It was an impressive sight. From the factories and poor areas of Caracas tens of thousands of Chavistas poured onto the streets in red shirts and baseball caps, waving flags and placards. These were the people who defeated the counter-revolution two years ago, and their enthusiasm for the Revolution remains undimmed.

The meetings began with music and a few warming-up speeches. Then Chávez spoke. It was interesting to observe the relations between Chávez and the masses. There can be no doubt about the intense loyalty felt by the poor and downtrodden masses to this man. Hugo Chávez for the first time gave the poor and downtrodden a voice and some hope. That is the secret of the extraordinary devotion and loyalty they have shown him. He aroused them to life and they see themselves in him. This has earned him the undying hatred of the wealthy and powerful, and the loyalty and love of the masses.

That explains the equally extraordinary hatred the ruling class shows towards Chávez. It is the hatred of the rich for the poor, of the exploiter for the exploited. Behind this hatred is fear – fear for the loss of their wealth, power and privileges. This is a gulf that cannot be bridged by fair words. It is the fundamental class division of society. And it has not been eliminated by the defeat of the coup and the subsequent bosses' lockout. If anything, it has grown in intensity.

As usual, Chávez spoke at great length, covering many issues, national and international. Significantly, he drew a clear distinction between the government and the people of the United States, appealing to the former for support against Bush and the imperialists. As he spoke, I was able to watch the reaction of the masses on the big screen behind the president. Old people and youngsters, men and women, the overwhelming majority working class, listened intently, straining on every word. They applauded, cheered, laughed and even wept as they stood there. This was the face of an aroused people, a people that has become aware of itself as an active participant in the historical process – the face of a revolution.

And Chávez? Chávez clearly draws his strength from the support of the masses, with whom he identifies fully. In his manner of speaking – spontaneous and completely lacking in the stiff formality one expects from a professional politician – he connects with them. If there is sometimes a lack of clarity, even this reflects the stage in which the mass movement finds itself. The identity is complete.

First encounter

Immediately after the mass rally, the international delegates were invited to a reception inside the palace of Miraflores. It is not an easy place to get in and out of. Security is very tight because of the constant threat of assassination. Bags are searched and searched again. Passports are checked minutely. Guards with mirrors inspect the underside of all vehicles. It takes a long time, but these precautions are absolutely necessary.

Chávez again addressed the meeting, and one wonders where he gets his energy from. He speaks at length about the day of the coup when he was arrested and reveals certain details that nobody knew up to that point. Afterwards, he was surrounded by a lot of people wanting to shake his hand and exchange a few words. It was a bit like a rugby match, but eventually I managed to get close enough to introduce myself: "I am Alan Woods from London, the author of *Reason in Revolt*."

Grasping my outstretched hand firmly, he looked at me with curiosity: "What book did you say?"

"*Reason in Revolt*".

A broad smile lit up his face. "That is a fantastic book! I congratulate you." Then looking around him he announced: "You must all read this book!"

Not wishing to take up any more of his time at the expense of other people who were waiting, I asked if we could meet.

"Of course we must meet. See my secretary." He pointed to a young man at his side, who promptly informed me that he "would be in touch".

I was going to leave, to allow others to meet the President, when he stopped me. He now seemed to be oblivious of all around him and spoke with obvious enthusiasm: "You know, I have got that book at my bedside and I am reading it every night. I have got as far as the chapter on 'The molecular process of revolution'. You know, where you write about Gibbs' energy." It appears that this section has made a considerable impact on him, because he quotes it continually in his speeches. Mr. Gibbs has probably never been so famous before!

This is no accident. The Venezuelan Revolution has now reached a critical point where the outcome must be determined in one sense or another. The chapter he referred to deals with just such a critical point in chemistry, where a certain amount of energy, known as Gibbs' energy, is needed to bring about a qualitative transformation. Chávez has grasped the fact that the revolution needs to make this qualitative leap, and this is why that passage in the book attracted his attention.

The following day I was completely occupied. I spoke at a meeting of a hundred people in a debate about the fundamental problems of the revolution, in which I advocated the expropriation of the property of the oligarchy, the arming of the people and workers' control and management. I quoted Lenin's famous four conditions for workers' power, and the bit about the limitation on the salaries of officials proved particularly popular.

I was answered by a Colombian member of parliament, who put a completely reformist position. He is a former guerrilla (they are always the most fervent reformists). I answered him quite firmly – to the obvious delight of the audience – quoting Tawney's celebrated dictum: "You can peel and onion layer by layer, but you can't skin a tiger claw by claw". In the end the poor chap looked quite dazed.

In the evening I was joined by Manzoor Ahmed, the Marxist Member of Parliament from Pakistan. Poor Manzoor had just come off a plane after an exhausting journey of 33 hours. Nevertheless, he seemed fresh as he addressed the main plenary session in an inspirational speech where he drew a parallel between the Venezuelan Revolution and the Pakistani Revolution of 1968-69.

As Manzoor explained what had happened when Bhutto failed to carry through the revolution to the end, I was watching the faces of the people around me. Most of them were worker activists of the Bolivarian Circles. They were clearly enthralled by what Manzoor was saying, interrupting with cries of "That's right! That's what we want! About time this was said!" When Manzoor finally drew the conclusion "You cannot make half a revolution, the revolution must be finished", the audience broke into wild applause. Manzoor was given the only standing ovation of the evening.

The second encounter

The next day I phoned Chávez's secretary to ask about the appointment. The reply was not encouraging: "The President is very busy. A lot of people want to see him."

"Well, let's get this straight: is the meeting going to take place – yes or no?"

"I think it will be impossible."

I drew the obvious conclusion and went to discuss with two oil workers leaders from Puerto la Cruz over lunch.

In the middle of lunch, I was surprised when Fernando Bossi entered the restaurant and came up to our table. He is an Argentinean and the head of the Bolivarian Peoples' Congress, spreading all over Latin America.

"Alan, be ready by half past five. The President will see you at half past six."

The palace of Miraflores is an elegant neo classical building probably built in the 19th century and with an air reminiscent of the Spanish colonial era. In the centre there is a large patio surrounded by columns. Although the meeting was initially scheduled for half past six, it was past ten o'clock by the time I was called. As I stood waiting I was struck by the sound of the local crickets, so much louder and more strident than the ones I am used to in Spain.

I was told to expect an interview of between twenty and thirty minutes, which seemed perfectly adequate to me. The person before me was Heinz Dieterich, a German now living in Mexico, and an old friend of Chávez. He was with the President for 40 minutes, and profusely apologised for keeping me waiting. I told him I did not mind. However, there was a long gap before I was finally called. I supposed that Chávez was tired after a long day and wanted a rest, or maybe he was having something to eat.

These speculations were incorrect. I later discovered that Hugo Chávez is not a man who tires easily. He starts work every day before 8 o'clock and works until about three in the morning. Then he reads (he is a voracious reader). I don't know when he sleeps, yet he always seems to be bubbling with energy and talking endlessly about all sorts of things. This does not make him an easy man to work with, as his personal secretary told me: "I would do anything for him, but there is never a moment's peace. Sometimes I can't even go to the toilet. I start to walk in that direction and somebody shouts: 'the President wants you!'"

The reason I was kept waiting is that the President wanted to read all the material of the Hands off Venezuela campaign. As I walked into his office, he was sitting at his desk, with a huge portrait of Simon Bolivar behind him. On the desk I noticed a copy of *Reason in Revolt* and a letter I had sent him. The letter had been heavily underlined in blue.

Chávez greeted me very warmly. Here was no "protocol" but only openness and frankness. He began by asking me about Wales and my family background. I explained that I was from a working class family, and he replied that he was from a family of peasants. "Well, Alan, what have you got to say?" he asked. Actually, I was more interested in what he had to say – which was very interesting.

First I presented him with two books: my history of the Bolshevik Party (*Bolshevism, the Road to Revolution*) and Ted Grant's *Russia – from Revolution to Counter-revolution*. He looked extremely pleased. "I love books," he told me. "If they are good books, I love them even more. But even if they are bad books, I still love them."

Opening the Bolshevism book he read the dedication I had written, which reads: "To President Hugo Chávez with my best wishes. The Road to Revolution passes through the ideas, programme and traditions of Marxism. Forward to Victory!" He said "That is a wonderful dedication. Thank you, Alan." He began to turn the pages and stopped.

"I see you write about Plekhanov."

"That's right."

"I read a book by Plekhanov a long time ago, and it made a big impression on me. It was called *The Role of the Individual in History*. Do you know it?"

"Of course."

"The role of the individual in history", he mused. "Well, I know none of us is really indispensable," he said.

"That is not quite correct," I replied. "There are times in history when an individual can make a fundamental difference."

"Yes, I was pleased to see that in *Reason in Revolt* you say that Marxism cannot be reduced to economic factors."

"That is right. That is a vulgar caricature of Marxism."

"Do you know when I read Plekhanov's book *The Role of the Individual in History*?" he asked.

"I have no idea."

"I read it when I was a serving officer in an anti-guerrilla unit in the mountains. You know they gave us material to read so that we could understand subversion. I read that the subversives work among the people, defend their interests and win their hearts and minds. That seemed quite a good idea!"

"Then I began to read Plekhanov's book and it made a deep impression on me. I remember it was a beautiful starlit night in the mountains and I was in my tent reading with the light of a torch. The things I read made me think and I began to question what I was doing in the army. I became very unhappy.

"You know for us it was no problem. Moving about in the mountains with rifles in our hands. Also the guerrillas had no problems – they were doing the same as us. But the people who suffered were the ordinary peasants. They were helpless and they had a rough time. I remember one day we went into a village and I saw some soldiers torturing two peasants. I told them to stop that immediately, that there would be none of that as long as I was in command.

"Well, that really got me into trouble. They even wanted to put me on trial for *military insubordination*. [He put special emphasis on the last two words]. After that I decided that the army was no place for me. I wanted to quit, but I was stopped by an old Communist who said to me: 'You are more useful to the Revolution in the army than ten trade unionists.' So I stayed. I now think that was the right thing to do.

"Do you know that I set up an army in those mountains? It was an army of five men. But we had a very long name. We called ourselves the Simon Bolivar people's national liberation army." He laughed heartily.

"When was that?" I asked.

"In 1974. You see, I thought to myself: this is the land of Simon Bolivar. There must be something of his spirit still alive – something in our genes, I suppose. So we set about trying to revive it."

I had no idea that the present position in the Venezuelan army was the result of decades of patient revolutionary work. But it is the case. Chávez went on, as if thinking aloud:

"Two years ago, at the time of the coup, when I was arrested and being led away, I thought I was going to be shot. I asked myself: have the last 25 years of my life been wasted? Was it all for nothing? But it was not for nothing, as the uprising of the paratroop regiment showed."

Chávez remembers the coup

Chávez spoke at some length about the coup. He related how he was kept in complete isolation. The rebels wanted to pressurise him into signing a document, resigning from office. Then they would have let him go into exile in Cuba or somewhere. They wanted to do what they have done recently with Aristide in Haiti. He was not to be killed physically but morally, to be discredited in the eyes of his followers. But he refused to sign.

The plotters used all kinds of tricks to get him to resign. They even used the Church (about which Chávez speaks very caustically).

"Yes, they even sent the Cardinal to persuade me. He told me a pack of lies:

that I had no support, that everyone had abandoned me, that the army was firmly behind the coup. I had no information, and was completely cut off from the outside world. But I still refused to sign.

"My captors were getting very nervous. They were getting lots of phone calls from Washington demanding to know where the signed resignation letter was. When they saw the letter not forthcoming, they became desperate. The Cardinal pressed me to sign in order to avoid civil war and bloodshed. But then I noticed a sudden change in his tone. He became polite and conciliatory. I thought to myself: if he is talking like this, something must have happened.

"Then the phone rang. One of my captors said: 'It's the minister of defence. He wants to speak to you. I told him I would not speak to any golpista. Then he said: 'But it is *your* minister of defence.' I tore the phone out of his hand and then I heard a voice that sounded like the sun. I don't know if you can say that, but anyway, that is just what it sounded like to me."

From this conversation I was able to form an impression about Chávez the man. The first thing that strikes one is that he is transparently honest. His sincerity is absolutely clear, as is his dedication to the cause of the revolution and his hatred of injustice and oppression. Of course, these qualities in and of themselves are not sufficient to guarantee the victory of the revolution, but they certainly explain his tremendous popularity with the masses.

He asked me what I thought of the movement in Venezuela. I replied that it was very impressive, that the masses were clearly the main motive force and that all the ingredients were present to carry the revolution through to the end, but that there was something missing. He asked what that was. I replied that the weakness of the movement was the absence of a clearly defined ideology and cadres. He agreed.

"You know, I don't consider myself a Marxist because I have not read enough Marxist books," he said.

From this conversation I had the distinct impression that Hugo Chávez was looking for ideas, and that he was genuinely interested in the ideas of Marxism and anxious to learn. This is related to the stage that the Venezuelan Revolution has reached. Sooner than many people expect, it will be faced with a stark choice: either liquidate the economic power of the oligarchy or else go down to defeat.

It is possible that events will convince Chávez of the need to make a sharp turn to the left. He recently made a speech in which he called for the arming of the people. He is clearly frustrated with the constant sabotage and provocations of the opposition inside and outside parliament. He has listed the methods of sabotage used by the judges, the opposition parliamentarians, the Metropolitan Police, the bureaucrats of PDVSA, etc. If the revolution is going to advance, these obstacles must be removed. In order to remove them, the mass movement must be mobilised, organised and armed.

There is resistance to this at the tops of the movement. The reformist and social democratic elements are weak or non-existent in the rank and file but strong at the top. This is bitterly resented by the Chavista rank and file, which is becoming frustrated at the lack of decisive action against the counter-revolution.

Under these circumstances the ideas of Marxism, represented by the Revolutionary Marxist Current – *El Militante-Topo Obrero* – are getting a powerful echo.

The Hands off Venezuela Campaign

The conversation then turned to our international solidarity campaign Hands off Venezuela, about which President Chávez expressed the greatest enthusiasm. He asked me what I thought about the International Gathering. I told him that it was an excellent idea but that there were weaknesses. Almost all the delegates from Europe were just individuals, mostly academics and intellectuals representing nobody but themselves. Chávez's reaction indicated that he knew this was the case.

I said: "What can such people do? They will go home and organise a seminar about how marvellous the Bolivarian Revolution is. With such solidarity you will not get very far. What the revolution needs is a serious campaign in the international labour movement."

"But the intellectuals can do something after all. They can get us some publicity."

"I agree, I do not propose to exclude them. But the main basis of support for the Venezuelan Revolution must be the working class and the international labour movement."

The President was in complete agreement on this point. He then began carefully to read the 16-page list of signatures of people supporting the Hands off Venezuela Campaign.

As he read out the names, his face showed that he was deeply moved.

"Look at this!" he said to his secretary. "I told you so. These are not just individuals. There are shop stewards, trade union secretaries, workers' leaders. This is what we need!" He then paused for a moment.

"Look, some have even written messages. Here's one. Alan, what does *Rabochaya Demokratiya* mean?" "It's Russian. It means *Workers' Democracy*."

Chávez then translated the text of the message into Spanish. It said:

To the working men and women of Venezuela
Comrades!
At this time, when the rapacious claws of US imperialism, in collaboration

with the reactionary forces inside Venezuela, are stretching out towards the Bolivarian republic, attempting to privatise the oil wealth of the country and to plunge the workers and peasants of Venezuela into even greater misery, we Russian (Soviet) Marxists express our solidarity with the class struggle of the workers of Venezuela against the forces of reaction.

As is shown by the successful experience of the Russian Revolution of 1917, it is possible to defeat the plans of the imperialists only through the formation of workers councils (Soviets), a workers militia, and the nationalisation of industry under workers control.

A successful revolution in Venezuela and the foundation of a workers state will be a beacon for the workers and the poor people of Latin America and the whole world. Workers of the world, unite!

"That is a really wonderful message," said Chávez, visibly moved. "I feel I must write to thank them. I must write to all of them. How can I do it?"

"You could write a message on our website" I suggested.

"That is what I'll do!" he exclaimed.

The President glanced at his watch. It was eleven o'clock.

"Do you mind if I put the television on for just a moment? We are starting a new news programme and I would like to see what they've done."

We watched the news for about five minutes. It was a programme about Iraq.

"Well, Alan, what did you think of it?"

"Not bad at all."

"We're planning to launch a television service that will be broadcast all over Latin America."

No wonder the US imperialists are having sleepless nights about Hugo Chávez.

About George W. Bush, Chávez expresses himself in terms of the deepest contempt. "Personally, he is a coward. He attacked Fidel Castro at a meeting of the Organisation of American States (OAS) when Fidel was not present. If he had been there he would not have dared to do it. They say he is frightened to meet me and I believe it. He tries to avoid me. But one time we were together at an OAS summit and he was sitting quite near to me." Chávez chuckled to himself.

"I had one of those swivel chairs and I was sitting with my back to him. Then, after a while, I spun the chair round so I was facing him. 'Hello, Mr. President!' I said. His face turned colour – from red to purple to blue. You can tell the man is just a bundle of complexes. That makes him dangerous – because of the power he has in his hands."

At the end of our meeting, Hugo Chávez expressed his firm support for the Hands off Venezuela Campaign. He also gave his personal backing to the publication of a Venezuelan edition of *Reason in Revolt*, with the possibility of other books in the future. We parted company on the best of terms. It was about half past eleven. But as I was about to go, he asked me about Manzoor Ahmed, the Marxist MP from Pakistan:

"Is he here?" he asked.

"Yes, he arrived yesterday."

"But why hasn't he come to see me?"

"I suppose he hasn't been invited."

The President's face darkened for a moment.

"Well you tell Manzoor from me that he must not think about leaving Venezuela without coming to see me. Where's my appointments book?" Chávez began to flick impatiently through the pages. Every spare minute was filled with meetings. He frowned for a moment, then brightened up: "Well, we will have to meet tomorrow night after dinner. You will both be there? Good. So let's say ten o'clock at night."

An improvised speech

The following evening the foreign delegates were once again assembled in a hall inside the President's palace. Again there must have been about 200 people present, together with television cameras. I had arrived a little late and sat at the back of the crowded hall. After some minutes a man from the President's office came up to me and tapped me on the shoulder: "Mr. Woods, be ready to speak in five minutes."

I was not at all prepared for this, but I walked up to the microphone in front of the television cameras, next to the table where President was sitting. I spoke about the world crisis of capitalism and explained that all the wars, economic crises, terrorism, etc., were only individual manifestations of this organic crisis of capitalism. I pointed out that the only way to solve the problems of humanity was through the abolition of capitalism and the establishment of world socialism. I explained that in the 200 years since the death of Bolivar, the bourgeoisie of Latin America had turned what ought to be an earthly paradise into a living hell for millions of people.

In conclusion I pointed to the colossal potential of the productive forces that was being wasted because of the two major barriers to human progress – private ownership of the means of production and "that relic of barbarism the nation state". I pointed to the enormous achievements of science and technology that were sufficient in themselves to transform the lives of the majority of the planet.

At this point I said: "It seems the Americans are now preparing to send a man to Mars. I believe we should support this proposal on one condition – that the man in question is George W. Bush and that he is on a one-way ticket."

At this the hall erupted into laughter, and Chávez shouted above the din: "And Aznar – don't forget Aznar."

To which I replied: "Mr. President, let us not speak ill of the dead!" My speech was the only political speech of the evening and was very well received.

As usual, Chávez spoke last and he spoke for a long time, during which he mentioned my speech on several occasions. At regular intervals someone would come in with a despairing note from the caterers whose food was being ruined by the delay. But Chávez was in full flight and nobody could stop him. He would glance at the unfortunate messenger and say: "What! You again!" And then continue as if nothing had happened.

Like all Venezuelans he has a huge sense of humour. At one point, after he had been speaking for quite some time, he called out:

"Are you still there, Alan?"

"Yes, I am still here."

"Are you asleep?"

"No, I am wide awake."

[Pause] "Who is this Gibbs?"

"A scientist".

"Oh, a scientist." And then he continued as before.

The reference to Gibbs (or Hibbs as he pronounces it) had most of the audience mystified and I had to spend a little time telling people how it was spelt.

It was nearly midnight when we finally sat down for dinner. I was with my friend and comrade Manzoor and was not pleased that they had put us on different tables, even though they were next to each other. I called to a young lady from the Protocol Department and explained that I wished to change my place and sit next to Manzoor, explaining that he did not speak Spanish and would feel lonely. "That's alright, we will send an interpreter." I indicated my disagreement and proceeded to sit down next to my friend.

In no time at all a rather formidable young lady appeared – apparently the head of the Dreaded Protocol. "Mr. Woods," she said, in a voice that seemed to accept no argument. "Please come with me." Like lamb to the slaughter I meekly accepted my destiny, though with a final appeal to her better nature. She did not appear to have one, so I sat looking round at my fellow guests. To my considerable surprise, there was President Chávez, together with his young daughter. We were entertained by a group of musicians playing Venezuelan music with guitars and harps and other traditional instruments, which he pointed out to me, obviously enjoying himself tremendously.

The dinner finished at about one-thirty or even later. But that is early for Chávez, and we still had to meet together with Manzoor. Just before two o'clock we were escorted to a large room, as always adorned with huge portraits of

Bolivar. In addition to Chávez and his secretary was the Minister of Foreign Affairs – an indication of the importance given to this interview. For once I thought the President looked a bit tired, but anyway he proceeded to ask Manzoor detailed questions about Pakistan and Afghanistan.

Nothing seems to lessen his insatiable appetite to know more about the world we live in. On the other hand, his secretary and minister looked more than ready for bed.

Manzoor presented him with a traditional embroidered shawl from Sindh and some beautifully worked vases – a present from the Pakistani metal workers. He placed the vases in strategic places in the room and put on the shawl, in which he was photographed. For Chávez such things are not small details. He recounted his meeting with Manzoor in great detail the following day on the radio. For this man, every international gesture of support is enormously important and valuable.

A few last words

What more can I say? I do not usually write in such detail about individuals, and I am conscious of the fact that some people consider such things to be out of place in Marxist literature. But I think they are mistaken, or at least a bit one-sided. Marx explains that men and women make history and the study of those individuals who play a role in making history is a valid part of literature – including Marxist literature.

Personally, I have never been very interested in psychology, except in the very broadest sense of the word. All too often, second rate writers try to cover up their lack of real understanding of history by claiming to delve into the deepest recesses of the mind of certain individuals to discover, for example, that Stalin and Hitler had an unhappy childhood. This is then supposed to explain why they later became ruthless dictators who tyrannised over millions. But in reality such explanations explain nothing. There are many people who have unhappy childhoods but not many who become Hitlers or Stalins. To explain such phenomena one must understand the relations between classes and the objective socio-economic processes that shape them.

Nevertheless, up to a certain point, an individual's personality has an effect on the processes of history. For me, what is interesting is the dialectical relationship between subject and object, or, as Hegel would have expressed it, between the Particular and the Universal. It would be very instructive to write a book on the exact relationship between Hugo Chávez and the Venezuelan Revolution. That such a relation exists is not open to doubt. Whether it is positive or negative will depend on what class standpoint one defends.

From the standpoint of the masses, the poor and downtrodden, Hugo Chávez is the man who brought them to their feet and who has inspired them, by his undoubted personal courage, to acts of unparalleled heroism. But the story of the Venezuelan Revolution is not yet finished. Various endings are possible – not all of them pleasant to contemplate. The masses are still learning, the Bolivarian movement still developing. The tremendous polarisation between the classes will end in a showdown in which all parties, tendencies, programmes and individuals will be put to the test.

From my limited contacts with Hugo Chávez, I am firmly convinced of his personal honesty, courage and dedication to the cause of the masses, the oppressed and exploited. I already thought that this was the case even before we met, and everything I have seen and heard confirms me in this belief. But, as I have said many times, personal honesty and courage, in and of themselves, are not sufficient to guarantee the victory of a revolution.

What is necessary? Clear ideas, a scientific understanding, a consistently revolutionary programme, policies and perspectives.

The only guarantee of the future of the Bolivarian Revolution consists in the movement from below – the mass movement which, headed by the working class, must take power into its own hands. That demands the rapid construction of the Revolutionary Marxist Current, the most consistently revolutionary section of the movement.

I believe that a growing number in the Bolivarian movement are looking for the ideas of Marxism. I am sure that this applies to many of its leaders. And Hugo Chávez? He told me that he was not a Marxist because he had not read enough Marxist books. But he is reading them now. And in a revolution people learn more in 24 hours than in 20 years of normal existence. In the end, Marxism will draw to itself all the best elements in Venezuelan society and fuse them together in one invincible fighting force. On that road lies the possibility of victory.

Chapter Six

Marxists and
the Venezuelan Revolution

London, May 4th, 2004

"Whoever expects to see a 'pure' social revolution will never live to see it. Such a person pays lip-service to revolution without understanding what revolution is". (Lenin)

There are Marxists of all kinds: some have read a lot, some not so much. Some have taken the trouble to penetrate the essence of the Marxist method, to make a careful study of dialectics, while others have merely skated over the surface, limiting themselves to a kind of vulgar economic determinism that may be useful as agitation but is really quite alien to Marxism.

Reading the writings of such "Marxism" one always has the impression of entering into the dark basement of a public library that has remained closed for many years. It is full of bits of undigested knowledge, but airless, dusty and sterile. This is Marxism stripped of dialectics – that is, stripped of its revolutionary soul. This kind of "Marxism" is essentially quite compatible with reformism and passivity, since, for all its radical terminology, it never leaves the armchair and the slippers.

This deviation is particularly common in Britain, where it has a very long lineage going back to Hyndman. In part, this reflects the British tradition of narrow empiricism and aversion for broad theoretical generalizations, in part also the pressure of reformist ideas and Labour Movement routinism, which is never able to see the wood for the trees.

Revolutionaries must have a "feel" for the movement of the masses and have revolution in their soul. By contrast, bookish pedants see the historical process as a question of "objective forces" that determine everything in advance. Such people are not revolutionaries but eternal observers whose standpoint has far more in common with Calvin's notion of predestination than the revolutionary dialectic of Marxism.

The idea of predestination played a progressive role in the early stages of the bourgeois revolution in Holland and England in the 16th and 17th centuries, but is nowadays hopelessly antiquated. Marxist dialectics leaves plenty of room for the creative role of men and women in the historical process. But it also explains that men and women are never completely free of the objective circumstances of the historical period in which they live.

A revolutionary must have an understanding of the dialectical method that takes its starting point, not from abstract definitions and axioms, but from living reality, in all its concreteness, richness and contradictions. He or she must take the movement of the masses as it is, as it has historically developed, and strive by all means to enter into contact with it, to establish a dialogue with it, and to fertilise it with the ideas of Marxism.

A revolutionary who was not prepared to follow the masses through this contradictory process but instead tried to preach to them from the sidelines would not be a revolutionary at all but only a pitiful formalist. A mechanical and doctrinaire attitude to the mass movement would rule out any possibility of influencing it.

The subjective factor

Marxism has never denied the role of the individual in history, and individuals or groups of individuals can play an absolutely decisive role at certain junctures of the historical process. What Marx did explain – and in this he was absolutely correct – was that *in the last analysis* the viability of a given socio-economic system depends on its ability to develop the productive forces. The general crisis of world capitalism at the present time at bottom reflects the inability of capitalism to develop the productive forces to the extent that it did in the past.

This undeniable fact provides the broad historical context on which the great drama of world politics is being played out. It determines the general processes absolutely and establishes its limits. But within these general processes there can be all kinds of crosscurrents, ebbs and flows, in which the character of individuals can and does play a decisive role. In fact, it is the weakness of the subjective factor on a world scale that is having a decisive effect, delaying and distorting the movement in the direction of socialist revolution.

The most important factor in the present situation is the absence of a strong and authoritative Marxist leadership on a world scale. The tendency of genuine Marxism has been thrown back for decades and at present represents a small minority. It cannot yet lead the masses to victory. But the problems of the masses are excruciating. *They will not wait until we are ready to lead them.* They will try by all means to change society, to strive to find a way out of the impasse. This is particularly true of the ex-colonial countries of Africa, Asia and Latin America, where there is no possibility of carrying society forward on a capitalist basis.

In the absence of a mass Marxist tendency all sorts of peculiar variants are possible – in fact they are inevitable. A creative approach is necessary to understand the nature of such developments, distinguishing at every stage what is progressive and what is reactionary.

For the sectarian mentality, a revolution *must conform to a pre-established scheme*: for instance *it must be led by a Marxist party.* Now we are far from disputing the vital importance of the revolutionary party and leadership in the revolution. But in order to build such a party, it is necessary to have a realistic appraisal of the stage the movement has reached, and our role within it. We will return to this point later.

The problem with this approach is that it deals, not with living processes, but with abstract formulae, definitions and universal norms. *That is to say, it is idealist and not materialist, metaphysical and not dialectical.* It establishes *an ideal norm* of what a revolution is, and systematically rejects anything that does not conform to this norm. In the mind of an idealist, this is perfect. But such ideal perfection frequently clashes with reality, as we have known ever since Plato.

For the purposes of a definition, we all know what a human being is: it is either male or female, has two eyes, two legs, and so on and so forth. But in real life, some humans may be born with one eye or one leg, or none, and even the sex of some humans cannot be precisely determined. In fact, departures from the norm are frequently encountered in nature and in everyday life, and we must learn to deal with them or else suffer a great deal of mystification and inconvenience.

The success of the revolution would indeed be guaranteed if there existed a mass Marxist party that could give the necessary guidance to the leading layers of the class, and arm them with a political programme. But the building of such a party cannot be achieved by decree. The revolutionary vanguard can only win the majority by submitting to the test of events and the approval of the masses. It can never be achieved by preaching to the masses from the sidelines. And before we can reach the masses it is first necessary to understand the nature of the mass movement, the stage it is at, the different (contradictory) tendencies within it, and in which direction it is moving. *That is to say, a dialectical approach is needed.*

The first law of dialectics, however, is absolute objectivity: when approaching a given phenomenon we must not proceed from *preconceived ideas or definitions* but from a careful examination of the facts – *not examples, not digressions but the thing itself.* If we are to understand the events in Venezuela, and the role of the movements and individuals in these events, it is necessary to start with the events themselves. *A definition in the dialectical sense must be drawn from a careful examination of facts and processes, not imposed upon them from without.*

This was the method of Trotsky. In his Preface to the *History of the Russian*

Revolution Trotsky writes:

"The history of a revolution, like every other history, ought first of all to tell what happened and how. That, however, is little enough. From the very telling it ought to become clear why it happened thus and not otherwise. Events can neither be regarded as a series of adventures, nor strung on the thread of a preconceived moral. They must obey their own laws. The discovery of these laws is the author's task."

The above lines represent an excellent example of the dialectical method of analysis. By contrast, formalistic thinkers do not bother their heads with a careful study of facts and processes. They do not have to work hard to discover the laws of motion of a given revolution, because they already know (or imagine that they know) the laws of revolution in general. Thus armed, they do not need to waste time studying the facts. They merely apply their preconceived ideas and definitions to the facts, like a chemist who applies a litmus paper to a fluid. If the paper turns red it is an acid, if it turns blue it is an alkali.

Such a method is simple – *childishly* simple, in fact, and therefore *very suitable for little children*. Armed with such potent knowledge, the formalist can decide in advance whether to recognise the events in Venezuela (or any other country on the terrestrial globe) as a revolution or not. From the Olympian Heights, *they refuse to give the Venezuelan Revolution a birth certificate*. Fortunately, the revolution does not know about this excommunication and cares even less about it.

What is a revolution?

The weakness of the position of the sects in relation to Venezuela (insofar as they have even bothered to notice it) is that they base themselves on preconceived ideas as to what a revolution "*ought to be*" while betraying a complete ignorance of what revolution *is*.

What is a revolution? This self-evident question is rarely asked. But unless we ask and answer it, we shall never be in a position to determine what is now happening in Venezuela – or anywhere else. A revolution, as Trotsky explains in the *History of the Russian Revolution*, is a situation where the masses begin to take their destiny into their own hands. This is certainly the case in Venezuela now. The awakening of the masses and their active participation in politics is the most decisive feature of the Venezuelan Revolution and the secret of its success.

In the same Preface, Leon Trotsky – who, after all, knew a few things about revolutions – answers in the following way:

"*The most indubitable feature of a revolution is the direct interference of the masses in historical events*. In ordinary times the state, be it monarchical or democratic, elevates itself above the nation, and history is made by specialists in that line of business – kings, ministers, bureaucrats, parliamentarians, journalists. But at those crucial moments when the old order becomes no longer endurable to the masses, they break over the barriers excluding them from the political arena, sweep aside their traditional representatives, and create by their own interference the initial groundwork for a new regime. Whether this is good or bad we leave to the judgement of moralists. We ourselves will take the facts as they are given by the objective course of development. *The history of a revolution is for us first of all a history of the forcible entrance of the masses into the realm of rulership over their own destiny.*" (Leon Trotsky, *The History of the Russian Revolution*, Preface, my emphasis)

In normal periods the masses do not participate in politics. The conditions of life under capitalism place insurmountable barriers in their way: the long hours of labour, physical and mental tiredness, etc. Normally, people are content to leave the decisions affecting their lives to someone else: the local councillor, the professional politicians, the trade union official, etc.

However, at certain critical moments, the masses burst onto the scene of history, take their lives and destinies into their hands and become transformed from passive agents into the protagonists of the historical process. One would have to be particularly blind or obtuse not to see that this is precisely the situation that now exists in Venezuela. In recent years, but especially since the attempted coup of April 2002, millions of workers and peasants have been on the move, fighting to change society. If this is not a revolution, then we will never see one. Only the most woodenheaded sectarian could fail to understand this.

It is necessary to understand that the masses, whether in Venezuela or any other country, only learn gradually from their experience. The working class has to go through the experience of the revolution and the social crisis in order to distinguish between the different tendencies, programmes and leaders. It learns by a method of successive approximations. As Trotsky explains:

"The different stages of a revolutionary process, certified by a change of parties in which the more extreme always supersedes the less, express the growing pressure to the left of the masses — so long as the swing of the movement does not run into objective obstacles. When it does, there begins a reaction: disappointments of the different layers of the revolutionary class, growth of indifferentism, and therewith a strengthening of the position of the counter-revolutionary forces. Such, at least, is the general outline of the old revolutions." (Ibid.)

And he adds:

"Only on the basis of a study of political processes in the masses themselves, can we understand the role of parties and leaders, whom we least of all are inclined to ignore. They constitute not an independent, but nevertheless a very important, element in the process. Without a guiding organisation, the energy of the masses would dissipate like steam not enclosed in a piston-box. But nevertheless what moves things is not the piston or the box, but the steam." (Ibid.)

These remarks exactly fit the situation in Venezuela, where the movement of the masses from below constitutes the principal motor-force of the revolution. It is impossible to understand the process by confining oneself to an analysis of the leaders, their class origins, statements and programmes. This is really like the froth on the waves of the ocean, which are only a superficial reflection of the profound currents beneath the surface.

"The dynamic of revolutionary events is *directly* determined by swift, intense and passionate changes in the psychology of classes which have already formed themselves before the revolution." (Ibid.)

In the absence of a mass revolutionary Marxist party, the forces of revolution have gathered around Chávez and the Bolivarian movement. Hugo Chávez is the man at the centre of the storm. No matter what one thinks about this man, he has broken the dam and opened the floodgates. He alone has dared to confront the power of the oligarchy and defy the might of American imperialism. Even his declared enemies and critics cannot deny that he has shown colossal courage. And in giving a courageous example he has conjured up tremendous forces that have lain dormant in the depths of Venezuelan society for generations. This is a fact of tremendous importance.

For the first time in the almost 200 years history of Venezuela the masses *feel* that the government is in the hands of people who wish to defend their interests. In the past the government was always an alien power standing against them. They do not want to see the return of the old corrupt parties. The masses, the poor shanty town dwellers, the unemployed, the workers, the peasants, the Indians, the blacks, have been stirred out of their apathy and brought to their feet. They have discovered a new meaning in life, a new sense of human dignity, a new hope. Overnight, they have become Chavistas, although they do not understand very well what this means.

Maybe the masses have only the vaguest idea of what they really want, but they have a very clear idea of what they do not want. They do not want a return to the old order, the old parties and the old bourgeois leaders. They have had a taste of what it means to be free and they do not wish to return to the old slavery. With every fibre of their being, they yearn for a fundamental change in the conditions of their lives. For them, this is what Chavismo means. And this great dream of a change in their lives is summed up in their minds in one man – Hugo Chávez.

Many people are surprised with the fervour – almost a religious fervour – with which the masses regard their President. They would be ready to suffer hunger and poverty, to sacrifice all their possessions, to risk their lives (as they did two years ago) for him. This represents a tremendous power and explains how it is that Chávez has been able to defeat all attempts to overthrow him. The real secret of his success lies not within himself but in the masses, and it is the strength of the masses that determines the whole course of the revolution and is its fundamental motor-force.

Chávez's enemies on the right cannot understand the reason for this. They cannot understand it because they are organically incapable of understanding the dynamics of the revolution itself. The ruling class and its intellectual prostitutes can never accept that the masses have a mind and personality of their own, that they are a tremendously creative force that is capable not only of changing society but also of administering it. They can never admit such a thing because to do so would be to admit their own bankruptcy and confess that they are not a necessary and indispensable social agent endowed with a God-given right to rule, but a superfluous and parasitic class and a reactionary obstacle to progress.

Sectarians incapable of understanding

But it is not only the bourgeois enemies of the revolution who display a complete incapacity to understand the Venezuelan Revolution. Many on the Left (including so-called Marxists) have shown a similar inability to understand what is happening. Having proclaimed themselves the Leaders of the working class, they are mortified by the spectacle of the masses' enthusiastic support for Chávez and are mystified by it. They grumble in corners, mumbling something about *"populism"*, but show their complete inability to connect with the real movement of the masses. But then, that is the main feature of sectarians everywhere.

What none of these ladies and gentlemen have understood is the dialectical relation between Chávez and the masses. They have in common a formalistic and mechanistic approach to the revolution. They do not see it as a living process, full of contradictions and irregularities. It does not conform to their preconceived schemes of how a revolution ought to be, and therefore they turn their backs on it in disgust. They behave like the first European who saw a giraffe and exclaimed: "I don't believe it!"

Unfortunately for our formalistic friends, the revolution does not develop smoothly, it does not go according to any preconceived plan, it does not perform like a well-rehearsed orchestra following the conductor's baton. It follows its own rules and obeys its internal laws, laws that do not come from a revolutionary cookbook, but which are rooted in the contradictions of society that gradually work themselves out through the collective action of the masses themselves who do not learn from textbooks but through experience of the struggle and a painful process of trial and error.

"But Chávez is a bourgeois", they protest. These people always think in simplistic terms: black or white, yes or no, bourgeois or proletarian. Old Engels had this kind of formalistic mentality in mind when he quoted from the Bible: "Let thy communication be: Yea, yea, nay, nay, for whatsoever is more than these cometh of evil." Such demands for a clear-cut definition appear at first sight to be reasonable and wise. But it is not possible in all circumstances to demand clear-cut definitions.

Even as a sociological definition, the above characterisation is incorrect. The social background from which Hugo Chávez comes is not the bourgeoisie but rather the middle class. He calls himself a peasant. However, this does not exhaust the question from a Marxist point of view. The middle class is not a homogeneous class. In its upper layers, the wealthy lawyers, doctors and university professors, it stands close to the bourgeoisie and serves it. In its lower layers, the small shopkeepers, small peasants, the lower ranks of the intellectuals, it stands close to the working class and, under certain circumstances, can come over to the side of the socialist revolution.

However, the class origin of the leaders also is not conclusive when deciding the class nature of a particular party or movement. What ultimately determines the class nature of a political movement is its programme and policies, and its class basis. We can broadly describe the programme and policies of the Bolivarian movement as those of petty bourgeois revolutionary democracy. As such, it does not go beyond the limits of a very advanced bourgeois democracy. The revolution has carried out an ambitious programme of reforms in the interests of the masses, but has not yet abolished capitalism. This constitutes its major weakness and the greatest threat to its future.

The question of the state

"But the state is still bourgeois!" our formalistic friends insist. Insofar as the oligarchy has not yet been expropriated, insofar as a large part of the economic power remains in its hands, then Venezuela remains capitalist and we must define the class nature of the state accordingly. Moreover, a large part of the old bureaucracy remains in place: the judiciary has been inherited from before, the Metropolitan Police acts as a state within the state, the loyalty of sections of the middle officers is unclear. This means that a qualitative change has not yet taken place, and therefore the present situation can yet be reversed. However, this cannot be done without a ferocious conflict and civil war.

However, the general definition of the state as a bourgeois state tells us nothing about real class balance of forces or the concrete reality of the state, or the way in which the situation is moving. *In reality, the state in Venezuela is no longer controlled by the bourgeoisie*. That is why the oligarchy is obliged to resort to extra-legal and extra-parliamentary methods to regain control. The majority of the armed forces, including an important section of the officers, support the Revolution. This creates enormous problems for the counter-revolution and potentially favourable conditions for those who wish to carry the revolution through to the end.

Earlier we asked *what is a revolution*? It is necessary also to ask the question: *what is the state*? This question was answered long ago by Lenin (following Engels) when he said that the state, in the last analysis, is *armed bodies of men* – the army, the police, etc. In normal periods the state is controlled by the ruling class. But in exceptional periods, when the class struggle reaches a peak of intensity, the state can acquire a large degree of independence, lifting itself above society. That is the position now in Venezuela.

The final argument of the sectarians refers to the armed forces. *"We must not have anything to do with army officers."* This is really not an argument at all but only a stupid prejudice. The idea that it is not possible to win over the army to the side of revolution is absurd. If this were true, there could never have been a single revolution in the whole of history. But the army is made up of men and women in uniform and men and women can be influenced by the events in society. (To have to make such comments is rather embarrassing, but it seems that one can take nothing for granted nowadays.)

In every great revolution in history, the army is affected by the movement of the masses. It tends to split on class lines. *If that were not the case, revolution in general would be impossible.* The revolutionary ferment affects not only the soldiers and NCOs but part of the officers. Under especially favourable circumstances, a large part of the officers can be affected and refuse to fight for the old regime or even pass over to the side of the revolution, like Tukhachevsky, who was a tsarist officer.

Moreover, it has happened more than once that a revolutionary movement first started at the top, with a revolt of a section of the officers, and then spread to the masses. This is particularly the case where the old regime was exposed as utterly corrupt and bankrupt. The history of Spain in the 19th century is full of such events, which were known as *pronunciamientos*, and which frequently opened the floodgates of revolution. However, there are more recent examples of the same process.

The Portuguese Revolution

The idea that the Bolivarian Revolution is absolutely unique is not correct. Of course, it has specific peculiarities, but it is far from being unique. As a matter of fact, every revolution has features that are common to all revolutions. If that were not the case, it would be impossible to learn anything useful from the study of past revolutions – but this is very far from the case. Exactly 30 years ago in Portugal we saw a remarkably similar process to the one in Venezuela at the present time.

After more than half a century of fascist rule, the people of Portugal overthrew the hated Caetano dictatorship and entered the road of revolution. How did this begin? It began as a coup carried out by left wing army officers. This is in complete contradiction to the normal situation, where the army officers almost always played a counter-revolutionary role. Here the opposite was the case. Ted Grant wrote in 1975:

"The real peculiarity of the Portuguese Revolution in comparison with any revolution of the past is the involvement of the mass of the lower and middle officers – and even some of the generals and admirals – in the revolution.

"If the powers of the state as Marx and Lenin have explained reduces itself to the control of armed bodies of men, then the decay of the Portuguese regime is shown in a naked form. The bourgeoisie staked all on the ultimate weapon of a ferocious and totalitarian repression of the masses. Over two generations, witnessing its consequences, the bourgeoisie lost its support also in the middle class and by contagion even in the greater part of the officer caste. The senseless war in Africa played its part but that is not the entire explanation. The even more lunatic massacre during the 1914-18 war did not lead the [Russian] officer caste in its overwhelming majority to abandon Tzarism. They did not hesitate to go over to the counter-revolution and support wars of intervention against their own country.

"In 1918 the German Revolution was opposed by the bulk of the officer caste. The counter-revolution of Hitler was supported by the overwhelming majority of the officers.

"In the Spanish Revolution of 1931-37, 99 percent of the officer caste went over to Franco. And to come nearer home, in 1926 the big majority of the officer caste supported Salazar.

"There has been a titanic swing of the political pendulum to the left. During the past three decades the petty bourgeoisie have swung left too – as the student movement demonstrates – and in Portugal the impasse of capitalism and the hatred of the cliques of monopoly capital, who coined money out of the blood and suffering of the people and the soldiers, has been reflected in the isolation of the very rich circles. They supported and benefited to the last moment from the totalitarian or authoritarian regime. The hatred of these odious parasites extended to layers of the officer caste. This is an indication that capitalism has worn out its historic mission and is becoming further and further a fetter on production. Thus in Portugal *even the general staff was split* as the episode of the unhappy Spinola demonstrates."

These lines could have been written yesterday – in relation to the Venezuelan Revolution. The Marxist tendency explained these phenomena decades ago, but they remain a closed book to all sectarians and formalists, who are therefore quite unable to understand the Venezuelan Revolution, let alone intervene in it. They are blinded by their own formalistic method that prevents them from seeing what is going on under their noses. They constantly refer to definitions and ready-made quotations from the Marxist classics ("*we must smash the old state*", etc.), which in their hands become transformed from scientific statements into *empty clichés* or *religious incantations*. Instead of helping us to understand the real process, they act as a barrier to understanding.

In his 1975 document on the Portuguese Revolution, Ted Grant wrote:

"Marx had written that in the heavy and apparently obscure writings of Hegel could be seen the revolution at a certain stage in history. Now the inventive genius of history had presented us with the spectacle of the revolution moving through the vehicle of military generals and admirals! This is because capitalism had exhausted itself in Portugal – a country semi-colonial and semi-imperialist – with no way forward after the loss of empire under capitalism. At the same time the road of open bourgeois military dictatorship has been utterly discredited with even sections of the military caste as the result of the 50-year experience of dictatorship.

"But the main reason for the enormous role of the military has been the paralysis of the workers organisations by the lack of a genuine Marxist party and Marxist leadership. In reality from the beginning of the revolution – *real power has been in the hands of the workers and soldiers* – the Armed Forces Movement has filled the vacuum caused by the failure of leadership of the SP and CP organisations."

Nature abhors a vacuum, it is said, and the same is true of society and politics. In the absence of a mass revolutionary Marxist party, other tendencies can and will fill the political vacuum under certain concrete conditions. But once the officers in Portugal had begun the process, once the floodgates were opened, the masses and the working class poured through them and set their stamp on the revolution. All the conditions existed for a peaceful revolution in Portugal, especially after the defeat of the reactionary coup of general Spinola in March 1975. This was very similar to the coup of 11th April in Venezuela, and it ended in the same way, as Ted explains:

"When there were mass demonstrations by the workers, the forces of the counter-coup melted away. The paratroopers and commandos are always the most conservative force in the Army, composed usually of the most adventurous and wild elements of the population, and usually an elite force of crack troops, the most reliable and the last to crack like the Cossacks in Russia. Now the paratroops assured the demonstrators 'we are no Fascists.' They fraternised with the workers and the troops of the Artillery Regiment. Some gave away their rifles to demonstrators as proof of their good faith.

"Within hours of the coup the air base had been taken over. Spinola and many of the clique of officers supporting him fled to Spain. The coup fizzled out. It could be reckoned in minutes rather than days. It is perhaps the most ludicrous and comic attempt at counter-revolution in history. *But it was a fiasco precisely because of the red hot atmosphere of revolution which affected not only the workers and peasants but practically the entire rank and file of the Armed Forces. There was not a single regiment in all Portugal which was willing to be used for the purpose of the counter-revolution.*"

Again, the same lines would apply exactly to Venezuela two years ago. One only has to change the names. As in Portugal, it would have been possible to carry out a peaceful transformation of society after the collapse of the coup. But this was not done, and a highly favourable opportunity was wasted. This fact, in itself, shows the need for a consistent revolutionary leadership with a clear strategy and line. Such errors will be paid for in the future and the bill will not be cheap.

Our sectarian friends will cry triumphantly: "This proves why we cannot trust the officers!" But it is not a question of trust. That is a moral category, not a scientific one. What is decisive is not the moral character of the leaders but the programme and policies. Many of the officers in Portugal were very honest men who sincerely sided with the masses. Many of them even wanted to carry through a profound social transformation in Portugal, but they did not know how to carry it out.

The real responsibility for the failure of the Portuguese Revolution lies, not with the left wing army officers, but with the reformist policies of the leaders of the Communist and Socialist Parties who between them wrecked the revolution. In passing we must add that the ultra left pseudo-Marxist sects also played a lamentable role and were incapable of providing an alternative for the workers and the radicalised officers who were, in fact, looking for one.

Crisis of capitalism

The reason why such developments can take place is the organic crisis of capitalism on a world scale. Twenty-nine years ago Ted Grant wrote:

"One of the key factors in the development of revolution is the demoralisation of the ruling class itself. Now in the decisive countries of capitalism, splits and fissures are opening up in the ruling class. They look with dread to the processes taking place in Europe and the World. The most powerful of all, the United States capitalists, who looked towards a century of world domination, and being the policeman of the colonial and capitalist countries, are as demoralised as the rest."

These lines are perfectly applicable to the present situation.

The world situation is characterised by a general turbulence. Far more than in 1974, there has been an accumulation of deep contradictions. This is certainly a period of upheavals, sharp changes and sudden turns in all continents and all countries. The capitalists are finding it extremely difficult to pull the world economy out of recession. Only the United States has experienced some kind of growth, and this is extremely fragile and based on consumer spending, credit and unprecedented debt.

On a world scale the capitalist system is in a deep crisis. There are many symptoms – wars, terrorism, political, social and diplomatic instability – but these are all manifestations of the central crisis. The apologists of Capital try to present this as a conjunctural crisis, a minor adjustment or "correction". It is no such thing. The convulsions we see everywhere are a reflection of the impasse that capitalism is in. At bottom, this expresses the revolt of the productive forces against the twin barriers of private ownership and the nation state.

The crisis expresses itself with special force in the former colonial countries of Asia, Africa and Latin America. They are all experiencing unprecedented convulsions – economic, financial, social and political. There is not a single stable bourgeois regime in the whole of Latin America.

If there existed powerful Marxist parties, the workers of Argentina, Bolivia, Peru, Ecuador, could have taken power easily in the last period. But no such parties exist. To the degeneration of the Second and Third Internationals, we must also add the total incapacity of those sectarian organisations that lay claim to the banner of Trotskyism, which have made all kinds of errors of both an opportunist and ultra-left character, and have long since abandoned any right to be taken seriously as a revolutionary force.

In the absence of a strong Marxist party, it was inevitable that the revolution in the underdeveloped capitalist countries would manifest itself in all manner of peculiar ways. This is the result of the delay in the socialist revolution in the advanced capitalist countries. The workers and peasants of Asia, Africa and Latin America cannot wait. They need to seek a solution for their most pressing problems now. And if there is no Marxist party ready to hand, they will have to seek some alternative. There is simply no answer to this logic.

In his theory of the Permanent Revolution, Trotsky explains that, under modern conditions, the tasks of the bourgeois-democratic revolution cannot be carried out without the expropriation of the bourgeoisie. The only way to save society from stagnation, hunger and misery was to abolish landlordism and capitalism. It was the impossibility of fully developing the forces of production under capitalism-landlordism which gave the drive to the colonial revolution. *On the road of capitalism there was no way forward.*

In the absence of a Marxist party, other forces can come to the fore. We saw this in Portugal in 1974-75 when a group of radicalised army officers overthrew the fascist dictator Caetano and opened the floodgates of revolution. In his article, comrade Ted writes:

"Consequently, because the development of productive forces is hampered by the elements of capitalism and big business which are subordinate to, and collaborators of, imperialism, they are swept away. In a twisted version of the permanent revolution this lower officer caste becomes – for a period – the unconscious agent of history, in carrying through the necessary tasks of the statification of the economy."

Of course, this statement flies in the face of the idea, which in certain "Marxist" groups has become a prejudice something like the Arc of the Covenant for orthodox Jews or the doctrine of Papal Infallibility for devout Catholics, to the effect that army officers are inevitably reactionary and that all military coups are right wing. If we set out from these simple propositions, then not only Chávez, but also the leaders of the Portuguese Revolution, stand condemned in advance. Alas! History is not so simple that it can be made to fit into such neat patterns. However, to adapt an old English proverb, simple things please simple minds.

The Portuguese Revolution went very far. In fact, *The Times* of London even published an editorial article with the title: Capitalism is dead in Portugal. This should have been the case. Under the pressure of the working class the Armed Forces Movement nationalised the banks and insurance companies, which in practice meant nationalising about 80 percent of the economy. Unfortunately, the gains of the revolution were undermined by the leaders of the Socialist and Communist Parties, and the whole situation was lost.

Now we are seeing a similar phenomenon in Venezuela. For generations, the people of Venezuela were misruled by bourgeois parties that represented the interests of the oligarchy and imperialism. Then in 1996 they found they had an alternative in the shape of a new political movement – the Bolivarian movement formed by Hugo Chávez. Chávez's programme was a modest one: against corruption, for reforms, etc. But it immediately brought him into conflict with the oligarchy and imperialism.

What we are witnessing in Venezuela is a peculiar variant of the theory of the Permanent Revolution. *It is impossible to consolidate the gains of the revolution within the limits of the capitalist system. Sooner or later, the choice will have to be made: either the revolution liquidates the economic power of the oligarchy, expropriates the bankers and capitalists and moves in the direction of socialism, or the oligarchy and imperialism will liquidate the revolution.*

Chávez and the masses

In a situation when the old order is in a deep crisis, when there is clearly no way out except a fundamental change, but where there is no mass revolutionary party, all kinds of peculiar variants are possible. Under such circumstances, a revolutionary ferment can reach the most unexpected quarters. We have already pointed out that to characterise Hugo Chávez as a bourgeois is sociologically inexact. But even if it were true, it would not automatically rule out an evolution in the direction of socialist revolution and a proletarian policy. Let us again call the founder of scientific socialism to our aid. In the *Communist Manifesto* Marx writes the following:

"Finally, in times when the class struggle nears the decisive hour, the progress of dissolution going on within the ruling class, in fact within the whole range of old society, assumes such a violent, glaring character, that a small section of the ruling class cuts itself adrift, and joins the revolutionary class, the class that holds the future in its hands. Just as, therefore, at an earlier period, a section of the nobility went over to the bourgeoisie, so now a portion of the bourgeoisie goes over to the proletariat, and in particular, a portion of the bourgeois ideologists, who have raised themselves to the level of comprehending theoretically the historical movement as a whole." (Marx and Engels, *Manifesto of the Communist Party, Bourgeois and Proletarians*)

How clearly Marx expressed himself! To anyone who has really absorbed the method of Marx, as opposed to repeating mechanically a few undigested clichés, what is happening in Venezuela presents no great difficulty. Nor is it the first time that we have witnessed similar phenomena. A few days ago our website reproduced Ted Grant's article *The Iberian Revolution, Marxism and the Historical Development of The International Situation* written in May 1975. It commences with the following words:

"Marxism would be a very simple theory if all that was necessary was a slavish repetition of the ideas of the past. Sectarians and opportunists of all the different cliques and sects ignore the methods and principles, which retain their validity and from which invaluable lessons can be drawn from the works of the great teachers. They repeat a few phrases gleaned from the past, which they think, turn them into brilliant strategists. The works of Marx, Engels, Lenin and Trotsky form a precious heritage and we must encourage young comrades to study them assiduously. But they do not provide blueprints for the process of history."

The acid test for revolutionaries is their attitude to revolution. The pseudo-Trotskyist sects were completely incapable of orienting and re-orienting to the development of events. They do not understand that without a Marxist party all kinds of things are possible. As Ted correctly said of these self-styled "Trotskyist" cliques: "They have become more and more remote, with not the slightest possibility of becoming mass working class organisations."

The reaction between the objective and subjective factors in history is a highly complex and contradictory one. Only the dialectical method can help us unravel the contradictions of the situation in Venezuela. In the absence of a genuine Marxist current, other trends inevitably make their appearance. And to the degree that the working class does not take the lead, other classes come to the fore. This is really not so difficult to understand!

The relationship between Hugo Chávez and the masses is a very complex and dialectical one. I had occasion to see this for myself when I attended the mass rally on 12th April in the centre of Caracas. There was no mistaking the colossal enthusiasm and devotion they show. But the secret of this is not to be found in Chávez's personality, but in class relations. The masses see themselves reflected in Chávez. They identify themselves with him as the man who first awakened them to political life and who has given voice to their aspirations. They personify the Revolution in him. For them, Hugo Chávez and the revolution is one and the same thing.

Of course, one thing is the perception of the masses, and another thing is the objective logic of events. In a revolution events move with lightening speed, and the leadership finds it difficult to keep up with the furious pace of events. The pendulum swings steadily to the left for a whole period. All parties, tendencies, programmes and individuals are put to the test. That is why the progress of the revolution is marked by the rise and fall of leaders and parties, in which the more radical wing tends to displace the more moderate elements.

The whip of the counter-revolution

The masses do not go into a revolution with a prepared plan of social reconstruction, but with a sharp feeling that they cannot endure the old regime. The first stages of the revolution are inevitably characterised by a confused and incoherent outlook. There is a sense of euphoria, of triumph, and of an irresistible advance. This is accompanied by the idea of unity, that "we are all together" in a kind of universal march towards freedom and social justice.

However, this is an illusion. The revolution inevitably comes up against the barriers of the existing social order and the existing institutions. This leads to clashes. Every action provokes an equal and opposite reaction – this law holds good for revolutions as well as elementary mechanics. Chávez's victory at the polls did not signify a social revolution, but it completely upset the old order and produced a general social ferment. The oligarchy, realising that they could not bribe or pressurise Chávez, decided to remove him by force. This led directly to the counter-revolutionary coup of 11th April 2002.

Exactly two years ago the counter-revolutionary forces of the Venezuelan oligarchy staged a coup with the backing of right wing army officers. Chávez was arrested and a "democratic dictatorship" was proclaimed. But the masses rose up with their bare hands and overthrew a reactionary government, preparing the way for a new advance of the revolution. And once again the masses were joined by the revolutionary section of the army. The reaction collapsed like a house of cards in 48 hours.

Marx pointed out that *the revolution needs the whip of the counter-revolution to advance*. In Venezuela every counter-revolutionary attempt has served to provoke a colossal movement of the masses that has swept all before it. On each occasion the mood of the masses has become harder, more determined and more militant. The demand for decisive action to finish off the counter-revolutionaries once and for all is becoming louder and more insistent: "*Mano dura!*" ("Give it to them!") – this is the call from below.

After the defeat of the coup it would have been possible to carry out a socialist revolution swiftly and painlessly. Unfortunately, the opportunity was lost and the reactionaries were allowed to regroup and organise a new attempt in the so-called strike (in reality a bosses' lockout) that did serious damage to the economy. The new attempt was defeated by the workers, who seized control of the factories and oil installations and kicked out the reactionaries. Once again the possibility existed of a radical transformation without civil war. And once again the opportunity was lost.

The situation is now completely polarised to the left and the right. A gaping abyss has opened up between antagonistic classes: rich and poor, *Chavistas* and *Escualidos*, revolutionaries and counter-revolutionaries, face each other in a state of permanent hostility. Society lives in a state of constant alarms and agitation. The air is thick with rumours of coups, conspiracies, foreign aggression. The atmosphere is electric, as before a thunderstorm. Sooner or later the storm must break.

The masses are learning quickly in the school of the revolution. They are drawing their conclusions. The main conclusion is that the revolutionary process must be pushed forward, it must confront its enemies and sweep all obstacles aside. This burning desire of the masses, however, is coming up against the resistance of those conservative and reformist elements who are constantly urging caution, and who, in practice, want to put the brakes on the revolution. The destiny of the Revolution depends on the solution of this contradiction.

The revolution in danger

The Venezuelan Revolution is now faced with a stark choice. The revolution is surrounded by enemies, both internally and externally, who are striving to overthrow it. In order to defeat the forces of counter-revolution, a clear programme and policy is needed. This can only be provided by the Marxist tendency.

The Venezuelan Revolution now stands at the crossroads. The masses have defeated reaction on three occasions in the last two years. But the forces of reaction have not been decisively defeated. The oligarchy continues to control key points of the economy and is constantly intriguing against the revolution. Washington is actively participating in these counter-revolutionary intrigues. Bush has declared that he will not rest until Chávez is overthrown. Recently an American general stated publicly that Venezuela represents a threat to the United States. All these are danger signals.

US imperialism is bogged down in Iraq. This makes it difficult for it to stage a direct military intervention in Venezuela, even on the scale of its Haitian adventure. But it has many other options. It is attempting to get the Organisation of American States (OAS) to organise a blockade of Venezuela, along the lines of the blockade of Cuba. So far, this has not succeeded. But there is a more urgent threat from neighbouring Colombia.

US imperialism wants to use Colombia as a base for its operations in Latin America. Under the pretext of a "war on drugs", Washington has poured arms, money and "military advisers" into Colombia.* This has completely upset the military balance in the region. The monstrous Colombia Plan is a disguise for imperialist intervention on a massive scale. This represents a grave threat to the Venezuelan Revolution. Just before he was ejected by the Spanish people, Aznar agreed to send a large shipment of tanks to Colombia. Since tanks are useless for an anti-guerrilla struggle, this move can only have one interpretation: the tanks are intended for use against a neighbouring state. The name of that state is Venezuela.

In recent months evidence has been accumulating of the activities of Colombian right wing paramilitary groups on Venezuelan soil. These are the notorious fascist death squads that for decades have been killing, torturing and terrorising the population with the covert support of the state and the Colombian armed forces. They are now acting as the hired mercenaries of the CIA. Their objective is the assassination of Hugo Chávez and the organising of violent provocations to justify an armed conflict between Venezuela and Colombia.

We have explained in previous articles that US imperialism is preparing to organise some kind of provocation on the border with Colombia. After the ignominious collapse of its referendum campaign, the internal opposition is in disarray, with one of its components breaking away, accusing the others of plotting another coup, and so on. The revolution is in danger. But as in the Great French Revolution of the 18th century, so in Venezuela today, the external threat can serve to push the revolution still further.

* Zapatero, the new Prime Minister cancelled the sale.

Class balance of forces

The class balance of forces inside Venezuela is still extremely favourable for carrying out a classical proletarian revolution. What is required is an energetic application of the united front policy. This by no means signifies either the dissolution of the workers' movement or the dissolution of the Marxist wing into a general "people's front." It means only that the working class and its vanguard is duty bound to enter into a fighting agreement with the revolutionary petty bourgeoisie, the poor peasants, the urban poor, and all other revolutionary elements in the population for an all-out struggle against imperialism and the oligarchy.

Does such a policy enter into contradiction with the aim of a socialist revolution? Only a hopeless doctrinaire would say so. Such a person has not the slightest idea what the socialist revolution is. Let us refer to Lenin on this subject:

"The socialist revolution is not one single act, not one single battle on a single front; but a whole epoch of intensified class conflicts, a long series of battles on all fronts, i.e., battles around all the problems of economics and politics, which can culminate only in the expropriation of the bourgeoisie. It would be a fundamental mistake to suppose that the struggle for democracy can divert the proletariat from the socialist revolution, or obscure, or overshadow it, etc. On the contrary, just as socialism cannot be victorious unless it introduces complete democracy, so the proletariat will be unable to prepare for victory over the bourgeoisie unless it wages a many-sided, consistent and revolutionary struggle for democracy." (*The Socialist Revolution and the Right of Nations to Self-Determination*, Jan-Feb., 1916.)

What do these lines mean? The socialist revolution is unthinkable without the day-to-day struggle for the improvement of the position of the working class and the exploited masses. Only in such a struggle can the proletariat gather and weld together the mass forces necessary to carry out the socialist transformation of society. This includes not only the struggle for higher wages, a reduction of the working day, more houses, hospitals and schools, etc., but also the struggle for democracy. In the course of this struggle, the working class has the opportunity to win the leadership and to place itself at the head of the nation. Without it, this will never be possible in a thousand years.

In Venezuela the secret of success is the militant unity of the socialist proletariat with the revolutionary democracy – the poor peasants, urban poor, and the revolutionary petty bourgeoisie in general. The enemies of the revolution constantly strive to break this unity. The Marxists strive to maintain it. But this does not signify that we must accept the leadership of the petty bourgeoisie or sink our differences with it. To use the Spanish expression – "*juntos pero no revueltos*" – "together but not mixed up."

The Bolivarian movement is not a monolithic Stalinist party, but essentially a broad movement of the masses, in which there are different currents and tendencies. The left wing, reflecting the revolutionary aspirations of the masses, wishes to press forward with the revolution, overcome the resistance of the oligarchy and arm the people. The right wing (reformists and social democrats), in practice, wishes to call a halt to the revolution, or at least to slow it down and arrive at a compromise with the oligarchy and imperialism.

In reality, the latter option does not exist. There is no compromise possible with the enemies of the revolution, any more than oil can be mixed with water. The whole logic of the situation is moving in the direction of an open confrontation between the classes. Upon the decision of this conflict the destiny of the revolution depends.

What attitude should the Marxists take in this concrete situation? Should we remain aloof, arguing that, since the revolution is "bourgeois", we should have nothing to do with it? But that would be equivalent to remaining neutral in the struggle between revolution and counter-revolution. *Such a position would be a betrayal of the revolution and the working class*. It would completely discredit any group or party that advocated it. They would be considered – with every justification – deserters and traitors.

To those who constantly remind us that the Marxists and the working class must retain their independence, we answer: You are reminding us of the ABCs of Marxism. We are grateful for this reminder, but we also wish to point out that after the ABC there are many more letters in the alphabet. It is of course necessary for the proletariat to maintain its class independence at all times and under all circumstances. That is why we call upon the workers of Venezuela to strengthen and build their class organisations – the trade unions, the factory committees, workers' control, etc.

The same basic principle holds good for the Marxist tendency. We are for collaboration with other tendencies in the revolutionary movement – but the prior condition is: no mixing up of banners, programmes or ideas. We must at all times maintain the ideas, programme and policies of Marxism and fight for them within the broad movement. That is to say, the only correct position is:

1) Unconditional defence of the Venezuelan Revolution against the oligarchy and imperialism.

2) Critical support for the revolutionary democracy and Hugo Chávez against the oligarchy and imperialism.

3) Within the general mass movement (the Bolivarian movement) we support the left wing against the reformists and social democrats.

4) Within the left wing the Marxists will defend their ideas, policies and programme and fight to win the majority by example, work, and the superiority of

our ideas.

5) Within the broad movement, we will fight to build strong independent organisations of the proletariat and extend their influence, beginning with the unions.

The need for a Marxist party

"We must build the party! We must build the party!" the sectarians repeat like a drunken parrot. But when asked how exactly the Venezuelan Marxists are supposed to build the party, the parrots suddenly fall silent. "Why, by *declaring* it, of course!" This is quite amusing. So three men and a dog (or a drunken parrot) gather in a café in Caracas and proclaim the revolutionary party. Good. What then? "We call on the masses to join us!" Excellent. And what if the masses do not join you, preferring to remain in their mass Bolivarian organisations? "Well, that's *their* problem!"

These tremendously "clever" people who imagine that the participation of Marxists in the Bolivarian movement represents the abandonment of the struggle for a revolutionary Marxist party *merely show that they have not the slightest idea of how such a party will be built – either in Venezuela or in any other country*. In this proposition there is not an atom of liquidationism or opportunism, but only an application of the genuine methods of Marx, Engels, Lenin and Trotsky. Let us quote a famous passage from the founding document of our movement, the *Communist Manifesto*. In the section Proletarians and Communists we read:

"In what relation do the Communists stand to the proletarians as a whole? The Communists do not form a separate party opposed to the other working-class parties.

"They have no interests separate and apart from those of the proletariat as a whole.

"They do not set up any sectarian principles of their own, by which to shape and mould the proletarian movement.

"The Communists are distinguished from the other working-class parties by this only:

"(1) In the national struggles of the proletarians of the different countries, they point out and bring to the front the common interests of the entire proletariat, independently of all nationality.

"(2) In the various stages of development which the struggle of the working class against the bourgeoisie has to pass through, they always and everywhere represent the interests of the movement as a whole.

"The Communists, therefore, are on the one hand practically, the most advanced and resolute section of the working-class parties of every country, that section which pushes forward all others; on the other hand, theoretically, they have over the great mass of the proletariat the advantage of clearly understanding the lines of march, the conditions, and the ultimate general results of the proletarian movement."

One would have thought that this was clear enough for a child of average intelligence to understand. Unfortunately, there are some very "clever" Marxists who do not possess this level of intelligence. Having perused the writings of some self-styled Marxists, Karl Marx once protested that if this was Marxism, he was no Marxist. We know just how he must have felt. But Marx, Engels, Lenin and Trotsky really should not be blamed for the nonsense written in their name, any more than Jesus Christ should be blamed for Venezuelan bishops.

The logic of this position was long ago described by Shakespeare in his play *Henry IV, Part One*, when the Welshman Owain Glyndower, a man with a lot of courage but mystical tendencies, tries to convince the prosaic Englishman Hotspur of his magic powers:

G: "I can call spirits from the vasty deep."

H: "Why so can I, and so can any man. But will they come when you do call for them?"

The proposition that it is possible to build a serious revolutionary party in Venezuela outside the mass movement is impossible to take seriously. We prefer to base ourselves on the methods worked out by Marx and Engels over 150 years – methods that, like all the fundamental ideas of Marxism, retain all their validity today. It is absolutely necessary to unite the forces of Marxism with the mass movement.

The working class must at all times preserve and build its own class organisations, its unions, factory committees, etc. At the same time it will work to build a mass movement that encompasses the widest layers of the non-proletarian and semi-proletarian masses. The Marxist wing of the movement will maintain its full political independence – its own papers, magazines, books and leaflets – and full freedom to defend its point of view. It will loyally work to build the movement and to draw in the widest layers of workers and youth, at the same time as it fights to win over the advanced elements to its programme, policies and ideas.

We do not seek to impose ourselves on the movement. We do not present it with ultimatums. Our aim is to build it, to strengthen it, to push it forwards and at the same time to arm the leading layer with the necessary ideas, programme and policy that can lead to the defeat of the oligarchy and imperialism and clear the way for the socialist transformation of society, for, as Lenin explains, a consistent fight for democracy will inevitably lead to the expropriation of the oligarchy and the transformation of the democratic revolution into a socialist revolution.

At present, this view may be a minority view. That does not worry us. We will accept that we are a minority and act accordingly. But we will continue to advocate the expropriation of the oligarchy and the arming of the masses as the only guarantee of the salvation of the revolution, and events will prove us right. We will defend our ideas, and we invite all other tendencies to do the same. Only Stalinists and bureaucrats fear open debate. Marxists and honest revolutionary democrats do not.

We stand firmly on the basis of the movement of the revolutionary masses. On the basis of their experience the masses will learn the correctness of our ideas, slogans and programme. That is the only road to success! We will leave the final word to that grand old man of Marxism, that remarkable theoretician, Ted Grant, who wrote the following about the mass organisations:

"From within their ranks, among the working class fighters will come the forces of Marxism-Leninism. Outside of the mass organisations nothing of lasting substance will be created."

Chapter Seven

Foxes and Grapes –
Sectarian stupidity and the
Venezuelan Revolution

London, July 23rd, 2004

One hot summer's day a Fox was strolling through an orchard till he came to a bunch of Grapes just ripening on a vine which had been trained over a lofty branch. "Just the thing to quench my thirst," says he. Drawing back a few paces, he took a run and a jump, and just missed the bunch. Turning round again with a One, Two, Three, he jumped up, but with no greater success. Again and again he tried after the tempting morsel, but at last had to give it up, and walked away with his nose in the air, saying: "I am sure they are sour."

Aesop, *The Fox and the Grapes*

The attitude to revolution is the acid test for revolutionaries. Yet surprisingly many of those who call themselves Marxists have proved organically incapable of understanding the Venezuelan Revolution or intervening in it. Two years ago, when the attempted coup against the Chávez government was defeated by the revolutionary movement of the masses, the response of most of the Left internationally was a deafening silence. They had nothing to say. Apparently, they could not even find Venezuela on the map.

This should not surprise us. The sectarian groups that are always fiddling and fussing on the fringes of the workers' movement in all countries are far too busy constructing mass revolutionary parties of two men and a dog to bother their head about the real movement of the working class, whether in Venezuela or anywhere else.

So it is a matter of some surprise when all of a sudden these ladies and gentlemen wake up and begin shouting about the Venezuelan Revolution. Well, not exactly about the Venezuelan Revolution, but rather about the terrible crimes of Alan Woods and *Marxist.com* in relation to the Venezuelan Revolution. For such groups, you see, the real movement of the working class is not very interesting. Instead, they spend every minute of their lives studying the websites of other left groups to see where they can attack them.

Instead of attacking the reactionaries, capitalists and imperialists, it is far more interesting to spend one's time attacking the real enemy – other groups on the Left. It reminds people of the famous scene in the film *The Life of Brian*, where one small group is obsessed with fighting another. Such groups are really only fit to be laughed at, although their publications are far inferior to a Monty Python film script. In and of itself they are of no interest. But unfortunately it gives Marxism and, sad to say, particularly Trotskyism, such a bad name among honest workers and youth everywhere.

The Marxist tendency has many enemies: the hungry wolves of imperialism and capitalism and their reformist allies in the labour movement. These are serious enemies, and most of our time is taken up fighting them. Then there are the sects, who run after us barking and snapping at our heels like a little dog. Normally we just ignore them. But occasionally – very occasionally – we are obliged to deliver a well-aimed kick to rid ourselves (at least for a while) of a small irritation.

In recent weeks, certain sections of the sectarian fraternity have been whipping themselves into a fury (they must always be furious about something) about Alan Woods' visit to Caracas and meeting with President Chávez. This has sent them into a paroxysm of rage. They see such actions as a betrayal of the working class, socialism and the revolution. Around this incident they have erected a whole mythology. Of course, they have plenty of time for such activities, which serve as a substitute for serious work.

What are the facts? Alan Woods, the editor of the British Marxist magazine *Socialist Appeal* and *Marxist.com*, was invited to attend an international forum in solidarity with the Venezuelan Revolution last April. No conditions of any sort were attached to this invitation. The author of these lines had complete freedom to defend his point of view – the point of view of revolutionary Marxism – before a large and very varied audience, including workers, trade unionists and revolutionaries from all over Latin America.

I did not hesitate to accept. I have no reason to regret this decision, which opened many possibilities for the revolutionary Marxist tendency throughout Latin America. As a matter of fact, I believe that we had no right to refuse such an offer. None of the groups that are now frothing at the mouth about this visit were invited to this meeting. This is the main reason for their fit of indignation. In the hypothetical event of their having received such an invitation, would they have accepted? We shall never know. But it does not matter, because, anyway, we all know from Aesop that the grapes were sour.

Now the question arises: why was Alan Woods invited and his critics not? The reason is not hard to find. We were invited because, unlike our sectarian friends, *we have actively intervened in the Venezuelan Revolution from the very beginning.* Our articles, which have put a consistent Marxist and revolutionary case, have been widely circulated inside Venezuela. Our ideas are well known in revolutionary circles and have had a certain impact. What echo have the ideas of our critics had in Venezuela? None at all. But then, it is difficult for a *deafening silence* to have any echo of any kind.

Now at long last, they have found a voice. They have purchased a school atlas and discovered that there is a country called Venezuela. Ah well, better late than never! But the purpose of this sudden interest in geography is not to intervene in the Venezuelan Revolution. No! It is to attack Alan Woods and the comrades of the Revolutionary Marxist Current, who are actively striving to build a Marxist tendency in Venezuela.

Marxism and sectarianism

What are we accused of? It seems that *In Defence of Marxism* and *Socialist Appeal* are so enamoured with the "Bolivarian Revolution" in Venezuela to the extent that we provided a "Marxist" gloss for pro-Chávez politics. The fact that our friends place the revolution in inverted commas already tells us a great deal about where they are coming from. In common with all the other sects *they refuse to acknowledge the existence of a revolution in Venezuela.* That is their starting point.

We have already dealt with this in the article *Marxists and the Venezuelan Revolution.* In this article we pointed out that, as Trotsky explained, the essential feature of any real revolution is the active participation of the masses, which take the road of revolution, seeking a way out of the crisis. This is the decisive feature of the Venezuelan Revolution, and one that not one of the sects has understood. The magnificent movement of the Venezuelan workers, peasants and urban poor is an inspiration to the workers and youth of the whole world. They saved the revolution two years ago and they have been the main motive force ever since.

It is the elementary duty of Marxists to stand with the masses against imperialism and counter-revolution. Yes or no? To this the sectarian has no answer. He is too busy searching for sticks and stones to throw at the revolutionary Marxists to notice anything as trivial as the mass movement. Real Marxists, on the contrary, take their starting point from the mass movement, orient towards it, enter into a dialogue with its most advanced elements and try to win them over to a consistently revolutionary class line.

The sectarian is like a man who wishes to learn to swim by reading books about swimming. He learns all the strokes by heart and can give you a very complete lecture on the art of swimming, complete with diagrams on anatomy, equations on the resistance of the water, a thermometer to measure the correct temperature of the water, etc. But when the time comes to take the plunge, he suddenly turns away, complaining that the water is too cold, the conditions are not right and a hundred other reasons that prevent him from swimming.

However, when such a man sees someone actually swimming in the water, his indignation knows no bounds: "This is intolerable! That man is using the wrong stroke. In fact, he should not be swimming there at all. I should be there instead of him. I'm sure I could do this much better – *if only I could actually get into the water!"* Of course, such people will never actually learn to swim. But they will always give you the best possible advice on how it should be done and mercilessly criticise any perceived deviation from the correct style and stroke.

In an effort to discredit the Marxists, the sects have taken a lot of time reading every line of our articles on Venezuela. We are delighted to see such a degree of attention, and hope that our friends have learned something useful from all this reading. But, based on past experience, one is not too confident in this respect.

One of these critics, having read every dot and comma of my articles, ends up with a slight problem. He cannot find a single thing to criticise in what I have actually written, and is compelled to resort to the murky realms of psychoanalysis in order to find fault. It is quite amusing to read a "criticism" in which every other line says: "Alan is quite right to say this" and "Alan is quite right to say that" – but of course, "he does not really mean it". This is really scraping the bottom of the barrel!

Active intervention needed

If one is writing articles that hardly anybody reads – which is always the case with sects – you can afford to write anything that comes into your head. It really makes no difference – as with the articles of our critics. But the revolutionary Marxist tendency, which I have the honour of representing has been actively intervening in the movement of the masses in Venezuela, winning workers and youth, and building the Revolutionary Marxist Current. Our articles are read by a large number of activists every week. This means that we have to think carefully what we write. Our critics, on the other hand, are under no such constraints and can be as irresponsible as they like.

We have always taken a firm and principled stand in relation to the Venezuelan Revolution from the beginning. We have never deviated a single millimetre from a consistent revolutionary class position. Nor can our critics quote a single line to show that we have. Right from the beginning we have pointed out that the Venezuelan revolution has begun, but it is not finished, and it cannot be finished until the power of the Venezuelan oligarchy is broken.

This means the expropriation of the land, banks and big industry under work-

ers' control and management. It means the arming of the people. It means the setting up of action committees linked up on a local, regional and national basis. It means that the working class must organise independently and strive to place itself at the head of the nation. And it means that the Marxist tendency must strive to win over the majority of the revolutionary movement.

We have explained this a thousand times. We have written it in articles and documents. I personally have defended these views in large public meetings in Venezuela, in a meeting of 200 leading activists of the Bolivarian Circles in Caracas, and on Venezuelan radio and television. Our views are widely known in Venezuela and internationally. They are posted on our website which receives an average of 20,000 successful page visits every day from all over the world.

It is frankly difficult to know what more we can do to explain our position. Yet our critics are not satisfied. Why are they not satisfied? Because, they say, *we are too friendly to Chávez.* They refer disdainfully to the interview that I had with Hugo Chávez, which they triumphantly point to as incontrovertible proof of "*betrayal*".

We would like to satisfy everybody, of course. But alas, this is not always possible. How can we satisfy our critics? What position do they advocate? *They would like us to denounce Chávez as a bourgeois Bonapartist!* This proposal shows just how far removed these people are from reality. It would immediately cut us off, not just from the masses, who are firmly behind Chávez, but also from the activists, most of whom remain loyal to Chávez, even if they have growing doubts and criticisms

The sects imagine that to criticise always means to *denounce*. That is why their articles and documents are always full of the most hysterical denunciations of everyone, except themselves. Every labour leader is described a traitor. Every strike will be betrayed before it has even begun, and so on and so forth. Hugo Chávez is a traitor (and this must be shouted from the rooftops). Alan Woods is a traitor. In fact, everyone is a traitor, except myself and the little sect to which I belong.

Not long ago I had a conversation with a religious fanatic who assured me that on the Day of Judgement, only the members of his particular group (I cannot remember which sect it was) were destined to go to Heaven. I pointed out that therefore everyone else in the world would go to Hell, and that, this being the case, the outlook for several billion men, women and children was rather bleak. To this, he merely shrugged his shoulders. It seemed to me he did not even understand what I was saying.

One has a similar feeling when reading the material of the political sects. They have a similar psychology. No doubt they feel much better after having verbally abused everyone else. They can then retire to bed with a splendid feeling of superiority and not a care in the world. However, this kind of thing alienates honest workers and fills them with disgust. It is not the method of Marxism but only a crude caricature that serves to discredit Marxism. It is completely counterproductive. The workers are alienated by these tactics, which actually serve to drive them into the arms of the very leaders they have denounced.

We have not and will not adopt such tactics. *It is necessary to distinguish Marxism from other trends in the mass movement, but this is not done by bawling and shouting insults.* Our criticism has a political character and is posed in a positive way. We follow the advice of Karl Marx, who, when he had to work with the English reformist trade union leaders on the General Council of the First International, said that he was always "*mild in manner but bold in content.*"

Our method is not the shrill denunciations of the sects but that which Lenin advocated in 1917 – patiently explain! That is the real method of Bolshevism. That is the only way to proceed, whether in Venezuela or anywhere else.

Tactics in ex-colonial countries

Our critics object, in principle, to my meeting with Chávez and our friendly attitude to the Chavista movement. It would be impossible for a serious Marxist to pose the question in this way. Such an attitude would be a complete violation of everything that Lenin and Trotsky ever wrote on the colonial revolution. Lenin and Trotsky explained that in colonial and semi-colonial countries it was an absolute obligation of the Marxists to support anti-imperialist movements, to enter into contact with them, to establish militant agreements with them and to try to push them to the left, while simultaneously working to build up the independent forces of the proletariat.

Of course, in participating in a united front the prior condition is that the proletarian tendency must at all times retain complete organisational and political independence. It must retain the freedom of criticism. Lenin explained that when one is fighting alongside allies, it is necessary always to keep one eye on the enemy and the other eye on the ally, who at any time can break ranks and leave you in the lurch. All that is true and is really ABC for the Marxists.

In general, the class relations in semi-colonial nations are more complex than in the advanced capitalist countries. Side by side with the proletariat there are a large number of petty bourgeois and semi-proletarian layers, peasants, unemployed, street vendors, shantytown dwellers, etc. In order to prepare the conditions for the socialist revolution, it is necessary for the proletariat not only to develop its own independent organisations, but also to establish firm links with these layers and to impel them in a revolutionary direction. Without such work, the proletarian revolution would be only an empty phrase.

In Venezuela the overwhelming mass of these layers (and the big majority of the working class) are Chavistas. If the Venezuelan Marxists are not to be condemned to complete isolation and impotence, they must work to establish links with the Bolivarian movement, to push it to the left and try to win it to the policies and programme of Marxism.

"But this means winning over the rank and file, not the leaders!" This argument of the sects is as false as everything else they write. The masses in Venezuela follow their leaders and have faith in them. They are not yet convinced of the ideas of the Marxists. That will come from their experience, and we have to patiently go through their experiences with them, patiently explaining what is necessary at each stage.

The idea that it is possible to separate the masses from their leaders by simple denunciations and ultimatums is foolish in the extreme. It is the notorious "theory" put forward by the German Stalinists in their ultra-left phase in the early 1930s of the so-called united front from below, which Trotsky firmly rejected. They said to the Social Democratic workers: "We invite you to join us in a united front, but your leaders are all bourgeois traitors, so you must leave them behind." It does not require much imagination to know how the Social Democratic workers reacted to this offer.

When our critics object to my meeting with Chávez and our joint work with the Chavistas, what are they trying to say? Are they saying that it is impermissible in principle for Marxists to enter into a dialogue with the leaders of a revolutionary democratic movement in a semi-colonial country, standing at the head of millions of workers, peasants and poor people? Are we saying that in a semi-colonial country, it is impermissible for Marxists to form a united front with such people, to enter into a militant agreement for the purpose of the struggle against imperialism and the oligarchy? This is really the height of childishness.

The Marxists do not advance the united front as a manoeuvre or a trick to fool the masses, but as an honest proposal for joint activities to achieve an agreed aim, such as the struggle against imperialism. We agree that this is necessary, and we will participate in each and every activity that contributes to the success of the anti-imperialist struggle. But we point out that the only way to defeat imperialism and consolidate the gains of the (bourgeois democratic) Bolivarian revolution is by expropriating the oligarchy. That is to say, we maintain that the only way to achieve the tasks of the bourgeois democratic revolution in Venezuela is by transferring power to the working class, in alliance with the poor peasants and the urban poor.

We have maintained this position consistently from the beginning, and have advocated it from every available platform. It goes without saying that most of the work of the Venezuelan Marxists is at rank-and-file level. But where it is possible to put forward our arguments to the leaders of the Bolivarian movement –

including Hugo Chávez – we will not hesitate to do so.

Our attitude to Chávez

Trotsky said that the colonial revolution can throw up some outstanding leaders, and Hugo Chávez is one of these leaders. That is why the imperialists have bent all their energies to removing him. In the referendum campaign, the Venezuelan Marxists are fighting shoulder to shoulder with our Bolivarian comrades to defeat the counter-revolutionary opposition. We defend Chávez because his removal by the reactionaries would deal a shattering blow against the revolutionary forces in Venezuela and all Latin America. This is a concrete example of the united front in action.

But does this mean that there are *no differences* between Hugo Chávez and the Marxists? This does not follow at all, and we have never said such a thing. In the course of our conversation, Chávez told me that he was not a Marxist. I told him that I was. The standpoint of Hugo Chávez is that of petty-bourgeois revolutionary democracy. That of Marxism is proletarian revolution.

Under the specific conditions of the Venezuelan Revolution – the starting point of which is the struggle against imperialism, for national self-determination, for the right of the Venezuelan people to own and control their own natural resources and decide their own destiny without outside interference – it is both possible and necessary for these two trends to collaborate. But the differences remain, and must be settled one way or another in the future.

Insofar as the revolutionary democracy fights against imperialism, we can and must work with it and try to push it to the left, while building an independent revolutionary proletarian current. But by their very nature, even the best of the revolutionary democrats will tend to compromise and halt halfway. They do not have a clear class vision of the anti-imperialist struggle and try to unite "the nation" on the basis of a programme which, despite its radical aspects, does not go beyond the capitalist system.

This is the fatal weakness of petty-bourgeois revolutionary democracy, and one that ultimately can lead to surrender to the oligarchy and imperialism. That danger is clearly present now. However, this outcome is not set in stone. The dynamics of the Venezuelan Revolution is determined above all by the balance of class forces. The magnificent movement of the masses has intervened at each decisive stage to defeat the counter-revolution and push the revolution forward. We must base ourselves on the mass movement, on the unerring revolutionary instincts of the workers, peasants and urban poor, and attempt to give a clear organisational and political form to these instincts.

"Woods was received by President Chávez for a private audience that lasted well over an hour", growl our critics. Yes, that is true, and that fact reveals something, does it not? *It shows that the Marxist tendency is taken seriously in Venezuela, in a way that other groups are not. It shows that the Hands off Venezuela campaign has earned us respect, which others have not earned and do not deserve.*

Let us be clear. The task of building the forces of Marxism takes place not at the top but in the rank and file, where the Revolutionary Marxist Current is working very successfully. But that does not mean that it is incorrect to enter into contacts with the leaders of the Bolivarian movement, to open a dialogue with them and, to the degree that it is possible, to attempt to influence them. To what degree such discussions will have an effect it is impossible to say. That will depend, not on conversations, but on the class balance of forces and the way the revolution develops.

A lot of fuss has been made about what was really a very limited contact between the leader of the Bolivarian Revolution and the editor of *Marxist.com*. It has even been suggested that I have become (or aspire to become) one of the President's advisers. I believe the President has plenty of advisers – not all of whom are giving him the best advice, it is true. I have received no invitation to join this team, and do not expect to receive one. Nor do I think that my influence over the President's actions amounts to much. Certainly, some of his recent speeches reflect influences that are very far distant from any opinions of mine.

Having made that clear, I am entitled to ask whether it is wrong in principle to attempt to influence the leaders of a revolutionary movement involving millions of workers and poor peasants. If anyone thinks so, I beg to differ. If it is possible to influence Chávez or any other leader of the Bolivarian movement, we should certainly attempt to do so, as Lenin and Trotsky did on many occasions. *However, that is not our main task. Our main task is to work patiently at rank and file level, building the Marxist tendency. That must always be kept firmly in mind.*

There are different currents in the movement, which is far from homogeneous. In the last analysis, these currents reflect antagonistic class interests. It is necessary to adopt a careful attitude to the different tendencies in the Bolivarian movement. The leadership is under the pressure of imperialism and the opposition, and one wing – the reformist wing – reflects that pressure. But there is also powerful pressure from the rank and file of the movement, from the workers and peasants, and that finds a reflection in the left wing.

There is a sharp conflict at the top of the Bolivarian movement between the right wing, Social Democratic, reformist tendency, who are striving to halt the revolution and do a deal with the oligarchy and imperialism and the left wing Chavistas, who want to carry the revolution to the end. Hugo Chávez has sometimes reflected the pressures of the left wing and the masses. But at other times he has bent to the extreme pressure of the reformist wing. Everyone knows that it is not an easy thing to get to see the President, and that an audience of almost an hour and a half is almost unprecedented. It is also no secret that the reformist bureaucracy in the palace was very unhappy about this meeting and attempted to prevent it from taking place.

Was there any principled reason for not meeting the President? None at all. There were no conditions, and no restrictions on what could be said. It gave me an opportunity that few have had to form my own opinion about the man and his ideas. I later wrote about my impressions in *Encounters with Hugo Chávez*. This article was seized upon by the sects to "prove" that I have given an "unqualified endorsement" to Chávez.

The article, which provokes this outburst of indignation, does not provide an analysis of Chávez or Chavismo but is a more or less journalistic account of my meeting with the President. It is rather literary and descriptive than theoretical. There is a place for such literature on a Marxist site, but that is not the place to look for a rigorous account of our position on Chávez and Venezuela. That can be found in many other writings, such as *Theses on Revolution and Counter-revolution*.

Distorted and dishonest

However, if our critics had taken the trouble to quote even this article fairly, instead of taking isolated phrases, torn from their context and presented in such a way as to give a distorted and dishonest impression of our views, they would have seen that we put forward the revolutionary Marxist policy very clearly. Right at the beginning of this article I wrote the following lines, which I quote in full so there can be no possible ambiguity:

"I also had the opportunity to meet and talk with the President of the Bolivarian Republic, Hugo Chávez. As a writer and Marxist historian I am used to writing about men and women who have made history. But it is not every day that one has the opportunity to observe a protagonist of the historical process at close quarters, to ask questions and to form an impression, not from newspaper reports but from personal experience.

"I should like to make a few things clear before proceeding to my subject. I approach the Venezuelan Revolution as a revolutionary, not as an external observer, and certainly not as a sycophant and a flatterer. Flattery is the enemy of revolutions because it is the enemy of truth, and revolutions need above all to know the truth. The phenomenon of 'revolutionary tourism' I find profoundly abhorrent. It is particularly out of place in the case of Venezuela, because here the revolution finds itself in the greatest danger. Stupid speeches that constantly assert the wonders of the Bolivarian Revolution, but conveniently ignore the dangers it still faces, are false friends of the revolution in whom no reliance can be placed.

"A successful revolution always has many 'friends'. Those middle class elements who are attracted to power as flies to a honey pot, who are ready to sing the praises of the Revolution as long as it remains in power, who do nothing useful to save it from its enemies, who weep a few crocodile tears when it is overthrown, and the next day pass onto the next item on Life's agenda – such 'friends' are worth two a penny. A real friend is not someone who always tells you that you are right. A real friend is someone who is not afraid to look you straight in the eye and tell you that you are mistaken.

"The best friends of the Venezuelan Revolution are the revolutionary Marxists. They are the people who will move heaven and earth to defend the Venezuelan Revolution against its enemies. At the same time, the true friends of the revolution – honest and loyal friends – will always speak their mind without fear. Where we consider that the right road is being taken, we will praise. Where we think mistakes are being made, we will give friendly but firm criticism. What other kind of behaviour should be expected of real revolutionaries and internationalists?

"In speech after speech in Venezuela – including several televised interviews – I was asked my opinion about the Venezuelan Revolution, and answered in the following sense: 'Your revolution is an inspiration to the workers of the whole world: you have accomplished miracles; the driving force of the revolution, however, is the working class and the masses, and that is the secret of its future success. However, the revolution has not been finished and will not be finished unless and until you destroy the economic power of the bankers and capitalists. In order to do this, the masses must be armed and organised in action committees, organised at all levels. The workers must have their own independent organisations and we must build the Marxist Revolutionary Tendency'."

In these lines, which have been widely published in English and Spanish all over the world, there is not a hint of opportunism. They accurately reflect the true content and spirit of the programme of revolutionary Marxism that we have consistently defended. The assertion that in some way my meeting with Chávez represented an abandonment of these ideas and principles is a complete invention of ill-intentioned people.

Alas! Some people are never satisfied. Once they begin to grumble there is no end of it. That is their privilege. Grumbling costs nothing and is one of life's little pleasures when you have nothing else to do. They do not like what I write about Chávez in my article, where I write that "Hugo Chávez for the first time gave the poor and downtrodden a voice and some hope." And, "from my limited contacts with Hugo Chávez, I am firmly convinced of his personal honesty,

courage and dedication to the cause of the masses, the oppressed and exploited."
These are *my personal impressions* of Hugo Chávez, who, as a man, I found to be honest and courageous. I see no reason to change that view. But do these lines really signify an unqualified endorsement of Chávez? They signify no such thing. Our attitude to Chávez has all along been one of *critical support*. That is to say, we will support Chávez to the degree that he strikes blows against imperialism and the oligarchy, but we will criticise him when he vacillates or makes concessions to imperialism and the oligarchy.

Our policy is firmly in line with the Leninist policy of the united front: march separately and strike together. We do not give anyone a blank cheque. Following the advice of Lenin, we keep an eye on our allies. At no time do we forget that we represent two different tendencies that can and must collaborate but which at a given stage will diverge.

The power of Marxist ideas

Our critics are even more displeased by the favourable attitude shown by Hugo Chávez towards certain books. He is, as he told me, an avid reader, and has stated on several occasions that he was impressed by my book *Reason in Revolt*. The fact that the President has given his personal support to the publishing of the Venezuelan edition of *Reason in Revolt* is mentioned, as though this were something suspicious or reprehensible. On the contrary, it is a very positive development, and only a hardened sectarian could complain about it.

Why did President Chávez not speak favourably about any other Marxist group? Not because of their "revolutionary intransigence", but simply because none of them had lifted a finger to support the Venezuelan Revolution against imperialism or taken the slightest interest in it – until now. They claim that Chávez "flattered" me in his programme Alo Presidente, when he made favourable mentions of *Reason in Revolt* and also *Bolshevism – the Road to Revolution.*

It is true that the President made some complementary comments about my book *Reason in Revolt* and also quoted approvingly from these books on the programme. Whether or not this constitutes flattery I do not know. I do know, however, that these books have been very well received by many people. I do not take this as praise for myself, but as *a confirmation of the power of the marvellous ideas of Marxism*. As for myself, flattery and insults leave me equally unmoved. The cause of the socialist revolution is too important for us to worry about such trivia.

What we have here is absolutely typical of the method of the sects. It is not a serious scientific method. It has nothing in common with Marxism. It is trivial and superficial. It is based on a string of anecdotes and gossip, which is meant to be a substitute for serious argument and analysis. It is not meant to clarify or to raise the political level of the reader. It is only meant to denigrate, to insult and to ridicule – and they do not even know how to do that effectively. In short, one can learn absolutely nothing from this. It is only a horrid lesson on how not to work, speak or write.

As the author of a number of Marxist books, I would like to say the following. The fact that the President of Venezuela quoted from Marxist books on television before millions of people should be a matter of satisfaction to any left-wing activist who is not complexly blinded by sectarian prejudice. Irrespective of what opinion one has of Hugo Chávez, the propagation of Marxist literature to a broad audience of millions – mainly workers and peasants – was a very progressive development, which can only benefit the Venezuelan Marxists who are working to win the majority of the revolutionary movement.

I might add that many workers, trade unionists and activists who saw the programme later commented favourably on it and expressed their wholehearted congratulations to me. That is important. The whining of the sects is not.

The Hands Off Venezuela Campaign

Our amiable critics also attack the "Hands Off Venezuela" (HOV) Campaign, arguing that it provides *a left cover for Chávez*. They complain that the HOV statement requires signatories to agree to the "defence of the revolutionary process" in Venezuela and its website is subtitled "in solidarity with the Venezuelan Revolution".

But wait a second! Everybody knows that the US intervention in Venezuela is directed against the government of Hugo Chávez. The struggle in Venezuela is a struggle between two camps. On the one hand there are the counter-revolutionary forces (the "opposition") led by the bankers, capitalists and landlords, with the support of the millionaire press, the Church and all other reactionary forces. On the other hand there is the working class, the peasants and the urban poor who support Chávez and the Bolivarian movement.

The question is therefore not abstract but very concrete. And to a concrete question one must always give a concrete answer. We ask our critics a straight question: In the struggle between the chavistas and the counter-revolutionary opposition, is it permissible for the Marxist tendency to be neutral? Yes or no? In the present referendum campaign, what advice should the Marxists give to the working class?

Let us spell it out in very simple terms, so that even a sectarian can understand: *to be neutral in this struggle would be a betrayal of the revolution, the working class and socialism. It would completely discredit the Marxists in the eyes of the masses and render impossible the building of a revolutionary party in Venezuela.* And although our critics are always talking about the revolutionary party (they are very good at talking), they are only good at building revolutionary parties in the clouds. In this sinful earth, however, they show *that they have not the slightest idea of how the party can be built.*

As Marxists we do not confine our activities to endless discussions over a cup of coffee but we strive to intervene in the real movement. That is why we set up the Hands Off Venezuela Campaign. When was this campaign established and for what reason? It was set up as a response to the counter-revolutionary bosses' lockout (incorrectly described as a "strike" by the media) in order to mobilise the world labour movement in support of the Venezuelan revolution.

This campaign has had quite an important echo in the workers' movement internationally, as a glance at our website will immediately show. I believe it was, at least until recently, the only significant attempt on the Left internationally to mobilize solidarity for the Venezuelan revolution. What was the response of our critics to this? Nothing – just the same deafening silence. They did not lift a finger to aid the people of Venezuela but confined themselves to pontificating about Chávez, as they are still doing today.

The sects accuse us of dissolving working class politics in Venezuela into "Chavism", or at least in providing a Marxist justification for the same. This is quite incredible. Our friends have an amazing ability to read and read and not understand a single word of what they have read. In all our articles and documents and speeches we have stressed the need to maintain the political and organisational independence of the proletariat in the Venezuelan Revolution.

There is absolutely no truth in the allegation that we are "for dissolving working class politics in Venezuela into Chavism." But in order to build the Marxist tendency it is necessary to gain the ear of the workers, starting with the active layer. It is necessary to express our ideas in such a way that they will get an echo. The overwhelming majority of the workers in Venezuela support the Bolivarian movement and insofar as they are active, are active in and around it. For a sectarian, of course, what the workers think is irrelevant. They do not write for the workers but only for themselves and other like-minded groups. Precisely for that reason they will never build anything.

In order to reach the workers and revolutionary youth of Venezuela it is absolutely necessary to participate in the mass movement, which in Venezuela is the Bolivarian movement. Outside this movement there is nothing, and as the ancient Greeks pointed out: "From nothing comes nothing." If what the sects mean by "not dissolving the working class into Chávism" means that we must build the revolutionary movement outside the movement of the masses, we can only shrug our shoulders and say: "After you, gentlemen!"

Apart from their exquisite methods of polemicising, the timing of these people is really tremendous. They demand that we denounce Chávez *right in the middle of the recall referendum, when all the forces of reaction are united to bring down the govern-*

ment and install a counter-revolutionary regime by constitutional means. That would be a severe blow, not just to the Venezuelan Revolution but also to the revolution throughout Latin America. Only a blind man could fail to understand this. And there are none so blind as they who will not see.

The building of a revolutionary party is an art that cannot be learned from a cookbook. It requires not only a firm and principled line, but also tremendous tactical and organisational flexibility and a good sense of timing: every vegetable has its season, as my good friend and comrade Ted Grant likes to say. It is necessary to understand at every moment what tasks are on the order of the day. At this moment, it is necessary to mobilize all the forces of the mass movement, to strain every muscle, to defeat the counter-revolutionaries in the referendum. All future developments depend on this.

What have our critics got to say about the referendum? Not a lot. They fiddle and fuss about this or that quotation by Alan Woods, but on the urgent tasks of the Venezuelan Revolution they have, as usual, nothing to say. They cannot (one presumes) support the opposition. On the other hand, if they support Chávez, would they not be committing the unpardonable sin of "providing Chávez with an unqualified endorsement" and providing a "Marxist left cover for dissolving the working class into Chavismo"? In short, they end in a complete mess.

The irresponsible phrase-mongering of the ultra-lefts, which sounds so nice in the cafes and bars of London and Paris, does not sound so good in Caracas. Where is the "independent proletarian policy" in the referendum campaign? A referendum is not an election. You cannot call for an independent workers' candidate. You can only vote yes, no or not vote. What should we do? Should we perhaps call on the workers to abstain? But abstention is no position, and the mass of workers would see it (quite correctly) as assisting the reaction.

The only correct policy is to participate actively in the movement to defeat the opposition, while at the same time opposing the attempts of the right wing reformists to reach a deal with the opposition, and demand that the revolution must not be halted halfway but strike a decisive blow against imperialism and the oligarchy.

Reformist intrigues

What is needed is a political line that steers clear of both ultra-leftism and opportunism. In the given conditions in Venezuela, the only correct revolutionary policy, the only permissible line of action, is *critical support for Chávez.* Our critics complain because I described Hugo Chávez as an honest and courageous man, but I have said many times that, while President Chávez is a courageous and honest man, *courage and honesty are not enough to ensure the success of the revolution. A correct policy is necessary.* And our policies differ in important respects from those currently defended by Hugo Chávez.

Since Chávez is not a Marxist, he thinks it is possible to develop the country and to rid it from imperialist domination within the limits of capitalism. This is not possible. It is the fatal weakness in his programme, policy and perspectives and it is this that is the dividing line between us. For all his courage, he can be pushed, and is being pushed in different directions according to the pressures exerted.

When I spoke to him in April, there were certain indications that he was moving to the left. Certainly, I know for a fact that his militant anti-imperialist speeches were causing alarm among the reformist wing in the leadership. But in recent weeks the pressures of imperialism and the oligarchy have been enormously intensified. They are reflected through the right wing reformist faction that now has gained control of the palace of Miraflores and is exerting pressure on Chávez to modify his anti-imperialist stance. There are indications that they are succeeding.

There are clear signs that the right wing of the leadership has gone onto the offensive in the last two months and is now in the ascendant. The acceptance of the referendum – despite the well-known fact that the opposition did not get the requisite number of signatures – is proof of this. The vanguard of the Bolivarian movement were right to be suspicious of the referendum. Over generations, Washington has developed a formidable arsenal for maintaining and expanding its power on a world scale. Part of this arsenal – but only part – consists of rockets, tanks and bombers. But it possesses other, no less deadly weapons. Having failed repeatedly to remove Chávez by a frontal assault, they are resorting to behind-the-scenes manoeuvres and intrigues.

A pernicious role is being played by the Organisation of American States and by Jimmy Carter, the ex-President of the USA, who is pretending to "mediate" between Chávez and the opposition. Carter is a poisonous snake in the grass. This smooth-talking religious hypocrite, with his permanent smile and weasel words about democracy and human rights, is far more dangerous than George W. Bush, who at least has the merit of attacking from the front. Ex-President Carter, on the other hand, powerfully brings to mind the phrase of Shakespeare: "There are daggers in men's smiles."

Are the reformists attempting to reach some kind of secret deal with Carter and the OAS? It is possible. They would see this as "realistic politics". These elements distrust Chávez, who they see as excessively radical. They wish to isolate him from the masses and there is even talk of "Chavismo without Chávez." If so, the outlook is not good. It is no more possible for the revolution to do a deal with the counter-revolution than it is possible to mix oil with water. Of course, the President of Venezuela can discuss with whomever he likes, but revolutionaries must be on their guard and warn against any concessions to people like Carter and Cisneros.

Carter represents the left boot of US imperialism just as Rumsfeld represents the right boot. Although the President has not toned down his anti-imperialist speeches, it is clear that Chávez is under pressure from the oligarchy and imperialism. In addition there are the usual siren voices in the leadership of the Bolivarian movement calling for a "more cautious" approach, dialogue and negotiation, etc. All this is done in the name "of developing Venezuela, having a patriotic approach and in opposition to the oligarchy which has sold out to imperialism."

Fifth Column

The oligarchy has indeed sold out to imperialism. More than this, it constitutes a kind of Fifth Column of imperialism on Venezuelan soil. As long as the oligarchy continues to hold important levers of economic power in its hands, especially the banks, the gains of the revolution will never be safe. At a mass meeting one week ago, Chávez spoke, in very strong terms, of defeating the oligarchy. This was ecstatically received by the masses, which fervently desire the completion of the revolution.

Chávez has held meetings with employers – not small business but representatives of big business such as those from Daimler-Chrysler. Chávez has also met with Cisneros (the richest man in Venezuela and the owner of the mass media that supported the coup two years ago). The employers have made all sorts of demands and Chávez has made all sorts of offers to conciliate them. He says that the Bolivarian Revolution is not a communist revolution and does not threaten private property.

Here we see the fundamental difference between Marxism and the programme of even the most advanced petty-bourgeois revolutionary democracy. The notion that the Venezuelan Revolution can succeed while the capitalists and bankers continue to hold vital levers of economic power is a fatal mistake. *Under modern conditions the bourgeoisie of colonial or ex-colonial countries is incapable of carrying out the tasks of the bourgeois democratic revolution. Not a single one of the gains of the revolution can be guaranteed without the expropriation of the oligarchy.*

The refusal of Chávez to take decisive action against the oligarchy means that the whole thing can be thrown into reverse. Experience has shown that "moderation" will not persuade the enemies of the revolution to adopt a more favourable attitude. On the contrary, weakness invites aggression. The policies advocated by the reformists, who now have the upper hand in the palace of Miraflores, constitutes the main danger to the Bolivarian Revolution.

Despite everything, the mood of the masses remains overwhelmingly favourable to Chávez, but critical of the reformist leaders, such as those of the Comando Ayacucho which was unceremoniously ditched a few weeks ago, after having became completely discredited. While maintaining a principled stand, we must put forward slogans and demands that can get an echo in the mass movement, starting with the active layers. The Marxists cannot go too far ahead of the masses, or they would cut themselves off.

We must keep a sense of proportion – something the ultra-lefts never possess. We must not forget that our enemy is imperialism and the oligarchy. We are fighting to defeat that enemy and will willingly collaborate with any other forces that are doing the same. At the same time we will sharply criticize those elements in the leadership of the Bolivarian movement who are adopting a conciliatory attitude to the enemy, who are trying to halt the revolution and reach a deal with the oligarchy and imperialism. We must say concretely what measures are needed to carry the revolution forward.

We direct our fire against the reformist tendency that is strong in the upper layers of the movement but practically non-existent in the rank and file. This is what the most advanced elements in the vanguard want, but it is not enough for our ultra-left critics. They demand that we launch a frontal attack on the bourgeois Chávez! They demand that we proclaim the revolutionary party in Venezuela and break from the Bolivarian movement! They demand – they demand – in fact, there is no end to their demands. But since they have absolutely no forces to carry out these demands, and since we do not require their advice on swimming or anything else, we can safely ignore their demands and get on with our work building the forces of genuine Marxism in Venezuela and internationally, since we are the only tendency in a position to do it.

The Hands Off Venezuela Campaign has indeed been a great success. This fact was recognised by Chávez, when in March this year he publicly expressed his thanks to *In Defence of Marxism* expressing his "gratitude for your solidarity actions in favour of the Bolivarian Revolution". This, for some reason, is taken as further "proof" of our "betrayal". This stands the truth completely on its head. *To defend the Venezuelan revolution against imperialism and the counter-revolutionary oligarchy is not a betrayal. To fail to do so is.*

Let us speak clearly. This silence of these so-called Marxist groups at a time when the Venezuelan Revolution was struggling for survival was, and is, a scandal and a disgrace. If we agree that the main test for revolutionary organisations is their attitude to revolution, then we have to say that all the groups who today unite in attacking the Marxists for doing their revolutionary duty have failed miserably. That is precisely why they now feel the need to intensify their attacks – to cover their bare backsides and justify their total inactivity on the key question of Venezuela, the existence of which they have only just discovered.

Now they are scrambling desperately to climb on the bandwagon but it is too late. So they console themselves and their supporters (who are asking awkward questions) by ranting and raving about Alan Woods' alleged "complicity" with Chávez and Chavismo. Well, ladies and gentlemen, please carry on raving. No serious person will pay the slightest attention to you. Just stop wasting the time of people who are engaged in serious work.

The simple fact is that, like the fox in Aesop's fable, our critics are displeased because we have conducted an exemplary solidarity campaign, because we have managed to get the ideas of Marxism across to a very broad audience in Venezuela and internationally, because we are successfully building the forces of Marxism in the Bolivarian movement, in short, because we have been successful. And like the fox, they have no alternative now but to grind their teeth in impotent rage and mutter: "*these grapes are sour.*" To which we reply with Aesop's moral: *It is easy to despise what you cannot get.*

Chapter Eight

The targets are
Venezuela and Cuba:
New intrigues of US imperialism

Mexico City, 20th May, 2004

On May 1st, Fidel Castro denounced the United States before a million marchers in Havana. The Cuban leader also denounced the European Union as a mafia allied with Washington, and went on to criticise some Latin American governments, namely Mexico and Peru. Castro accused the two countries of joining the herd of hypocrites who voted to condemn Cuba at last month's meeting of the United Nations Human Rights Commission. Mexico was, he declared, now a mere pawn of the United States, its "prestige and influence gained in Latin America and the world... turned to ashes".

These comments were no more than the truth. Under the government of Vicente Fox, Mexico has become completely dependent on Washington, and a loyal ally for its foreign policy. Following Washington's dictates, Fox joined in the noisy chorus of condemnation of Cuba over "human rights". Mexico's relations with Cuba have therefore been tense since Fox's election victory in 2000.

These condemnations, coinciding as they do with the exposure of the systematic abuse of human rights by the US forces in Iraq, cut very little ice with most people here in Mexico, who are broadly sympathetic to Cuba and bitterly hostile to US imperialism. So when Fox demanded the recall of the Mexican ambassador from Havana and ordered the Cuban diplomats to leave, the response of the masses was anything but favourable. The diplomatic crisis between Mexico and Cuba has deepened the political crisis in Mexico and further undermined Fox and his right wing PAN government.

In 2002, the rift between the Fox government and Cuba became public when Castro walked out of a summit hosted by the Mexican president in Monterrey. Castro then released an audiotape of a phone call in which his host told him in no uncertain terms that he must leave early so as not to embarrass George Bush. The famous telephone conversation has become universally known in Mexico by Fox's graphic (and not terribly diplomatic) phrase "Come, y te vas" (You eat, then you leave).

However, the tensions between Mexico and Cuba are more complicated than this. For many weeks the political life of Mexico has been rocked by a scandal in which the present mayor of Mexico City, Andrés Manuel López Obrador, has been accused of involvement in a corruption scandal. News of the scandal every day fills the columns of the newspapers and the television screens, and is now at the very centre of the politics of this country.

The PAN government and its friends in the mass media accuse associates of López Obrador of receiving sizeable bribes from Carlos Ahumada, a Mexican businessman. Ahumada, a very shady character, apparently filmed himself paying these bribes to functionaries of the PRD (the centre-left party to which López Obrador belongs). However, the accusations have not got much of an echo among the people of Mexico, who are accustomed to believe (not without reason) that all Mexican politicians are corrupt and take bribes as a matter of course. The question is therefore why only the opposition PRD has been singled out for exposure.

The answer is not hard to understand and most Mexicans understand it very well. It is clearly part of a carefully worked-out strategy by Fox to bring discredit on the PRD and blacken the name of the popular mayor of Mexico City. The reason is that the popularity of Fox and the right wing PAN has plummeted. The old PRI party that governed Mexico for many decades is split and in crisis. Therefore it is quite possible that the PRD could win power in the Presidential elections in 2006.

This has implications that go far beyond the borders of Mexico. The prospect of a PRD government would be most unwelcome in Washington, which is attempting to eliminate all governments in Latin America and the Caribbean that do not blindly obey its commands. The removal of Aristide in Haiti through the direct military intervention of the US army was one indication of this aggressive policy. The attempts to overthrow Hugo Chávez in Venezuela are another. The increased pressure on Cuba is yet another.

The infamous Colombia Plan is calculated not only to increase the stranglehold of the USA on Colombia but on the whole of Latin America. Finally, the so-called Free Trade Agreement for the Americas (ALCA) is an attempt to get complete control of all the natural wealth, minerals and oil of the continent, and to conquer a monopoly of its huge market, free from competition from the European capitalists.

The fall of the Fox government would be a serious blow to these plans of US imperialism. The PRD is seen as a threat in Washington. Despite all the attempts of the PRD leaders to adopt a moderate stand and renounce radical policies, the US imperialists do not trust it. They fear the masses who stand behind the PRD – and in this they are not mistaken. They are terrified of a new version of Chávez on their frontiers. The hand of Washington is therefore clearly behind the recent scandal and the ever more strident attacks on the PRD.

For reasons known only to himself, Ahumada fled to Cuba immediately after the exposure of the corruption scandal in February. Cuba involved itself in Mexico's explosive political scandal when it deported him back to Mexico last week. Before deporting him, Cuban officials said that Ahumada had confessed to them that he was part of a conspiracy by Fox's people to bring the mayor down.

Mexico's government countered by accusing two Cuban Communist Party officials of spying during a recent visit to Mexico. Fox ordered the recall of the Mexican ambassador from Havana and the expulsion from Mexico of a number of Cuban diplomats and Communist Party members accused of carrying out "activities incompatible with their status". Peru also announced that it was withdrawing its ambassador from Havana.

Without precedent

This action is without precedent in the history of relations between Mexico and Cuba. Diplomatic relations between the two countries still exist, but only on a minimal level. Hitherto, relations were generally good. It is an unprecedented diplomatic crisis.

On May 6th the US State Department released a 500-page report, the outcome of a six-month policy review, on ways to step up American pressure against Cuba. Its proposals include restricting visits by Cuban Americans and cutting their remittances home by half; curbs on spending by Americans who travel legally to Cuba; and boosting support for anti-Castro elements and for propaganda broadcasts aimed at the island.

President Bush said the United States would also spend $59m (£33m) over the next two years to promote the goal of "a democratic Cuba" (read a capitalist Cuba), including US$18m to counter Cuba's jamming of anti-Castro broadcasts.

This latest attempt at bullying will not succeed. It has infuriated the Cuban people who staged a massive demonstration on the streets of Havana. About one million marched along the Malecón, Havana's harbour boulevard, in the protest. Posters portrayed George Bush wearing a Hitler moustache alongside a Nazi swastika, while others carried pictures of Iraqi prisoners abused by US soldiers, with the slogan: "This would never happen in Cuba."

Fidel Castro said the march was "an act of indignant protest, and a denunciation of the brutal, merciless and cruel measures" announced by Bush. The Cuban leader denounced and ridiculed the US President, George Bush, saying he was a fraudulently elected leader trying to impose "world tyranny". He vowed that Cuba would never become a neo-colony of the United States.

He went on to accuse the United States of fighting "wars of conquest to seize the markets and resources of the world", while Cuba was sending abroad thousands of doctors to save lives. He insisted that Bush had "neither morality nor any right at all to speak of liberty, democracy and human rights".

The lies of the Fox government and the new measures taken by US imperialism against Cuba have served to infuriate the Mexican public that is already tired of its anti-working class policies of neo-liberalism, downsizing and precarious jobs. Thousands of Mexicans spontaneously demonstrated at the Cuban Embassy this week. They understand clearly that their government is being shamelessly manipulated by US imperialism in the furtherance of its own reactionary policies and interests.

This is a fact. All these intrigues have been organised and orchestrated by the US State Department. It is very clear that all these events are interconnected and form part of a general plan of US imperialism to increase its domination of Latin America, silence all criticism and overthrow governments that refuse to bend the knee to George W. Bush.

The latest attempt to bully and isolate Cuba is partly – but not totally – dictated by electoral considerations. George Bush's hold on power gets shakier by the day. He needs to secure Florida in the Presidential election. This means adopting measures that will please the Cuban Mafia in Miami and other right wing groups. Several prominent members of the Cuban-American Mafia have top jobs in the Bush administration (although one, Otto Reich resigned this week as the special envoy to Latin America).

This miserable gang of mafiosi, thieves, drug dealers, cut-throats and pimps masquerading as respected businessmen and "democrats" are waiting in the wings for their return to Cuba where they hope to resume their crooked activities under the protection of the government of Washington, as in the "good old days" before the Cuban Revolution. As an insurance policy for their future well-being they pay millions into the coffers of the Republican Party. They naturally expect some kind of down payment on their investment, and their good friend in the White House has just obliged them.

Drunk with power

The recent intrigues are dictated by considerations that go far deeper than mere electoral tactics. After the fall of the USSR US imperialism has achieved a virtual monopoly of power in the world. Colossal power brings colossal arrogance. Drunk with power, the most reactionary circles of the US establishment are determined to impose American domination throughout the entire world.

This fact expresses itself most clearly in the policies of George Bush and the neo-Conservative faction that until recently controlled his actions. Despite the defeat that is staring it in the face in Iraq, the right wing clique that has seized control in the White House is already preparing new adventures and new explosions.

The right wing of the Bush administration and its friends in the Pentagon would probably like to prepare the ground for an invasion to secure "regime change" in Havana. They have learned nothing from Iraq and are probably calculating that with the attention of the world focused on the Middle East, a couple of little adventures in Latin America will not be noticed.

These people are really quite unbalanced. They would be prepared for anything, but they no longer have the influence they enjoyed before the debacle in Iraq. The neo-Conservative wing are losing ground. The war in Iraq that they planned and encouraged is ending in a complete debacle for the United States. The revelations of brutality and torture have completely demolished the last excuse for the invasion. Rumsfeld is fighting for his political life. Probably the neo-Conservatives will be made a scapegoat for George Bush's disastrous miscalculation in Iraq.

Does this mean that new adventures by US imperialism in Latin America are ruled out? Not at all. The politics of US imperialism in fundamentals are not decided by who is in the White House but by the interests of the imperialists and the big US corporations that they defend. Latin America is the backyard of US imperialism. Washington cannot afford to allow Cuba and Venezuela to live peacefully because they represent points of reference for millions of poor people, unemployed workers and landless peasants throughout Latin America.

Nor will a Democratic victory in the Presidential elections necessarily signify a fundamental change of course, as some people foolishly imagine. The declarations of Kerry about Venezuela are even more rabidly reactionary than those of Bush. His attempt to enlist the Republican John McCain as candidate for Vice President has exposed his real political agenda. There is no fundamental difference between him and the Republicans. Nothing whatsoever can be expected from this quarter.

The only way to expose and defeat the reactionary and aggressive plans of US imperialism is by mobilising the might of the world labour movement. The movement against imperialism and capitalism must be strengthened. Protests must be organised. Pressure must be applied. The lessons must be learned. Let us raise a universal cry that will be heard everywhere:

Hands off Cuba!

Hands off Venezuela!

Down with imperialism!

Chapter Nine

Theses on revolution and counter-revolution in Venezuela

London, May 21st, 2004

1) The Venezuelan Revolution is at the crossroads. Having twice defeated the counter-revolution, the revolution is faced with a new and furious offensive. This means that the counter-revolutionary forces are not reconciled to defeat. They are increasingly desperate, and their desperation makes them even more determined and violent. Moreover, they are combining legal and semi-legal methods of struggle (the "referendum" campaign), with preparations for armed struggle. The former is for the purpose of propaganda for foreign consumption and has a secondary significance. The latter constitutes the essence of their strategy. This is combined with a campaign of economic sabotage, the disruption of the food distribution chain and acts of rioting.

2) The arrest of Colombian paramilitaries in Venezuela indicates the existence of a well-prepared conspiracy to overthrow the government and assassinate Chávez. The dangers faced by the revolution are therefore very real. The time has therefore come to draw all the necessary conclusions and to take steps that will strike decisive blows against the counter-revolution.

3) Venezuelan society is now extremely polarised for and against the Bolivarian Revolution, to the right and left. On the left stand the Venezuelan workers, peasants and poor people, who are fighting to defend the revolution and carry it forward. On the right stand the Venezuelan counter-revolutionaries, led by the bankers, landlords and capitalists, who have succeeded in dragging behind them a large part of the middle class. The gulf between the two antagonistic camps is enormous. It cannot be bridged. All attempts at compromise are futile.

4) US imperialism continues to encourage, support and finance the forces of the internal counter-revolution, hoping that they can do the dirty work for it. But it has correctly concluded that the internal opposition is too weak to succeed on the basis of its own forces. Therefore, Washington is preparing a campaign of ter-

ror, using Colombian paramilitary forces that work in conjunction with the internal counter-revolutionaries. This amounts to a declaration of war.

5) Sooner or later, matters will be solved by a decisive victory of one side or another. The revolution has not yet passed the point of no return. All the gains made by the masses under the Chávez government can still be liquidated. The movement can be thrown far back. That is what the counter-revolutionaries are fighting for, while the workers are fighting to defeat them. The question of power has not yet been settled. In the not too distant future the decisive battle will have to be fought and won.

6) Who are the counter-revolutionaries? They are the same bourgeois who ruled Venezuela for decades. They looted and ruined the country, while filling their pockets and bank accounts with the wealth created by the working people. They are the local office boys of US imperialism. They are the same rotten and corrupt politicians and bureaucrats against whom Hugo Chávez rebelled, expressing the will of the Venezuelan people.

7) The programme of the counter-revolution is a mixture of lies, fraud and hypocrisy. They claim to stand for "democracy" but overlook the fact that Chávez has regularly won convincing majorities in every election. They claim to stand for the rule of law, but constantly violate the law – to the point of staging a coup to overthrow the democratically elected government. They claim to stand for order, but are constantly creating disorder and chaos as a cloak for their counter-revolutionary intrigues. They claim to be patriotic Venezuelans but have sold their country to US imperialism and have their fortunes in bank accounts in Florida. Now they are actively supporting an invasion of Venezuela by foreign counter-revolutionary forces.

8) In the struggle between revolution and counter-revolution, the counter-revolutionaries have one great advantage: the control of key points of the economy. During the so-called strike (in reality a bosses' lockout), the Venezuelan capitalists inflicted terrible damage on the economy. Total losses added up to over seven billion dollars. In addition to this, these so-called patriots have exported billions of dollars to banks in Florida, thus starving the Venezuelan economy of much-needed investment. Combined with this economic sabotage they are also disrupting the food distribution chain, controlled by three or four big monopoly companies, in order to create artificial price hikes and scarcity of basic foodstuffs. They are draining away the precious life-blood of Venezuela in an attempt to cause the maximum dislocation, unemployment and pain. They calculate that this will dampen the enthusiasm of the masses for the revolution. They also wish to cause chaos and disorder, in order to create the conditions for a coup by the army tops

to "restore order".

9) The decisive element in the equation is the working class. The workers of Venezuela have already begun to fight back against the bosses' offensive. They have taken the initiative, in some cases have occupied factories abandoned by the bosses, begun to introduce elements of workers' control in some companies, set up democratic unions, forced the bosses to pay unpaid wages and benefits. These initiatives should be taken up and generalised. They show the way forward.

10) A particularly pernicious role is being played by the so-called trade union leaders of the CTV. These corrupt and degenerate labour lieutenants of Capital have long ago sold their soul to the bosses and the CIA. They have abdicated any right to be considered a legitimate part of the labour movement. They should be driven out of the movement.

11) The building of the UNT is an urgent task. We must strengthen and build the democratic unions and provide them with a fighting programme. Build a mass trade union federation! Work out a programme of demands based on the immediate needs of the workers: the fight against factory closures and unemployment, the high cost of living, etc.

12) The UNT recently announced a campaign to organise 80 percent of the workforce into unions (which was publicly supported by president Chávez). This is a step in the right direction. By organising the unorganised layers, the revolution can cut the ground from under the feet of the old rotten right wing trade union bureaucracy. This initiative must be taken up energetically at all levels. At the same time, an appeal should be made to any workers who remain in unions affiliated to the CTV to fight to democratise those and join the UNT. In cases where this might not be possible new democratic unions should be set up, but always having the aim of organising the mass of the workers, and not only the most advanced layers.

13) To prevent sabotage, waste and corruption, the workers in industry must begin to exercise control over production. Corrupt officials must be dismissed. Managers, who side with the counter-revolution and sabotage production, must be given an ultimatum: either desist from such activities and serve the people, or be dismissed with loss of pension and all other rights. Serious cases of sabotage should be met with arrest and imprisonment. Corrupt and counter-revolutionary directors should be replaced by people who are honest and devoted to the cause of the revolution. This can only be done effectively by introducing workers' democratic control and management.

14) Can the workers run industry? Those sceptics who question the ability of the workers to run industry have had their answer. It was the workers who defeat-

ed the attempts of the bosses to sabotage the economy in the bosses' lockout twelve moths ago. The workers of the PDVSA have demonstrated their ability to run even the biggest and most complex industries. They have done so with a high level of skill and competence.

Skills to be put to use

15) In any case, the workers will not be alone. They will count on the help of the majority of honest engineers, scientists, technicians and managers, who are not saboteurs or counter-revolutionaries and who genuinely wish to see a prosperous and successful Venezuela. The people of Venezuela have enormous reserves of talent and creativity. They will attract to their side all that is best in Venezuelan society, including the cream of the intellectuals. The creative talents of the people under capitalism are crippled by a system that places the profits of a few above the interest of the majority. This is also true of those who occupy managerial positions at the lower level. In a socialist planned economy, their skills will be put to good use in applying the most modern technology and methods to boost productivity in the interests of all.

16) Workers' control will immediately bring to light all the corruption, waste and nepotism, the excessive profits and perks of the bosses. Open the books! Compel all companies to reveal their real profits. Let the workers have all the information about the fat profits and perks, the swindles and theft. This would dramatically reduce waste and channel these resources into production for the development of Venezuela. However, workers' control in and of itself cannot solve the fundamental problems of society. It is only a transitional step towards the nationalisation of the means of production and a planned economy.

17) The elements of workers' control already exist. Some factories closed by the bosses have been occupied by the workers. During the sabotage of the oil industry, even Hugo Chávez expressed his support for the slogan "Factory closed, factory taken over by the workers", though then the government did not really take any serious action to solve the problem of the workers who had occupied the factories. Isolated instances of workers' control can only succeed partially and temporarily. What is needed is an overall plan of production that can integrate the different sectors of the economy and branches of production. But such overall planning and integration immediately comes up against the barrier of capitalist anarchy (the "market"). No real progress can be made unless these obstacles are overcome.

18) The principal power of the counter-revolution consists in its ownership of the means of production. It continues to exercise control over key points in the

economy, which it uses to place a noose around the neck of the Venezuelan people. The only way to prevent this economic sabotage and to eliminate the waste and corruption that are the inevitable consequences of capitalism is to destroy the economic stranglehold of the bourgeoisie. As long as the counter-revolutionaries continue to hold economic power, the revolution will be fighting with one hand tied behind its back.

19) The land, banks, insurance companies and big industries must be nationalised. This can be done by introducing emergency legislation through the congress, backed up by an appeal to the workers to take over from below, to introduce workers' control to prevent sabotage by the bosses and ensure a peaceful and orderly transition to a planned economy. The President of the Republic can explain this step to the people by going on television to expose the scandalous profits of the bosses, the waste, corruption and nepotism, the systematic sabotage of the economy.

20) By nationalising the key points of the economy under democratic workers' control and management, it will be possible to introduce a genuine plan of production that will mobilise all the productive resources of Venezuela for the satisfaction of the people's needs: a crash building programme of houses, schools and hospitals can begin straight away, using the country's considerable oil revenue to finance an ambitious investment plan. Unemployment would be eliminated, and all citizens would have the right and obligation to work. Such a plan, which would guarantee an immediate improvement in the living standards of the immense majority, is only possible on the basis of nationalisation. You cannot plan what you do not control, and you cannot control what you do not own.

21) Unless decisive steps are taken to control the economy, the people of Venezuela will be faced in the future with growing economic chaos, unemployment and poverty. Venezuela's huge oil wealth will not be sufficient to prevent this. The bosses can use their economic power to sabotage and wreck the country's prosperity. But even without that, the attempt to combine measures of nationalisation with the market economy will produce distortions and particularly inflation that will cancel out the gains and provoke economic dislocation. The nationalisation of the key points of the economy is therefore an absolutely necessary and urgent measure of self-defence taken by the majority to protect its most vital interests and the most fundamental right – the right to life.

22) The first step must be the nationalisation of the banks. An important section of the Venezuelan banking system is under the control of two Spanish banking groups. Furthermore a large part of all the money that circulates in the financial system over a year is actually state-owned money, either directly or through

state-owned companies, particularly PDVSA. However the control over these financial resources is in private hands and is used to finance the counter-revolution and sabotage the economy. Without the nationalisation of the banks it will be impossible to plan the economy. Control of credit is one of the most fundamental levers of the modern economy. Without this, nothing can be accomplished. The state must know how much money there is, where it comes from and where it is going. Strict national accounting is the prior condition for a planned economy.

23) Nationalisation of the banks would allow the state to exercise real and not fictitious control over the economy, to control the flow of capital and investment into those fields that reflect the interests of the majority and the objective requirements of the economy. The bank employees themselves can play a key role in the nationalisation of the banks. They know all about the swindles and speculative movement of capital. They know how the counter-revolutionaries are using large sums of money for the purpose of sabotage and intrigues. An appeal must be made to the bank employees to control the movement of capital, ensure a smooth handover of the banks and prevent acts of sabotage.

24) The gains of the revolution are real and palpable. Important measures have been taken in the interest of the workers, the peasants and the poor, particularly the land reform and the health and education plans, which have reached millions. But all these gains are under threat. They can be reversed and they will be reversed if the counter-revolution gets back in the saddle. In order to guarantee the gains of the revolution, it must be made irreversible. This means a fundamental change in society. This poses the question of power.

25) Every revolution in history is ultimately settled by answering the question: who holds the power? Who is master of the house? Until this question is answered, the revolution is not finished. By beginning the Bolivarian Revolution, Hugo Chávez threw down a challenge to the old oligarchy. Their power was challenged but not completely overthrown. A colossal struggle began, which has still not been decided one way or the other. Upon the resolution of this struggle everything depends.

26) At bottom, the question of power can be reduced to one thing: Who controls the state power? That is the decisive question. The state in the last analysis consists of armed bodies of men – the army, the police, etc. In a normal capitalist regime, the bourgeoisie controls the state and uses it to oppress the majority of society and guarantee its power and privileges. It controls not only the army and police but also the judges, the bureaucracy and every other branch of the executive power.

27) However, there are exceptional periods in history, periods when the class

struggle reaches deadlock, when things are not quite so clear-cut. Venezuela is now passing through such a complex situation. Is the Venezuelan state a bourgeois state? As long as the bourgeoisie remains the ruling class, as long as it continues to own and control the key points of the economy, as long as its economic power has not been broken, Venezuela remains a capitalist country, and the state therefore remains a bourgeois state. This means that the revolution has not been carried out to the end, has stopped half way, and therefore can still be reversed.

28) The state is still a bourgeois state, but it is a bourgeois state with peculiar features. The most peculiar feature is that the bourgeoisie has – at least temporarily – lost control over key parts of its own state. This seems like a contradictory assertion, but it is only the expression of a real contradiction that exists in society. Venezuelan society is split right down the middle. The extreme class polarisation affects everything – including the state, which is itself split. A section of the army has gone over to the side of the Bolivarian Revolution. This includes the overwhelming majority of the ordinary soldiers, the non-commissioned officers, but also a significant number of the officers, like Chávez himself. This creates enormous difficulties for the Venezuelan bourgeoisie, which does not have the same grip on the army and the officer caste that exists, say, in Britain or the USA.

29) Many officers sincerely support the revolution. The upper echelons will have been purged following the collapse of the coup of April 2002. In general, the prevailing mood is unfavourable to the counter-revolution. The external threat posed by US imperialism and Colombia will have galvanised the natural instincts of the army to fight and rallied them round the President. The counter-revolutionaries, at least for the moment, find themselves in a difficult position. But from the outside it is difficult to say what the real balance of forces in the army is. This will only be made clear by events.

Courage and strength

30) In the last analysis, the correlation of forces inside the army is determined by the correlation of class forces in society. To the degree that the revolution advances and strikes decisive blows against its enemies, both internal and external, to the degree that the masses are roused and active, the revolutionary wing of the armed forces will take courage and be strengthened. But vacillations and retreats will dishearten the revolutionary wing and encourage the counter-revolutionaries.

31) Chávez and his supporters are leaning on the support of the masses to strike blows against the oligarchy and imperialism. They did not originally have

a socialist perspective, but only the notion of clearing out corruption and modernising Venezuela. They wanted a fairer, more just and equal society, but imagined that this was possible without breaking the bounds of capitalism. But this immediately brought them into conflict with the bourgeoisie and imperialism. The masses took to the streets and imparted an entirely different dynamic to the process. The mass movement has provided a stimulus to Chávez and in turn he has encouraged the movement in a revolutionary direction.

32) When Hugo Chávez founded the Bolivarian movement, he sought to clean out the stinking Augean stables that were Venezuelan political life. This was a limited and very modest objective – but it met with the ferocious resistance of the ruling oligarchy and its servants. It earned him the undying hatred of the wealthy and powerful, and the loyalty and love of the masses. Hugo Chávez for the first time gave the poor and downtrodden a voice and some hope. That is the secret of the extraordinary devotion and loyalty they have shown him. He aroused them to life and they see themselves in him.

33) That explains the equally extraordinary hatred the ruling class shows towards Chávez. It is the hatred of the rich for the poor, of the exploiter for the exploited. Behind this hatred is fear – fear for the loss of their wealth, power and privileges. This is a gulf that cannot be bridged by fair words. It is the fundamental class division of society.

34) The revolution stands for democracy. But a consistent struggle for democracy inevitably brings the revolution into conflict with the vested interests of the landlords, the bankers and capitalists and imperialism. That is to say, if the revolutionary democracy is to achieve its aims, it must be prepared to go beyond the boundaries of capitalism. It must take action to destroy the economic power of the oligarchy. Failure to do this will inevitably end in defeat, the victory of the counter-revolution and the complete eradication of democracy in Venezuela.

35) Though they swear by democracy in every other sentence, the Venezuelan oligarchy and imperialism are the enemies of democracy. They want a "democracy" in which anyone can say what they like as long as the wealthy minority decides what happens. The only class that is sincerely interested in democracy is the working class and its natural allies, the poor peasants and the urban poor. True democracy will only be achieved when the power of the oligarchy is destroyed forever and power is in the hands of the working people. What is needed is not the hollow fiction of bourgeois formal democracy, where real power is in the hands of the bankers and capitalists, but a genuine democracy of the working people, based on the nationalisation of the land, banks and big industries and a democratic plan of production.

36) The immediate programme must be: a) the amalgamation of the banks and the nationalisation of the banking system, b) the amalgamation of the insurance companies and the nationalisation of the finance sector, c) the abolition of commercial secrecy: open the books! d) workers' control and management of the PVDSA and all other big companies, and the nationalisation of all other sectors of the petrochemical industry, gas and energy, e) the organisation of the population into consumers' associations and co-operatives to control prices and distribution of food and other products, which can be carried out through the nationalisation of the monopolies which control the food distribution chain, f) the nationalisation of the land, the expropriation of the big estates and the formation of peasant co-operatives to run agriculture, g) the nationalisation of all big transport companies and the creation of a unified transport system, h) a state monopoly of foreign trade.

37) US imperialism is playing a game of cat and mouse with Venezuela. Having been defeated in two direct assaults, it is resorting to siege methods. It is putting pressure on other governments in Latin America to help it isolate the Venezuelan Revolution, which it regards as a dangerous focal point for the discontent of the masses throughout the continent. It is threatening to bring Venezuela to its knees with economic sanctions. At the same time it is actively preparing a campaign of terrorism and subversion.

38) Fearing to intervene itself, Washington is actively conspiring with the leading circles in Colombia, not just to isolate Venezuela, and to put pressure on it, but even to prepare direct intervention against the Venezuelan Revolution. It is constantly intriguing in the Organisation of American States (OAS) to interfere in Venezuela's internal affairs. The role of the OAS is like that of a "friendly neighbour" who advises a man who is being attacked by a gang of bandits to stay still and not shout so loud, as this will only provoke the robbers and disturb the whole neighbourhood. With "friends" like these, the people of Venezuela have no need of enemies!

39) It is, of course, necessary to make use of diplomacy in order to take every possible measure to prevent the isolation of Venezuela, to develop friendly relations, trade, etc., with Argentina, Brazil and, of course, with Cuba. However, it would be extremely short-sighted to base oneself on this. Governments can change, and they can be brought under the pressure of imperialism. There is no guarantee that this will not happen in the case of Brazil or Argentina.

40) In the last analysis, the only real allies of the Venezuelan people are the oppressed workers and peasants of Latin America. They can always be depended on to defend the Venezuelan Revolution, their governments cannot.

Ultimately, the real defence of the Venezuelan Revolution consists not in diplomacy but in a consistent revolutionary and internationalist policy aimed at spreading the revolution throughout Latin America and beyond.

41) President Chávez has courageously stood up to the imperialists. He has said: "If there is an imperialist intervention we will fight them for 100 years." Undoubtedly the masses would be prepared to make the greatest sacrifices for the revolution. They have been aroused to political life and have been given new hope and a sense of their own human dignity. Thus, the masses have tremendous reserves of revolutionary energy. This is something the imperialists and counter-revolutionaries are incapable of understanding. However, to rely exclusively on the willingness of the masses to make sacrifices is a mistake. The masses can sacrifice their "today" for the "tomorrow" only up to a certain point. This must always be kept in mind.

42) Ultimately, the economic question is decisive. In 2003 alone, Venezuelan GDP fell by 18 percent, despite the high price of oil. According to some calculations, living standards have fallen to the level of the 1950s. By these means the counter-revolution is trying to undermine support for the government, which it blames for the results of its own sabotage. So far, the plans of the counter-revolution have not succeeded. The masses remain fiercely loyal to the revolution and to President Hugo Chávez. But such a situation cannot last indefinitely.

43) For the time being, the Venezuelan economy has been helped by the rising price of oil. In 2003 the price of a barrel of Venezuelan oil ($25.65) was about 17 percent higher than a year earlier. President Chávez has attempted to alleviate the effects of the crisis by introducing price and exchange controls. Part of the income of the PDVSA has been diverted to social and housing programmes. Strict exchange controls have boosted the BCV's internal revenues from $13 billion in January to $22 billion now. The devaluation of the official dollar rate from 1,600 to 1,920 bolivars has also helped. The growth rate is sharply up, although this is partly a reflection of a natural recovery after the steep fall brought about by the bosses' lockout.

44) These measures have partially succeeded in alleviating the conditions of the masses. They have served to buy time. But there will be a price to pay. On a capitalist basis, such measures tend to produce inflationary consequences. The bolivar is falling sharply on the black market. Inflation is rising at 27 percent annually – the highest rate in the region. In the long run, this is unsustainable. Sooner or later it will be reflected in new and severe economic crises, shortages and unemployment. Thus, the fundamental problem remains.

Commanding heights

45) If the revolution does not advance, if it does not take over the commanding heights of the economy, the growth of unemployment and poverty can undermine the fighting spirit of the masses. For the time being, this does not seem to be the case. The economic recovery has provided a breathing space. The masses remain fiercely loyal to Chávez. The class balance of forces is still favourable to the revolution and unfavourable to the counter-revolution. But this can change. If the masses do not see a fundamental change, and above all decisive action against the counter-revolutionaries, frustration and disappointment can set in. The pendulum can swing back to the right.

46) Beginning with the less conscious, unorganised layers, a mood of apathy can set in among the masses. Seeing no real progress, the workers can become tired and disappointed. With every step backward, the reactionaries will take courage and pass onto the offensive. The vacillating elements can swing behind the counter-revolution. This mood can communicate itself to the state. Some of the "friends" of the revolution in the upper layers of the bureaucracy, the army and the police, can abandon the President and go over to the counter-revolution, alleging that the revolution has been taken over by "extremists" and is bringing nothing but chaos. The prostitute press will intensify its campaign of vilification and slanders. The stage will then be set for a counter-revolutionary coup under the banner of "Order".

47) The masses have expended enormous energies in carrying the revolution to where it is today. It has come a long way, but the decisive point has not yet been passed, and there is still a real danger that the whole process may be thrown into reverse. There is a growing awareness of this at rank and file level. Frustration is already growing among the activists. This is a warning. This frustration could lead to moods of impatience and ultraleft adventures on the part of a layer of activists who have moved far ahead of the rest of the class. This could have negative consequences for the revolution.

48) The reaction has been defeated, but it has not disappeared. It is waiting for a more favourable situation to act. The idea that it is possible to placate the counter-revolution by displaying "moderation" is extremely foolish and utterly counterproductive. The counter-revolution and imperialism cannot be placated by sweet words. This fact is shown by the scandal over the Colombian paramilitaries. Not "moderation" but decisive action is necessary.

49) The revolution has attracted many friends. Most of them are genuine and honest. But some of these "friends" are not acting in the interests of the revolution. They are not revolutionaries at all, but reformists. And it is the historical

destiny of reformism always to achieve results that are diametrically opposed to those that were intended. They are, of course, guided by the best of intentions. But the way to a very warm place is paved by such good intentions.

50) The reformists say that we must not do anything that will provoke the imperialists, we must be cautious, diplomatic, etc., etc. But the argument about "provoking" the imperialists is false to the core. The imperialists do not need to be provoked. They have been hostile to the revolution from the very first day. They have lost no opportunity to attack it. They have already organised two attempted coups and are preparing a third under the banner of the referendum. It is not this or that speech, or this or that action that provokes them – they regard the very existence of the revolution as a provocation. They will not be satisfied until it is destroyed.

51) The false "friends" of the revolution and the pseudo-Marxists argue that, since the Venezuelan Revolution is democratic and popular, not socialist, it cannot take action against private property. This is pure sophistry. The American Revolution of the 18th century was a bourgeois democratic revolution, yet the revolutionaries of 1776 did not hesitate to confiscate the property of the supporters of the English Crown. After the American Civil War, the United States government did not hesitate to confiscate the property of the Southern slaveholders worth billions of dollars in modern currency. These examples from American history show clearly that the demands of the revolution supersede the so-called sacred rights of property.

52) Since when did the property rights of an exploiting and oppressive minority carry more weight than the needs of the overwhelming majority? Democracy means the rule of the majority. And we stand for consistent democracy. The Venezuelan Revolution, following the excellent example of the American Revolution, will likewise not hesitate to take measures to eliminate the economic power of the counter-revolutionary minority.

53) An argument often used by the reformists is that it is necessary to win over the middle class and therefore we must not go too far in attacking capitalism. The first half of this statement is correct, but it directly contradicts the second half. It is both possible and necessary to win over a large section of the middle class, but we will never succeed in doing this if we accept the policies of the reformists, which can only alienate the mass of the petty bourgeoisie and push them into the arms of the counter-revolution.

54) The exploiting classes are a small minority of society. They could not rule without the help of a large number of sub-exploiters and sub-sub exploiters. Using their economic power and their control of the mass media, they have mobilised the

mass of middle class Venezuelans to oppose the revolution. Under the false flag of "democracy" they have organised street riots and clashes. Their shock troops are the sons of the rich – the "sifrinos" – wealthy parasites, fanatically opposed to the masses. The enraged petty bourgeois resent the concessions made to the poor, which they see as a threat to their own privileges. They make a lot of noise when required, but they are really just human dust, easily scattered to the wind when confronted with the movement of the masses.

55) However, the petty bourgeoisie is not a homogeneous class. There are contradictions within the middle class that can be expressed in splits in the opposition. The upper layers of the middle class are composed of privileged elements – prosperous lawyers, university professors, bank managers and politicians – who stand close to the oligarchy and are its willing servants. The lower layers – the small shopkeepers, small peasants, bank clerks, etc. – stand closer to the working class and can be won over. However, the way to win over the lower ranks of the petty bourgeoisie is not to make concessions to their leaders (really their political exploiters) but to take the offensive against the big bankers and capitalists, to show an attitude of absolute firmness and decision.

56) A section of the opposition consists of people who have been deceived by the counter-revolutionaries. They can be won over to the side of the revolution. The way to win them over, however, is by carrying out measures to expropriate the big capitalists and adopting measures in the interests of the small shopkeepers and small businessmen. They must be convinced that the revolution is invincible and that their interests are best served by joining forces with the working class against the big banks and monopolies.

57) The so-called bourgeois democracy is a gigantic fraud, behind which lurks the *dictatorship of big capital.* This dictatorship oppresses not only the workers but also the middle class. What is needed is not the hollow fraud of formal bourgeois democracy – in which real power is in the hands of the big banks and monopolies – but a real democracy – a democracy of the working people, based on the collective ownership of the land, the banks and industry.

58) It must be made clear that these measures of nationalisation are aimed only at the big capitalists, bankers and landowners. We have no intention of nationalising small businesses, farms or shops. These play no independent role in the economy, since they are utterly dependent on the big banks, supermarkets, etc. We will appeal to the small shopkeepers, etc., to support the programme of nationalisation, which is in their interests.

59) The nationalisation of the banks will enable the government to grant small businesses cheap and easy credit. The nationalisation of the big fertilizer

plants will enable it to sell cheap fertilizer to the peasants. And by eliminating the middlemen and nationalising the big supermarkets, distribution and transport companies, we can provide the peasants with a guaranteed market and a fair price for their products, while reducing prices to the consumer.

Dangerous advice

60) There are none so blind as they who will not see. Despite everything, there are still those who continue to advocate slowing the pace of the revolution in order to placate the counter-revolution and imperialism. They may be sincere in their views, but they are giving false and dangerous advice. It is not possible to stop the revolution half way. It is not possible to make half a revolution. Either the revolution is carried through to the end, or else it must perish.

61) The reformists consider themselves to be great realists. In reality they are the blindest utopians. They want a "more humane" capitalism. To demand that capitalism should be humane is to ask the tiger to eat grass instead of flesh. Not for nothing are the Venezuelan capitalists the bitterest enemies of the Bolivarian revolution. Not for nothing do they strive by all means to destroy it and overthrow Chávez. They can never be reconciled to the revolution. Fine words will not convince them. They must be defeated and disarmed. Their economic power must be terminated. There is no other way.

62) At the present moment, as Chávez himself has pointed out, the Venezuelan Revolution resembles Sisyphus, the character in Greek mythology, who pushed a heavy boulder to the top of a steep mountain, only to see it roll back again. With a little effort, the boulder can be pushed over the top of the mountain, and the problem would be resolved. But if we stop, the boulder will slide back and crush many people in the process.

63) Only the revolutionary movement of the masses from below prevented the counter-revolution from triumphing at the time of the 2002 April coup. The masses defeated the reactionaries and imperialists. At this point it would have been simple to inflict a decisive defeat on the reactionaries, who were divided and demoralised. If the President had lifted his little finger, it would all have been over. The working class could have taken power peacefully, without bloodshed or civil war. Unfortunately, that opportunity was missed. The revolution showed itself to be very moderate and cautious.

64) What was the result? Did this moderation and caution impress the counter-revolutionaries? Did it placate them? It did not. It encouraged them. The counter-revolutionaries regrouped and prepared a new offensive, the so-called strike that aimed to paralyse the economy. Everyone knows that this "strike" was organ-

ised and planned by the CIA with the help of the Venezuelan bosses and corrupt trade union bureaucrats. Again, this attempt was defeated by the revolutionary movement of the Venezuelan workers.

65) After the first coup Hugo Chávez tried to be conciliatory to the reactionaries. He tried to negotiate with them and even reinstated the old directors of the PVDSA. They rewarded him by organising the bosses' lockout that inflicted serious damage on the Venezuelan economy. What lessons can we draw from this? Do we conclude that a conciliatory attitude is the only way to disarm the counter-revolution and imperialism? Only a fool would say so. The real conclusion that must be drawn is that weakness invites aggression.

66) Experience has shown that the only firm base of support the revolution has is the masses, and in the first ranks of the masses, the working class. The masses wish to defend Chávez. How do they do this? Only by stepping up the movement from below, setting up action committees, learning how to use arms. The way to help Chávez is to wage an implacable struggle against the enemies of the revolution, to drive them from the positions of power they hold and prepare the way for a radical reorganisation of society.

67) In other words, the key to success consists in developing and strengthening the independent movement of the working class, and above all by building the revolutionary Marxist wing of the movement. Our advice to the workers of Venezuela is: trust only in your own strength and in your own forces! Trust only in the revolutionary movement of the masses! That is the only force that can sweep aside all obstacles, defeat the counter-revolution and begin to take power into its own hands. That is the only guarantee of success.

68) The reactionaries are now in a weak position, but a cornered animal can be dangerous. They are desperate, and this desperate mood of the opposition can lead to desperate methods. It is now quite clear that they are conspiring with Washington and its Colombian agents to assassinate Chávez and create chaos as the first step to a new coup. The greatest vigilance is required on the part of the mass movement to thwart the plans of the counter-revolution. Only decisive action by the masses can disarm the counter-revolution and render it harmless.

69) The only way to carry the revolution through to the end is from the bottom up. The most urgent task is the formation of action committees – committees for the defence of the revolution. But in the given situation, the committees must be armed. A people's militia is the slogan of the hour. The revolution can only defend itself against its enemies if it arms itself.

70) Chávez has called for the arming of the workers. He said: "Every fisherman, student, every member of the people, must learn how to use a rifle, because

it is the concept of the armed people together with the National Armed Forces to defend the sovereignty of the sacred soil of Venezuela." This is a thousand times correct. A people that is not prepared to defend its freedom arms in hand does not deserve to be free. The general arming of the people is the *sine qua non*, not only for the defence of the revolution against internal and external enemies, but for carrying the revolution through to the end and defending the democratic rights of the people.

71) The words of President Chávez should immediately be translated into deeds. In view of the threat posed by the internal and external enemies of the revolution, the government should set up special schools for the military training of the population. Competent officers loyal to the revolution must provide the necessary training in the use of arms, tactics and strategy. The only way to answer the threat of aggression is by the formation of a mass people's militia. Every workers' district, every factory, every village, every school, must become a bulwark of the revolution, prepared to fight.

72) The question of the state is the most fundamental question of all. The President himself has complained about the systematic sabotage of the bureaucracy – the sabotage of parliament by the philibustering of the opposition, reactionary judges, policemen, etc. How can the revolution base itself on the old bureaucrats and functionaries inherited from the past? How can it place its trust in judges that were appointed by the old regime? How can the old state bureaucracy purge itself? No devil ever cut off its own claws! What is necessary is to take a big broom and sweep out all this rubbish. A new social order demands a new kind of administration – a genuinely democratic administration that comes from the people themselves and reflects their wishes and aspirations.

73) The government has carried out a partial purge of the state. That is positive, but it has not gone far enough. It is necessary to remove all the conservatives, all the open and hidden allies of the counter-revolution from positions of power and influence. All power must be in the hands of dedicated revolutionaries whose loyalty to the cause of the people is proven beyond question. A serious purge can only be carried out from below, by the masses themselves. The masses are impatient to act, to push aside all the obstacles that are preventing the revolution from advancing and achieving all its aims. The key to success lies in developing and extending the mass movement and giving it an organised form.

74) The only way to carry the revolution forward is from the bottom up. The mass movement must be given an organised form and expression. This can only be done through the establishment of action committees, democratically elected in every workplace, workers' district, office, oil refinery and village. The committees

must be linked up at all levels – locally, regionally and nationally. Only in this way can the basis be laid for a new power in society: workers' power.

Take control!

75) The first task of the committees is to organise the struggle against the counter-revolution. They should patrol the workers' neighbourhoods, prevent crime and sabotage, arrest counter-revolutionaries and keep order. They should take over the control of transport and the supply of food and other basic necessities, control prices and root out speculation, corruption, profiteering and other abuses and ensure a fair distribution for all. In this way the masses can acquire experience in control, supervision, accounting and regulation, which will prepare them for bigger things when the time comes for them to participate in the running of society.

76) The Caracas Metropolitan Police and other police forces controlled by the opposition are known to be a centre of counter-revolutionary activity. They are operating as a state within the state, conducting provocations against the government, murdering people and causing chaos. This is completely intolerable. These reactionary forces must be disbanded and replaced by a popular militia under the control of the local revolutionary committees and the trade unions.

77) We stand for a genuine democracy – a workers' democracy, on the lines advocated by Lenin and put into practice by the Bolsheviks in 1917: a) free and democratic elections with right of recall of all state officials, b) a limitation on the salaries of officials, which should not be higher than that of a skilled worker; legitimate expenses can be paid, but must be open for inspection, c) the arming of the people, and the incorporation of the army into a popular militia, d) the involvement of the whole population in all the tasks of administration of industry, society and the state.

78) If the counter-revolution succeeds, the result will be a nightmare for the people of Venezuela. The smiling mask of "democracy" will immediately be discarded to reveal the ugly face of reaction. The bosses will be thirsting for revenge for all the defeats and humiliations they have suffered in recent years. They will want to teach the workers and the poor people a lesson they will never forget. They will exact a terrible revenge on the masses. They will crush the revolution in the dust, smash it utterly. This is a terrible prospect. But it is by no means inevitable. Everything depends on the working class and its leadership.

79) What is needed is a consistent revolutionary programme, based on scientific principles. That can only be provided by Marxism. To win this life and death struggle, sincerity and courage are not enough. Many times in history a brave

army with many soldiers has been defeated by a smaller army of trained troops led by capable commanders. The role of a revolutionary Marxist party is analogous to that of trained troops and experienced commanders.

80) It is entirely false to counter pose the struggle for democracy and against imperialism to the struggle for socialism. The struggle for revolutionary democracy will only succeed to the degree that it becomes a struggle against the dictatorship of Capital. Therefore, the struggle for democracy, if it is to succeed, must lead directly to the struggle for workers' power and socialism. There is no "middle way" and all attempts to find a middle way will necessarily lead to disaster. They will end in the liquidation of the revolution and the total destruction of democracy in Venezuela.

81) There are some people who call themselves Marxists, but who have in practice completely abandoned the revolutionary standpoint of Marxism. Their "Marxism" is purely abstract and academic in character and bears no relation to the real world of the class struggle. They produce all kinds of "clever" and "intellectual" arguments to show that Venezuela is not ready for socialism, or that the time is not ripe (for such people the time is never right), and a hundred other arguments to persuade the workers not to try to take power. In reality, they have no faith in the working class or the revolution. They fear the counter-revolution, they fear imperialism, they fear the sound of their own voice, and they wish to transmit this fear to the workers.

82) In reality, the situation in Venezuela is completely mature for the transfer of power to the working class. The bourgeoisie has revealed its complete incapacity to rule. On the other hand, the revolution has not been carried out to the end. The only possible consequence of this is chaos. The revolution has advanced to a point where the normal function of capitalism is impossible. The capitalists withdraw their money and organise a strike of capital. Only the lucky accident of rising oil prices allows the government to maintain something like normal economic life. But this highly unstable situation cannot last. The struggle between the classes threatens to produce stagnation and collapse. It must be settled decisively in one sense or another.

83) The argument that Venezuela is not ready for socialism does not bear close examination. Venezuela is a potentially wealthy nation, with a superabundance of oil and other materials. The working class constitutes a decisive majority of society. The workers have demonstrated enormous courage, creativity and revolutionary spirit. They have shown their will to change society, and to take control of industry. What is required is a bold lead.

84) Opportunistic elements, masquerading under the name of socialism, main-

tain that the working class is not conscious enough to carry out the socialist transformation of society. This is merely the expression of the snobbism of middle
class elements who have no knowledge of the working class or contact with it.
All the experience of the working class struggle in Venezuela in the last few years
demonstrates precisely the opposite. In so far as there is a problem of consciousness in the Venezuelan Revolution, it is not a problem of the working class but
of the leadership of the workers' movement which is lagging behind the class and
failing to draw the necessary conclusions.

85) Behind the counter-revolution stands the might of US imperialism. The
threads of all the intrigues, plots and conspiracies can be traced back to the US
embassy and the CIA. US imperialism is irreconcilably opposed to the Bolivarian
Revolution because it has aroused the mass of poor and dispossessed people, giving them new hope and a sense of their own power and dignity. Washington is
terrified because this is acting as a point of attraction and a beacon to the workers and peasants of all Latin America. They are determined to sabotage and crush
the revolution.

86) The attitude of Washington was shown in the first coup, when the US
government rushed with indecent haste to recognise the counter-revolutionary
bandits. This exposed the lying hypocrisy of their arguments about "democracy".
As always, the US imperialists only support "democracy" when it suits their
interests. When they do not like the way the majority votes, they support counter-revolutionary coups and dictatorships. The fact that the coup in Caracas
deposed a democratically elected government was only a small detail.

87) Everyone knows that the hand of Washington is behind every act of the
counter-revolution in Venezuela. Even a blind man could see this. Yet there are
still people who imagine that US imperialism will leave Venezuela alone if only
the revolution is halted. This is the logic of a little child who hears noises at night
and covers its head with a blanket. It imagines that if it is very quiet and closes
its eyes, it will be out of danger. But adult people know that the way to confront
danger is not by closing one's eyes.

88) Everyone agrees that imperialism is the most implacable enemy of the
Bolivarian Revolution. But what is imperialism? Imperialism is monopoly capitalism. It is a system of world relations based on the domination of the globe by
a handful of big corporations, most of them based in the USA. The military activities of imperialism are only an expression of the interests of these big corporations. The headquarters of imperialism is in Washington, but it has its local office
boys in Venezuela – the Venezuelan bankers and capitalists. The Venezuelan
bourgeoisie dances to Washington's tune. A serious struggle against imperialism

is therefore unthinkable without an implacable struggle against the local bourgeoisie.

89) US imperialism is clearly preparing new attacks against the Venezuelan Revolution. It is treacherously disseminating the lie that Venezuela is supporting the Colombian FARC guerrillas. This is a provocation that is intended to prepare the way for a future military intervention of the Colombian armed forces against Venezuela. The accusation that the Venezuelan government is guilty of supporting "narcoterrorism" is yet another indication that US imperialism is preparing to launch an armed aggression using the Colombian army and paramilitary groups. The recent declarations of the Colombian senate point unequivocally in the same direction. Now we have direct proof that the fascist thugs of the Colombian paramilitaries are already active on Venezuelan soil. They will be used as the shock troops of the counter-revolution. This perspective adds even greater urgency to the demand for the arming of the population.

Chaos and bloodshed?

90) In order to guarantee the future of the Venezuelan Revolution it is necessary to inflict a decisive defeat on the internal counter-revolution, to eliminate once and for all the Fifth Column that provides the US imperialists with a base for their operations against the revolution, that is constantly involved in sabotage and is actively conspiring with foreign counter-revolutionary terrorists to plunge the country into chaos and bloodshed. It is necessary to carry through the revolution to the end. That is the first step.

91) "But the Americans will invade!" our critics will exclaim. The logic of this argument is that if we do nothing, we will avoid the attacks of the counter-revolution and imperialism. The exact opposite is the case.

92) Naturally, we do not want a military conflict with either the USA or Colombia. But the way to avoid such a conflict is not to follow the advice of the reformists, but quite the opposite. The more decisive the attitude of the Venezuelan people, the more it shows that it is ready to fight, the less will be the appetite of US imperialism for a new military adventure. Conversely, the greater the vacillations, the more conciliatory the attitude, the greater will be the pressure of the warmongering faction in Bush's administration to intervene.

93) Despite its immense power, the room for manoeuvre of US imperialism is limited by the general world situation. It is bogged down in military adventures in Iraq and Afghanistan. The mood of the masses in the USA is increasingly critical. Therefore, it is unlikely that it would contemplate a direct military intervention in Venezuela, even on the scale of its intervention in Haiti. It understands that

Venezuela is not Haiti and it would be faced with massive resistance.

94) The power of US imperialism is vast, but it is not unlimited. In Iraq the American invaders are faced with a general uprising of the masses that they cannot defeat, despite all their tremendous military power. If they were faced with uprisings everywhere, they would not be able to intervene.

95) Napoleon stressed the vital importance of morale in war. It is not just a question of guns and military technology, but of the will to fight and win. The masses have already demonstrated that they are prepared to fight to defend the revolution. On two occasions they have defeated the counter-revolution. How much more enthusiastically would they fight once they had the power in their hands? Any attempt to stage an armed intervention against Venezuela would be met with strikes, demonstrations and uprisings. Iraq shows that it is impossible to hold down an entire people, when the people is armed and mobilised to fight. However, the best defence is an internationalist policy.

96) It is true that US imperialism has colossal power and reserves. But does the Venezuelan Revolution have reserves? Yes, it has huge reserves of support in the mass of downtrodden and oppressed people in Latin America and the working class of the whole world. That is why an internationalist policy is essential. Having taken power in its hands the Venezuelan workers must make an appeal to the workers of the rest of the continent to follow their example.

97) Everywhere in Latin America there is poverty, hunger and despair. A revolutionary appeal would not fall on deaf ears. The imperialists and reactionaries would be paralysed if there were a general revolutionary movement. This would have serious repercussions inside the USA itself, where the mood of the masses is already changing as a result of Bush's Iraq adventure.

98) The Bolivarian Revolution cannot succeed if it remains within the confines of capitalism. Nor can it maintain itself indefinitely within the narrow confines of the national state. The Bolivarian revolution can begin in Venezuela, but its ultimate triumph depends on the overthrow of the rule of the exploiters throughout Latin America and beyond.

99) The original vision of Bolivar – that great son of the Venezuelan people – was not a national revolution, but a revolution that would unite the peoples of all Latin America and the Caribbean. That was really the only way in which the continent could achieve genuine independence, freedom and prosperity. But Bolivar's vision was betrayed by the bourgeoisie and the Creole aristocracy. The greedy and corrupt oligarchies carried out the Balkanisation of Latin America, dividing it up into national states that often waged fratricidal wars for territory. This fatally weakened Latin America and brought it under the domination of

imperialism, draining its resources, destroying its huge potential and reducing its people to misery and despair.

100) Today Bolivar's vision of a united Latin America retains all its vitality. It is the only way forward. But it can never be realised on the basis of capitalism. The bourgeoisie has had almost 200 years to show what it can do, and it has been exposed as bankrupt. Only the proletariat, in alliance with the peasants, the urban poor and all other exploited classes, can realise this perspective. In order to do this, it must expropriate the landlords and capitalists and create a Socialist Federation of Latin America.

101) By uniting the vast economic resources of Latin America in a common socialist plan of production, the enormous economic potential of the continent can be realised for the first time. Compared to this, the miserable little schemes of the bourgeoisie, such as Mercosur, will be exposed as insignificant tinkering. In the space of two five year plans, enough resources would be generated to completely transform the lives of millions of men, women and children. That is the perspective we hold out to the masses of Latin America. It is the only cause worth fighting for. Once the masses realise the potential, they will fight with tremendous energy. Faced with a general revolutionary upsurge all over Latin America, the US imperialists would be rendered impotent. If they are not able to hold down Iraq, much less would they be able to hold down the whole of Latin America. Instead of intervening, they would be faced with revolutionary movements at home.

102) Sceptics will say this is utopian. But what is really utopian is the notion that by showing "moderation" we can avoid counter-revolution. The conditions for socialist revolution have matured in Venezuela, and are maturing all over Latin America. What is required is a courageous leadership that accepts this and acts accordingly. Those self-styled "realists" who are trying to halt the revolution half way, irrespective of their subjective intentions, are playing the game of the counter-revolution. What they advocate is the worst kind of utopianism.

103) The whole logic of the situation is impelling the working class to take power into its hands. This task would, however, be immeasurably easier if there existed a powerful Marxist tendency in the Bolivarian movement, impelling it in this direction. But the movement remains confused, its programme unclear. This confusion must be cleared away as soon as possible and the objectives of the movement spelled out with utmost clarity.

104) The forces of Marxism exist, but they are still too weak to provide decisive leadership. The most urgent task is to overcome this weakness as quickly as possible and unite all the forces of genuine Marxism as the only consistently revolutionary wing of the Bolivarian movement. The unification of *El Militante* with

El Topo Obrero marked an important step in this direction. But it is only the first step. Others must follow.

105) The greatest danger for the Venezuelan Marxists is impatience, sectarian and ultraleft moods. The revolutionary Marxist current is at present a minority of the mass movement. We cannot impose our solutions on it. We must resist the temptations to present it with ultimatums. We must be patient with the masses, working side by side with them to win their respect and confidence. Our slogan must be that of Lenin in 1917: Patiently explain!

106) We must constitute ourselves as an integral part of the mass movement – the Marxist wing of the Bolivarian movement. "But that means sacrificing the independence of the Party", the sectarians will exclaim. In reality, the independence of the Marxist wing is a political, not an organisational, question. We must remain absolutely independent in our ideas, programme, policies and methods. But we must also fight to carry these ideas into the mass movement, to fertilise it with the ideas of Marxism and to fight to win the majority. Conditions are ripe, since the concrete experience of the mass of working people in the last few years is already pushing them to draw the most advanced conclusions.

107) The first task is to win the advanced workers and the youth, who are active in and around the revolutionary organisations (Bolivarian Circles, revolutionary assemblies, democratic unions, etc). First we must win the advanced elements, and then through them we can reach the masses. We say to the activists of the movement: We Marxists are also part of the movement. We are ready to work for it, to build it, to strengthen it and to fight together with you against our common enemies. We do not seek to impose our ideas. All we ask is the right to defend our independent class standpoint and fight for our ideas within the movement.

108) There is no contradiction between building the Revolutionary Marxist Current and participating actively in the Bolivarian movement. In reality, the two things are inseparable. The Marxists must work and fight shoulder to shoulder with the masses, pushing the movement forward, and explaining at every stage what is necessary for the movement to succeed.

109) The first condition for our success is the education of the cadres. The only thing that separates us from the rest of the movement, apart from being the most militant and revolutionary elements, is our serious attitude to theory and ideas. Marxism is scientific socialism and a scientific standpoint is absolutely necessary if the working class is to succeed. We have a clear understanding of events nationally and internationally, a coherent method and strategy. By contrast, all the other trends are characterised by confusion, lack of clarity, ambigu-

ity and the complete absence of a coherent strategy. The consequences of this will be cruelly exposed as events unfold. The workers and youth will begin to understand through their own experience the superiority of Marxism.

110) Either the greatest of victories or the most terrible of defeats – that is the choice before the Venezuelan Revolution.

Chapter Ten

As August 15th approaches:
Why we are fighting for a "No"
next Sunday

London, August 11th, 2004

From the very beginning Marxist.com, the Hands off Venezuela campaign and the Revolutionary Marxist Current have fought against the attempts of the Venezuelan opposition, backed by US imperialism, to overthrow the democratically elected and progressive government of Hugo Chávez.

Why do we take this position? Because a defeat for Chávez in the referendum would be a heavy blow against the workers and peasants of all Latin America. It would be a victory for imperialism and the forces of reaction everywhere. The barricades have been drawn in this class war and it is necessary to take sides clearly and unambiguously.

The struggle for the socialist transformation of society consists of a series of battles. The workers and peasants are confronted with a number of partial struggles against the class enemy – the landlords, bankers, capitalists and imperialists. It is only by participating with the utmost energy and determination in such struggles that the masses can acquire the necessary experience to raise themselves to the level needed to carry out a decisive change in society.

The place of the revolutionary Marxists is side by side with our class brothers and sisters. We will always be in the first ranks of the struggle, striving to push the movement forward, while simultaneously attempting to win over the vanguard to the programme and perspective of the socialist revolution.

With unerring class instinct the workers and peasants of Venezuela have understood the need to inflict a decisive defeat on the oligarchy and imperialism in the referendum. It is necessary to keep the old reactionary gangsters out of the Presidential Palace! It is necessary to stop them from putting the clock back and to return to ruling Venezuela the old way. That is the immediate and most pressing task.

The opposition has nothing to do with democracy. Reactionary scoundrels like Pedro Carmona and Carlos Andres Perez describe themselves as "democrats", when in realty everyone knows that they are the sworn enemies of democracy, as shown by the coup of April 12th, 2002. Carlos Andres Pérez himself, who is in the Dominican Republic fleeing from corruption charges, said in a recent statement that the only way to remove Chávez is by violent means and that after that the country would need at least five years of dictatorship! As for Washington, George Bush (who has never won a fair election) backed the reactionary coup with indecent haste and no questions asked. The speeches of these gentlemen about "democracy" only serve to evoke loud laughter.

Had these reactionary gangsters succeeded in 2002, we know very well what kind of "democracy" they would have imposed upon Venezuela. We remember the two days of voluntary blackout of the local media when supporters and officials of the Chávez government were being hunted down, while the "democratic" media maintained a discreet silence.

For a long time the opposition has made no secret of its desire to see Chávez overthrown and even killed. These "Christian" ladies and gentlemen are motivated not by love of their country but by blind hate – class hate. They hate Hugo Chávez because they see him as the leader of the poor and exploited that they hate and fear. He has brought the masses to their feet and made them conscious of their power. This is the real reason for the implacable hatred with which the President is regarded by the rich.

Stranglehold of imperialism

The victory of the opposition would be a disaster for the working class and the masses of Venezuela. It would lead to the abolition of the progressive measures introduced by the Chávez government and increase the stranglehold of imperialism and of private monopoly capital over the Venezuelan economy. It would push the workers and peasants back into the old servitude from which they are struggling to emerge.

Behind the Coordinadora Democratica stands all that is rotten, retrograde and corrupt in Venezuelan society. Here are the landlords, bankers and capitalists who have sucked the blood of the people of Venezuela for generations and sold the country out to imperialism at bargain basement prices. Here are the hired agents of Washington. Here are the "gilded youth" and the retired actresses, the spoilt brats of the rich and the fascists, the reactionaries and gangsters of all shapes and sizes.

Here are the corrupt and reactionary managers of PDVSA, who did not hesitate to drag the country to the brink of bankruptcy and ruin by declaring a so-called strike "until the President resigns", and are now resorting to other means to attain the same end. Here are the corrupt "trade union" bureaucrats who have long ago sold their souls to the CIA and the oligarchy. Here are the prostitutes and liars of the millionaire press and television. Here are the cardinals and bishops who backed the coup in 2002 and used lies and blackmail to try to force the President to resign.

These are the forces that back the opposition and are calling for a "yes" vote on Sunday. What forces are on the other side?

On the side of Hugo Chávez are the working class fighting for decent wages and conditions, the peasants fighting for land, the unemployed fighting for work and bread, the working class women fighting for equality, the poor and oppressed fighting for housing and justice, the advanced intellectuals fighting for culture, the anti-imperialists fighting for freedom, the youth fighting for a future. Here are the true heirs of Bolivar, Marti and Che Guevara, side by side with those of Marx, Engels, Lenin and Trotsky: in one word, all the living elements of Venezuelan society.

In this class struggle, we are in no doubt where we stand.

Comrades! Workers and youth of Venezuela! Let us unite to smash the opposition on Sunday 15 August! And then let us continue the fight to carry the revolution through to the end!

In spite of the lies of the pro-opposition media and its scandalous manipulation of information, the opposition seems to be heading for a well-deserved defeat next Sunday. With just one week to go before the decisive Presidential recall referendum scheduled for Sunday, August 15th, a statistical review of all Venezuelan opinion polls (Mercanalisis, Opinion Research, Alfredo Keller, Hinterlaces and Evans) showed that President Chávez was in the lead. Published last Saturday, August 7th, 2004 in *VHeadline.com,* it indicated that "President Hugo Chávez Frias would continue in office after the results of the August 15th recall referendum are made known. Close on 14 million Venezuelan voters are registered to ratify Chávez Frias in the Presidency through January 10th, 2007 ... or, in the increasingly unlikely event that he loses the vote, to step down and schedule fresh Presidential election within 30 days."

Jesse Chacon, Venezuelan Minister of Information and Communications (MINCI), was quoted as saying that "all the pollsters ... including those who work for the opposition ... give the President an advantage of not less than 10 percent". This completely exposes the lies of the opposition and the capitalist media, which have been constantly plying the story that Chávez was a "dictator". The fact of the matter is that only a massive fraud next Sunday could bring about the overthrow of the President, who has the support of the overwhelming majority of the Venezuelan people.

Chacon thought that the differences were "irreversible at this point" despite fraudulent results published in some newspapers "... two opposition-controlled Caracas newspapers have been forced to admit that they have published bogus opinion surveys as part of their efforts to attack the presidency.

"The Minister says the vast majority of the general public has already made up its mind on how to vote in eight days' time ... only 10-15 percent remain undecided so the die is already cast!"

Let us hope that this is correct. In all probability it is. Ever since the start of the revolutionary process, the masses have shown a high degree of maturity and an instinctive grasp of political necessity. They have defeated every attempt of the counter-revolution. They have defied the guns and truncheons of the forces of reaction. They have brushed aside the lying torrent of propaganda of the media.

This time is no different. The attempt of the opposition to utilise the device of the recall referendum to stage a coup by constitutional means has yet again roused the masses to action. The campaign for a no vote has been actively supported by millions. This is the answer to all the cowards, cynics and sceptics. The masses have once again confronted the counter-revolutionaries and are blocking their path.

Is the result, then, a foregone conclusion? There are very few things in life that are absolutely certain, and even fewer in a revolution. The very fact that the recall referendum was called at all was the result of a massive fraud, in which the ranks of the opposition were miraculously swelled by a large number of dead people. Maybe the presence of so many cardinals and bishops were responsible for this miracle!

Such is the determination of the class enemy to eliminate President Chávez that the repeat of some such "miracle" next Sunday is not impossible. The workers and peasants must be on their guard! If the opposition "wins" through fraud, the people must take matters into their own hands. The only answer is direct mass action in the form of a general strike and an insurrection that will place power in the hands of the working people – the only truly democratic force in society.

Bolivarian movement

Let nobody fool himself. If – as seems likely – the masses win the referendum that will not mean the revolution is saved. On the contrary, the enemy will immediately launch a new and even more furious offensive against it. Those people in the leadership of the Bolivarian movement who argued that the acceptance of the referendum would satisfy the imperialists are wrong. The revolution will have to defend itself, and the only defence possible for a revolution is to go onto the attack.

The committees that have been set up to win the referendum campaign must be kept in being after August 15th. They must be broadened and made completely democratic, to include the widest layers of the working class and other oppressed layers. They must be linked up at local, regional and national level. Above all, they must be armed. Only the armed people can defend the Revolution against its enemies.

One thing is certain: as long as the oligarchy is permitted to retain key levers of economic power in its hands, it will continue to use its power to undermine the revolution, to insult, calumny and discredit the democratically elected government and to prepare for new coups, assassinations and violence.

Let us therefore mobilise all our forces to defeat the enemy on April 15th. But if we win, let us not waste our victory as we have done on previous occasions in futile attempts to negotiate and compromise with the enemy. Let us use our victory to advance and destroy the economic and political power of the oligarchy forever and carry the revolution out to the end in Venezuela and in the rest of Latin America.

❑ Defeat the counter-revolution!
❑ Vote "no" on August 15th!
❑ Down with imperialism and the oligarchy!
❑ Carry the revolution through to the end!

Despite the popular support that Hugo Chávez enjoyed in June 2004, the Electoral Commission gave in to the pressures of the OAS and the Carter Centre and accepted the signatures presented by the opposition to force a referendum. These signatures had been clearly collected by fraudulent means. To counteract this counter-revolutionary threat, during the referendum campaign the Venezuelan masses organised themselves into UBEs (Electoral Battle Units) and Electoral platoons. These bodies organised up to 1.5 million people on a community basis to canvas for the 'No' option.

Chapter Eleven

The recall referendum in Venezuela –
A crushing blow to the counter-revolution

London, August 16th, 2004.

At 4:03 this morning Venezuela's National Electoral Council (CNE) announced the result of the recall referendum on the government of the Venezuelan President Hugo Chávez Frias. A tally count of 94.49 percent of ballots from automatic voting machines revealed that the opposition had failed to obtain more votes than those who wanted Chávez to stay. 4,991,483 were in favour of him staying, representing 58.95 percent of those voting, and 3,576,517 against, representing 41.74 percent.

Immediately the opposition "categorically refused" to recognise the result. Nevertheless, it is clear that the "no" has won by an overwhelming majority. Early reports suggested an even bigger majority – 63 percent to 36 percent. This may be closer to the truth. Manual count of votes from rural districts and poor urban areas where Chávez has widespread support, and where automatic machines were not used, will probably increase the President's margin of victory.

The referendum has roused the masses. There was unprecedented voter participation because everyone knew what was at stake. As a result Venezuelans were queuing for up to 10 hours to vote. Our correspondent in Caracas wrote last night, giving a taste of the mood on the streets during the voting:

"The euphoria on the faces of the people and the street celebrations in poor areas of Caracas contrast with the angry mood in the areas of the *escuálidos*. In all areas there have been big queues to vote, but whereas in the poorer districts they are still waiting to vote, in the upper class and middle class areas the queues have already vanished. In some areas people have been waiting six or seven hours to vote."

The participation was around 70 percent. This historic voter turnout stands in stark contrast to the participation in elections in Britain or the United States. This is what happens when the people feel that they have something to vote for – and against. It is what happens when people feel that politics really matter and that voting can make a difference. What a contrast to the situation in the "western democracies" where in most cases people do not even bother to vote because they feel that, whoever is elected, it will make no real difference to their lives. Yet Bush and Blair think they have the right to lecture the people of Venezuela on democracy!

This outstanding victory in Sunday's referendum is the eighth electoral victory of Chávez and the Bolivarians in the last six years. Yet the opposition still persists in describing him as a "dictator". This flies in the face of the facts. Whatever you think about Hugo Chávez he is not a dictator. After almost six years in government, President Chávez has not only maintained his popular support but increased it. He won 56 percent in the 1998 elections and 59 percent in the 2000 re-election. Now his support is near 60 percent.

Defeated in every election, the opposition has tried to remove Chávez from power through a coup d'état in 2002, followed by a management-led shutdown of the state oil company PDVSA. When these attempts failed the opposition put all their weight behind the recall referendum to oust the democratically elected President before the end of his term.

This is ironical. The constitutional right to a recall referendum only exists thanks to the new Constitution drafted by an elected Constituency Assembly during Hugo Chávez's first year in office, and approved by popular referendum. The recall of elected officials was an idea proposed by Chávez to the Assembly, and it was supported by the majority and *rejected* by the opposition, which then hypocritically used that right to attempt to oust the President. By the way, if these "democrats" had won, the first thing they would have done is to abolish the right of recall referendum!

These gentlemen call themselves democrats but in practice show that "democracy" is only acceptable to them as long as their side wins. Right up to the last minute the opposition continued its manoeuvres. Before the official announcement was made by the CNE, a separate announcement was made by CNE board members Sobella Mejia and Ezequiel Zamora, questioning the result. It is an open secret that both Sobella Mejia and Zamora are aligned with the opposition. By such dirty tricks the opposition seeks to discredit the referendum and thus prepare the way for future acts of sabotage.

Once again the working class and poor people of Venezuela displayed an unerring class instinct. It was reported that in the working-class neighbourhood of Petare, people were queuing since 4 am. When it became clear that the opposition had been defeated, the mood of the masses erupted. The streets around the Miraflores Presidential Palace in Caracas were full of pro-Chávez demonstrators celebrating this new victory for the Bolivarian Revolution. *Venezuelanalysis.com* reports: "Chavistas have taken the streets of working-class neighbourhoods blowing horns and playing music. Fireworks and firecrackers can also be heard in working class sections of Caracas, resembling a New Year's celebration."

There is no doubt that this result represents a body blow to the counter-revolutionaries, a section of which was clearly reluctant to accept the result. Intense negotiations were reported to be taking place between the Carter Centre and the Organisation of American States (OAS) and the opposition coalition Democratic Coordinator to convince them to accept Chávez's victory.

It is quite natural that the masses should celebrate. They had yet again delivered a heavy blow against the counter-revolution and blocked it on the electoral plane. But strangely enough, Chávez opponents were also reported to be on the streets, ordered out by their leaders to celebrate their own "victory". Rank and file Chavista groups have denounced the call as a plan to cause public disruptions and possible roadblocks as was done earlier this year. An opposition leader's call for a "civil rebellion" to protest the delays in the voting process clearly confirm these fears.

The counter-revolutionaries were hoping to use the referendum to engineer new clashes and disorders. Their ever-present hope is to cause sufficient chaos to provoke a coup. This would have been the scenario especially if the result had been close.

Opposition leaders Humberto Calderon Berti and Cesar Perez Vivas from the COPEI party gave a press conference Sunday night to thank international observers present in this "historic election". The miserable expression on Berti's face told its own story. It was not supposed to be like this! The counter-revolutionaries hoped that their control of the mass media would give them a sufficient advantage to win the referendum. In addition they counted on the scarcely concealed support of Washington and most of the governments of Latin America, in the person of Jimmy Carter and the OAS.

We have still to hear the verdict of international observers, including former US President Jimmy Carter and the Organisation of American States. More than 400 international observers, including a mission from the Organisation of American States, descended upon Venezuela to "observe" the recall referendum process. This was really an unprecedented level of foreign interference in Venezuela's internal affairs. This recall referendum was the most closely monitored electoral process in the western hemisphere. There was certainly no such monitoring of the last US Presidential elections, which were rigged to allow George W. Bush to get possession of the White House. But such little contradictions do not bother Venezuela's foreign critics too much.

The best-known element in the "observer mission" is the Carter Centre, founded by former US President Jimmy Carter. This former peanut farmer made a mediocre President, but as a diplomatic manoeuverer he has excellent qualifications. President Chávez told me how Jimmy Carter wept when he learned of the appalling conditions of the Venezuelan poor. His ability to weep at given intervals is part of his inheritance from the US's Southern Bible Belt. No doubt his ancestors also wept for the plight of the poor at the same time as they enriched themselves on the backs of their black slaves. This special brand of Christian hypocrisy is a most useful weapon in the armoury of international diplomacy, and one that Mr. Carter has mastered to the utmost perfection.

Hypocrisy is, in fact, very much in demand in Venezuela at the present time. The counter-revolution cannot afford to appear publicly in its real guise, but must disguise itself as "true democracy", even though its real aim is to install a dictatorship in Venezuela. Numerous counter-revolutionary organisations have sprung up posing as "human rights" groups and so on. In order to deceive public opinion, things must be turned into their opposite: an election defeat must be presented as a victory, and a victory as a defeat, dictatorship must be presented as democracy and democracy as dictatorship, and so on.

One of those who specialise in this particular brand of hypocrisy and deceit is Súmate, which is supposed to be an objective non-partisan civil association but in reality it is a pro-opposition group, financed by Washington. The co-director of Súmate, Maria Corina Machado, was a participant in the 2002 coup that briefly overthrew Chávez – she signed the decrees of would-be dictator Pedro Carmona. She is currently being investigated for treason, for having received funds from a foreign government (the US) earmarked for ousting the Chávez government.

Súmate used its funds generously supplied by US donors to organise a large team of "volunteers" whose aim was to collect the largest possible number of "yes" votes in exit polls. These "objective results" could then be presented as "proof" that the opposition had won, and used as propaganda for organising disturbances when a Chávez victory was announced.

Despite its public image of an "impartial body", the Carter Centre is a tool of Washington. The Carter Centre relies on US government funding. And as the English proverb goes: he who pays the piper calls the tune. It is well known that the entire US political establishment opposes Chávez and supports the opposition.

In testimony before a US subcommittee hearing on March 15th, 2000, the Carter Centre's lead observer, University of Georgia political science professor Jennifer McCoy clearly placed the Venezuelan government in the category of *"new, subtler forms of authoritarianism through the electoral option..."* In her declared quest to "deter new hybrid democracies," McCoy called for continued US government support of the Carter Centre, claiming that such funding represented a "neutral and professional means to improve the electoral process."

Dr. McCoy has called for US pressure on the Chávez government, though there had never been any significant allegations of electoral fraud in either Chávez's 1998 election or in the plebiscites that his government sponsored in following years. She also portrayed the Chávez government in the same light as the Peruvian ex-dictator Alberto Fujimori!

Carter urges caution

The fact that the sympathies of Carter and the OAS were all on the side of the opposition is not seriously in doubt. However, the plans of the opposition to make use of the foreign "observers" were dashed by the mass response to the referendum campaign. The campaign itself was conducted in a scrupulously fair and democratic manner. None of the hoped-for irregularities were found.

Early on Sunday, after visiting several voting centres, Carter was forced to admit that the voting queues in Venezuela were "unprecedentedly long and orderly". Carter, who heads the Carter Centre mission to observe Venezuela's historic recall referendum, added that "from the first hours of the day we have visited several voting centres of Caracas and there are thousands of people waiting with plenty of patience and in peace." OAS Secretary General Cesar Gaviria stated on Sunday that the referendum results would be "trustworthy".

What else could these ladies and gentlemen say? The original intention of the OAS and the Carter Centre was to put pressure on the Caracas government to reach a "compromise" with the opposition, or, if possible, to rig the referendum in favour of the latter. If the result had been a close one, they might have tried to announce an opposition victory before the official result had been announced. This was probably the reason why the announcement of the result was delayed.

A section of the hardliners must have been demanding that the OAS and Carter should collaborate with such a manoeuvre. Some sectors of the opposition had apparently announced their intention to release the results of their own exit polls five hours before the voting centres were scheduled to close. This seems to have been the position of the opposition leader Enrique Mendoza. This would have been a clear provocation. But both the Carter Centre and the Organisation of American States have understood that it is pointless and counterproductive to try to deny the result of the referendum.

At half past one in the morning, officials from the Carter Centre and OAS emerged from a meeting with the National Electoral Council. They were desperately trying to convince the Democratic Coordinator opposition coalition to accept Chávez's victory. There must have been a heated exchange in the small hours of the morning. But Carter could not oblige the hard liners. He is undoubtedly an imperialist scoundrel, but he is not a complete fool. A blatant attempt to hand victory to the opposition through fraud would have immediately provoked an explosion that could not be controlled.

144 ◆ Revolution in Venezuela

Carter, a relatively astute representative of US imperialism therefore had to put pressure on the opposition to calm down. The Venezuelan newspaper *Diario Vea* stated that Dr. McCoy had indirectly criticized the opposition's decision to release early and unofficial results. Dr. McCoy reportedly declared that all political actors should wait for the announcement of results by the accredited governmental body, the National Electoral Council.

Both the Carter Centre and the Organisation of American States understood that it was pointless and counterproductive to try to deny the result of the referendum. But that was only a tactical decision. They understood that a coup was out of the question *at this moment in time*, because the class balance of forces was not favourable. Thus, a Chávez victory will have to be grudgingly accepted by at least one sector of the opposition. The best that they can hope for is to cast some doubt on the process, exaggerating irregularities, shouting fraud, etc. This they are already doing. In fact, they were already doing it before the referendum even took place.

What now?

As we predicted in our previous article, the imperialists understand that the time is not ripe for a new coup, which would lead to civil war – a civil war that they would certainly lose. *Therefore, they have decided to adopt a different tactic.* Having failed to take their objective by assault, they will resort to siege warfare. The struggle has not ended – merely passed onto a different plane. The counter-revolutionaries and their imperialist allies will wait until the correlation of class forces is more favourable. They will move again. But for now they must beat a tactical retreat and lick their wounds.

Does this mean that everything is solved and that the opposition has been decisively defeated? No, it means no such thing. What the referendum campaign has shown is that Venezuelan society is extremely polarized between right and left. This polarisation will not disappear after the referendum, but steadily increase. In that sense, *the referendum has solved nothing.* The counter-revolutionaries will regroup their forces and prepare for a new offensive once the conditions are more favourable.

On the international plane they will not cease their noisy campaign against the Venezuelan Revolution, or drop their claims that that Chávez has authoritarian tendencies. With the aid of organisations like Súmate, they will publish fake exit polls that directly contradict the official results to show that the result was based on fraud. They will continue to sabotage and obstruct the progress of the revolution, attempting to cause economic and social chaos. They will never be satisfied until Chávez has been overthrown and the gains of the Bolivarian revolution completely liquidated.

The latest victory of the Chávez government places the bourgeois opposition in a difficult position. This is the fourth time that a free election in Venezuela has given a decisive majority to Chávez. The Venezuelan bourgeoisie is getting increasingly desperate. The class war is intensifying all the time. The workers and peasants, encouraged by the result of the referendum, will demand more reforms and a deepening of the revolutionary process. The bourgeoisie and the imperialists will demand a halt and a reversal. The government will find itself ground between two millstones.

The massive voter participation on Sunday is a clear reflection of the extreme political polarization of Venezuelan society to the right and left. The immediate question was the permanence of President Hugo Chávez in office, but far deeper questions are involved, and these questions remain to be solved. It was necessary to win the referendum, but the referendum result will not solve these fundamental problems. It will only pose them in an even sharper way.

Those leaders of the Bolivarian movement, who argued that by holding the referendum the enemies of the revolution would be silenced, have been shown to be wrong. The internal and external enemies of the Venezuelan Revolution cannot be reconciled by elections, referendums and negotiations. They will only be satisfied when the revolution is defeated. Not to recognise this is the height of irresponsibility.

On previous occasions when the masses defeated the counter-revolution there was a golden opportunity to carry through the revolution to the end and finish the power of the oligarchy once and for all. But on each occasion the opportunity was thrown away. The leaders allowed themselves to be seduced by the siren voices that argued for "moderation" and "negotiation". The inevitable result was a new offensive of the counter-revolution.

It is time to learn the lessons! One cannot make half a revolution. As long as the oligarchy continues to maintain its hold on important sections of the economy, it will continue to act as a Trojan Horse of US imperialism, sabotaging and undermining the Bolivarian Revolution. It is time to ask ourselves the key question: can we allow the interests of a handful of rich parasites to decide the destinies of millions of people? Or will we put an end to this situation once and for all, expropriating the property of the counter-revolutionaries and taking the road of socialist democracy?

The 15th August will enter the annals of revolutionary history as a great victory for the working people – on one condition: that we do not waste it, that we do not hand the initiative back to our enemies, but strike blows against them that will destroy the basis of their power. That is the only way we can build upon our victory, and turn it into a decisive revolutionary transformation of society.

Chapter Twelve

The nationalisation of Venepal:
What does it signify?

London, January 21st, 2005

"Without succumbing to illusions and without fear of slander, the advanced workers will completely support the Mexican people in their struggle against the imperialists. The expropriation of oil is neither socialism nor communism. But it is a highly progressive measure of national self-defence. Marx did not, of course, consider Abraham Lincoln a communist; this did not, however, prevent Marx from entertaining the deepest sympathy for the struggle that Lincoln headed. The First International sent the Civil War president a message of greeting, and Lincoln in his answer greatly appreciated this moral support.

"The international proletariat has no reason to identify its program with the program of the Mexican government. Revolutionists have no need of changing colour, adapting themselves, and rendering flattery in the manner of the GPU school of courtiers, who in a moment of danger will sell out and betray the weaker side. Without giving up its own identity, every honest working class organisation of the entire world, and first of all in Great Britain, is duty-bound – to take an irreconcilable position against the imperialist robbers, their diplomacy, their press, and their fascist hirelings. The cause of Mexico, like the cause of Spain, like the cause of China, is the cause of the international working class. The struggle over Mexican oil is only one of the advance-line skirmishes of future battles between the oppressors and the oppressed."

(Leon Trotsky, *Mexico and British Imperialism*,
Socialist Appeal, 25th June, 1938)

Dramatic events are unfolding in Venezuela. The nationalisation of Venepal under decree number 3438 marks a sharp new turn in the situation. Venepal was one of the biggest paper mills in Venezuela. The company was abandoned by its owners when the lockout of 2002 took place. After two years of struggle and continuous occupation of the factory, it has been nationalised under workers-state control. This act represents a blow against the corrupt and rotten Venezuelan oligarchy and the imperialist robbers who stand behind it. It will be welcomed enthusiastically by the workers of all countries, in the same way that Trotsky welcomed the nationalisation of the Mexican oil industry by President Lazaro Cardenas in 1938.

Although in itself it does not yet mean a qualitative change in the class nature of the Venezuelan Revolution, this bold measure certainly signifies a step in the right direction. It indicates that the working class is intervening in the revolution with increasing determination, pressing for its independent class interests, demanding a break with capitalism and pushing the revolution forwards. This, and this alone, can guarantee the final and decisive victory.

The Venezuelan Revolution began as a national democratic revolution that did not go beyond the boundaries of capitalism and private property. Despite this fact, it immediately aroused the hatred and the implacable opposition of the Venezuelan oligarchy and its masters in Washington and of the bourgeoisie and reactionaries of Latin America and the rest of the world.

From the very beginning, the international Marxist tendency represented by Marxist.com has consistently defended the Venezuelan Revolution against its enemies. It is the elementary duty of all workers and progressive people everywhere to defend the Bolivarian Revolution against the conspiracies of imperialism and the oligarchy. *At the same time, the Marxists defend their own policies, ideas and programme. We stand firmly on the basis of the proletariat and, within the general process of the national democratic revolution, defend its independent class demands. Our slogan is that of Lenin: "march separately and strike together!"*

President Hugo Chávez, like Lazaro Cardenas, has shown himself to be a courageous champion of the poor and oppressed and a fearless fighter against imperialism. Until now he did not pose the question of socialism. But by boldly challenging the privileges of the ruling class and resisting the pressure of imperialism, he inevitably placed himself on a collision course with the forces of the old society. *This has a logic and a dynamic of its own.*

The whole logic of the revolution tends to exacerbate the contradictions between the Venezuelan landlords and capitalists on the one hand, backed by imperialism, and the Venezuelan workers and poor peasants, backed by the masses in Latin America and the world Labour Movement, on the other. Not to see this fact would be unpardonable stupidity. Not to see that the struggle must be fought out to the end and can only result in the decisive victory of one class over another would be reformist blindness.

The destiny of the Venezuelan Revolution will be decided by the class struggle. The final outcome is not yet sure. What is completely sure is that the only force that has saved the Revolution time and again from defeat is the masses: the workers and poor peasants, who have repeatedly demonstrated their unshakable loyalty to the Bolivarian Revolution, their willingness to fight and to make the utmost sacrifices to defend it against its enemies. This is the real base of the revolution, its true strength, its only hope.

Muddle headed reformists try to blur the differences between different classes in the Revolution. They speak of the "people" as a homogeneous bloc, when in reality it is an empty abstraction that conceals a sharp difference of interests. What does the Venezuelan worker have in common with the capitalists? What does the Venezuelan peasant have in common with the landlords? What does the Venezuelan small shopkeeper have in common with the bankers and moneylenders?

At every decisive turn in the revolution, the role of the different classes has become manifest. The bankers, landlords and capitalists have resisted the revolution, sabotaged it and attempted to overthrow it. And who saved the revolution at every stage? It was the masses, and the working class in the first place, who saved the revolution in the coup of April 2002, and it was the workers who saved it at the time of the bosses' lockout that was designed to paralyse the economy and bring it to its knees. Finally, it was the masses who rallied magnificently to the defence of the revolution in the August referendum that inflicted a crushing blow to the counter-revolution.

Colossal power

All these events were great victories that demonstrated the colossal power of the masses, once they are mobilised to fight for a better world. We celebrated these victories, but at the same time we warned that the war was not over, that the enemies of the revolution were not decisively defeated, and that they would regroup and organise new counteroffensives, one after the other.

Events in recent weeks have proved that we were right. Those who imagined that the referendum result would silence the enemies of the revolution have been proven wrong. The imperialists are not in the slightest interested in the rules of formal democracy. They see the Venezuelan Revolution as a serious threat to their most vital interests and will not stop until they have destroyed it. Condoleeza Rice was no sooner installed in her new position than she attacked Venezuela. That shows that Washington remains intransigently hostile to Chávez and the Bolivarian Revolution. No amount of fine words or diplomatic gestures will appease the US imperialists!

George Bush and his allies inside Venezuela will stop at nothing to eliminate

Hugo Chávez and liquidate the Venezuelan Revolution. The only real allies of the Venezuelan Revolution are the masses of workers and poor peasants of Latin America and the world Labour Movement. The kidnapping of a Colombian guerrilla by Colombian agents in collaboration with elements of the Venezuelan armed forces indicates what was evident to all but the blindest of the blind: that US imperialism and its puppets in Bogota have not abandoned their intrigues against the Venezuelan Revolution.

The counter-revolutionaries remain active. New conspiracies are being hatched. The kidnapping in Caracas showed that Washington is still using its puppets in Bogota to attack and undermine the Venezuelan Revolution. Its armed agents operate with impunity on Venezuelan soil. The fact that they were aided by elements within the Venezuelan armed forces indicates that counter-revolutionary elements still exist within the state and are conspiring with the enemies of the revolution at home and abroad.

The power of US imperialism is very great but it has definite limits. Washington cannot permit itself the luxury of intervening militarily in Venezuela at a time when it is bogged down in an unwinnable conflict in Iraq. But it can intervene indirectly, using Colombia and the OAS. After the scandal of the kidnapping, Peru, Mexico and Brazil have all hastened to offer their services to "mediate", that is, to place Venezuela in the accused bench for allegedly allowing foreign guerrillas to enter its territory, while drawing attention away from the criminal activities of the Colombian government and armed forces and their paymasters in Washington.

Against the power of imperialism and the oligarchy, the Bolivarian Revolution has its own powerful reserves of support: the power of the masses in struggle for their rights, the workers, the peasants, the revolutionary youth and the progressive intelligentsia. The US imperialists have the support of their hired mercenaries in Colombia and their despicable jackals in the OAS. But the Bolivarian Revolution has infinitely greater points of support – the oppressed masses of the whole of Latin America and the working class of the entire world.

Just as Simon Bolivar understood the need to carry the flame of revolution to the whole of Latin America, so the modern inheritors of Bolivar have the same mission. They can succeed where he failed – on one condition, that they do not allow themselves to be hypnotised by slavish respect for private property, bourgeois legality and the nation state.

Clarity is needed!

Genuine Marxists (as opposed to sectarian chatterboxes) have energetically supported the Venezuelan Revolution. But support for the Chávez government against imperialism and the counter-revolutionary oligarchy does not necessarily mean uncritical acceptance of everything that is done in Caracas. Like every successful revolution, the Bolivarian Revolution has attracted a large number of "friends" and admirers – some of whom only yesterday were its sternest critics. These are fair weather friends who will turn their backs on the revolution the moment it finds itself in difficulties. With "friends" like these, one does not need enemies!

These "friends of Venezuela" provide a regular chorus of praise and adulation. They insist that we should not criticise the government but simply nod in agreement. The workers and revolutionaries of Venezuela do not need flattery. As Lenin once said, talk, rhetoric and flattery have ruined more than one revolution. What is needed is an honest and frank appraisal of the revolution, its strong points and weaknesses, its successes and failures. Only on the basis of an honest discussion can the revolution learn and go forward. What is needed is clarity.

Unfortunately, the programme of the Bolivarians is not always very clear. Even the present measures in relation to Venepal are not entirely clear. The government has said that it will invest a lot of money in the company in order to make it viable. The state will be the owner at the beginning but there are hints that afterwards it will be given over to the workers as a cooperative as payment for the back wages that are owed to them. There has also been talk of co-management between the workers and the state (which could mean a whole range of different things, from workers being represented in the directors board, to workers control, etc).

It is necessary to clarify all these questions and to open a debate on the future direction, not just of Venepal, but of the Bolivarian Revolution itself. In this debate the Marxists will give critical support to the leaders of the national democratic revolution. We will say: *"This is a start, an important start – but only a start. The nationalisation of Venepal is very good, as far as it goes. But it does not go far enough. One swallow does not make a summer, and one nationalised firm does not make a socialist revolution. However, in order to succeed, the national democratic revolution must transform itself into a socialist revolution."*

Nevertheless, it is necessary to see the other side of the question. The real strength of Hugo Chávez and the Bolivarian Revolution was that it has brought the masses to their feet. Once the working class enters the arena of struggle, it acquires a dynamic and a movement of its own. The strength of the revolutionary movement in Venezuela lies not in its understanding of theory but in its daily practice. Its deeds speak louder than its words. Its actions far outstrip its consciousness. But sooner or later the masses will become conscious of the real meaning of their actions. They will come to understand the objective necessity of a radical break with capitalism. The recent speeches of President Chávez are already an anticipation of this.

Marx once pointed out that for the masses, one real step forward was worth a hundred correct programmes. And Lenin said that for the masses an ounce of practice is worth a ton of theory. The working class, whether in Venezuela, Britain or Russia, does not learn from books, but from experience. "Life teaches," says the Russian proverb. The workers learn from events, especially great events like the Venezuelan Revolution. They are learning fast through active participation. It was the pressure of the workers from below that led to the nationalisation of Venepal, and this in its turn will strengthen the tendency towards the statisation of the productive forces, towards a break with capitalism, towards a democratic socialist plan of production.

"Appetite comes with eating"

There is an old proverb: "appetite comes with eating". The nationalisation of Venepal is a big step forward. Its great merit is that is has broken the ice and opened the flood gates. Workers will be asking questions: why should nationalisation be limited to factories that are bankrupt or threaten to close? Why should the state always nationalise the losses and privatise the profits? In order that the nationalised enterprises should be viable, they must be part of a general plan of production. That will not be possible as long as key sections of the economy, such as banking and credit, remains in private hands.

The argument that the Bolivarian Revolution must not go beyond the boundaries of capitalism, must respect private property and so on, is sometimes put forward by certain Bolivarian leaders. It is presented as a very "realistic" point of view, as opposed to the supposed "utopia" of socialism. In reality, this argument itself is the most miserable form of utopianism. The idea that the revolution must confine itself within the iron straitjacket of capitalism is empty formalism. Life teaches us otherwise! At every step this argument clashes with the demands of reality.

The bosses express their bitter hatred of the revolution, they sabotage production, lay off workers, condemn their families to hunger and conspire with imperialism and the counter-revolution. The workers know this very well. They cannot understand how the interests of the revolution can be served by conciliating its enemies, allowing them to maintain their stranglehold over key points of the national economy.

For all these reasons the workers are demanding nationalisation and workers' control. They wish to help the Bolivarian government by fighting against its enemies, by driving out the landlords and capitalists, by concentrating power in the hands of the only people who really have the interests of the revolution at heart – the workers and peasants and their natural allies, the urban poor, the revolutionary youth, the soldiers, the women and the progressive intelligentsia.

Once the economic power of the bourgeoisie is broken, once the land, the banks and the industries are in the hands of the state, it would be possible to mobilise all the productive capacity of the nation in a common, democratically planned socialist economy. Very quickly it would be possible to win the war against poverty and misery, to raise the whole country to a new and higher level.

The Bolivarian movement has many strengths, and a number of important weaknesses. The main weakness of the Bolivarian movement is its lack of theory. Theory occupies a place in revolutions that military strategy occupies in war. A mistaken strategy in war will lead inevitably to mistakes in tactics and practical operations. It will undermine the morale of the troops and lead to all kinds of blunders, defeats and unnecessary loss of life.

It is the same in a revolution. Mistakes in theory will sooner or later be reflected in mistakes in practice. A mistake in everyday life can often be rectified. Everyday mistakes are not usually matters of life and death. But revolutions are life and death struggles and mistakes can be paid for very dearly. The task of the Venezuelan Revolutionary Marxist Current is to provide the necessary theoretical and programmatic clarity, not by pontificating from the sidelines, but by energetically participating in the movement, fighting in the front ranks and pushing it forward at every stage.

Imperialism and capitalism

The central problem facing not only the Venezuelan Revolution but the people of the whole world is imperialism and capitalism. The giant corporations are trying to control the whole world and plunder it for profit. They are supported by the big imperialist bullies, in the first place the USA, which enjoys unprecedented power and uses it to make and unmake governments and subject whole countries and continents to its will. *Not one of the problems facing the masses can be solved without an all-out struggle against capitalism and imperialism.*

It is impossible to achieve our ends without a radical break with capitalism. In order to solve problems like unemployment or the lack of houses and schools it is necessary for the government to introduce economic planning – to draw up an economic plan based on the needs of the majority, not the profit of the minority. But you cannot plan what you do not control and you cannot control what you do not own. As long as the land, the banks and the big industry remain in private hands, no solution is possible.

That is the central challenge that faces the Venezuelan Revolution at the present time. The revolution has begun, but it is not finished. As a matter of fact, the main task remains to be accomplished. What is the central problem? Only this: that a number of key economic levers remain in the hands of the Venezuelan oligarchy.

The problem here is both economic and political. The oligarchy will never be reconciled to the revolution. Although up till now its property has hardly been touched, although it still enjoys its wealth and privileges, although it still holds in its hands powerful means of communication in the shape of the main daily papers and TV channels, which is used to spew out a daily torrent of filth, lies and slander against the democratically elected government – despite all this, it is not satisfied. And it will never be satisfied until it has overthrown the government and crushed the masses under its feet.

Workers' control is a big step forward, and we must encourage it. It challenges the "sacred right" of the capitalists and bureaucrats to manage industry, while giving the workers priceless experience in administration and control that can be put to good use in a socialist planed economy. However, as long as key elements of the economy remain in private hands, as long as there is not a genuine nationalised planned economy, the experience of workers' control will inevitably have only a partial, one-sided and unsatisfactory character.

The President said yesterday that the expropriation of Venepal was an exceptional measure: "We are not going to take away land, if it is yours it is yours". But he also said that "*any factories closed or abandoned, we are going to take them over. All of them.*" And he added: "*I invite the workers' leaders to follow on this path*". These words will not fall on deaf ears. Workers in other occupied factories will take this as a signal to mobilise and demand that the Bolivarian government expropriate their owners. This is the correct road!

What is necessary is to nationalise the land, the banks and what is left of private big industry. That will enable us to plan the economy and mobilise the productive forces in the benefit of the majority. Hugo Chávez stood in two elections and obtained substantial majorities in both. He has a big majority in parliament. He has won a crushing victory in the referendum. What is to stop the government now from introducing an emergency law (*decreto ley*) nationalising the property of the oligarchy? It would be possible to explain to the country on television the reasons for this (there are a number of very sound reasons). At the same time, an appeal should be made to the workers and peasants not to wait for parliament (which tends to be slow) but to take immediate action, occupying the land and the factories.

Dialectics and revolution

Marxism is based on a definite method – the dialectical method. This explains that every process inevitably leads to a critical point (to use a phrase from physics) where quantity becomes transformed into quality. That is the essence of a revolution. There is a definite point where the power of the old ruling class is decisively shattered and the whole situation changes course. Unless and until this point is reached, the revolution cannot be said to be accomplished.

Sectarian blockheads have complained that we say that there is a revolution in Venezuela. These people talk a lot about revolution but they have not the slightest idea of what a revolution is. When a revolution is actually taking place before their very eyes they cannot even see it! The fact that for several years millions of workers and peasants have been mobilising to take their lives and destinies into their hands, fighting reaction in the streets, in the factories, on the estates and in the barracks – all this goes completely over their heads. They go scuttling back to their libraries to write "learned" articles quoting from Lenin and Trotsky. Not wishing to disturb their beautiful reveries, we will leave them in peace and get on with the pressing task of actually intervening in the revolution.

In Venezuela we can definitely say that the revolution has begun, but can we say that it has been completed? Can we say that there has been a decisive change in property relations and the state to the point that there can be no going back? Some people have actually said this. But this view is not only wrong but irresponsible and harmful to the revolutionary cause. Hugo Chávez himself rejected this when, in my presence, he compared the Venezuelan Revolution to the myth of Sisyphus in Greek legend. The masses heave and strain to push a massive boulder to the top of the hill, only to be pushed back again before reaching the summit.

This analogy is quite correct. The Venezuelan Revolution is not yet irreversible. Despite all the heroic efforts of the masses, and despite all their undoubted achievements, the boulder can still roll back down the hillside, crushing many lives in the process. The point of a qualitative change has not yet been reached in Venezuela and will not be reached until the nettle is grasped and the landlords and capitalists are expropriated. The nationalisation of Venepal is an important step in this direction. Now other, even more decisive steps are necessary.

President Hugo Chávez has consistently revealed an unerring revolutionary instinct. He has striven to express the revolutionary instincts of the masses. That is his great strength! It has been shown yet again with the nationalisation of Venepal. However, at the tops of the Bolivarian movement there are all kinds of people. The President is surrounded by advisers, not all of whom are firm revolutionaries. Not all of them share the President's faith in the masses. They incline towards compromise, concessions, and so-called realism – that is, they tend towards policies that, if accepted, would undermine the revolution and wreck it totally.

In his speech at the signing ceremony, Chávez said "here we are creating a new model, and that is why in Washington they are angry... our model of development implies a change in the productive apparatus. The working class must be united, learn and participate". He said correctly that *capitalism is a model based on slavery*, "and this is why in Washington they are angry, because we want to liberate ourselves from capitalism, in the same way that they were angry many years ago with the ideas of Liberator Simon Bolivar".

He added that some might be annoyed at what is happening in Venezuela, but *"they will continue to be annoyed by the revolutionary process, because no one is going to dislodge us from it."* That is the kind of lead the masses are looking for! It has nothing in common with the half-hearted and cowardly measures proposed by the reformists. The revolution cannot stop half way! It must go from strength to strength, striking blows against its enemies, or else it will fail.

President Chávez also said that the "role of the workers in this model is fundamental and this is the difference between this model and the capitalist model". He emphasised that *"it is necessary to change the productive relations.* "Capitalism wants to annihilate the workers... here we are carrying out a process of liberation of the workers, and this is why they are annoyed in Washington". The liberation of the workers from capitalist slavery is only possible through a fundamental alteration in the productive relations – *but this cannot mean anything else but the socialist revolution.*

That is a thousand times true. But it is also necessary to draw all the conclusions. *The Venezuelan Revolution is already coming into conflict with the narrow limitations of capitalism. It cannot accept these limitations. It must either break through them, tear them down and boldly strike out on a new course, or else it will in the end be forced into retreat and be defeated.*

As was pointed out by Jorge Martin, the measures of nationalisation must be extended to all sectors of the economy that are under monopoly and imperialist control, such as the banking system (the lion's share of which is in the hands of two Spanish multinationals), the telecom sector (in the hands of US multinationals), the food distribution sector (in the hands of a couple of Venezuelan companies owned by known coup organisers), and others.

Workers of Venezuela! Take the road of struggle! Occupy the factories under workers' control! Demand that they be nationalised! Drive out the counter-revolutionary bosses! The Venezuelan Revolution will triumph as a socialist revolution or it will not triumph at all.

The question is posed point blank: who shall prevail? There are only two possibilities before the people of Venezuela. Either the revolution will eliminate the power of the oligarchy, and then spread the revolution to the rest of Latin America, or the oligarchy, in conjunction with US imperialism, will eliminate the revolution. No third way is possible.

Chapter Thirteen

Chávez: "Capitalism must be transcended"

London, February 1st, 2005

"Everyday I become more convinced, there is no doubt in my mind, and as many intellectuals have said, that it is necessary to transcend capitalism. But capitalism can't be transcended from within capitalism itself, but through socialism, true socialism, with equality and justice. But I'm also convinced that it is possible to do it under democracy, but not in the type of democracy being imposed from Washington."

Hugo Chávez.

Two days ago, Venezuelan President Chávez gave a speech at the Gigantinho Stadium at the closing session of the World Social Forum in Porto Alegre, Brazil. In this speech, President Chávez gave further indications of the direction in which the Bolivarian Revolution is moving. This speech, reported in Venezuelanalysis.com (Caracas, January 30th, 2005), deserves to be studied by every conscious worker and revolutionary youth.

The Bolivarian Revolution started out as a national democratic revolution, aimed at freeing the people of Venezuela from the rule of a corrupt and degenerate oligarchy that acted as the local agency of imperialism. The Marxist tendency always stood firmly for the defence of the Bolivarian Revolution against its twin enemies, the oligarchy and imperialism, but also pointed out consistently that the only way in which the revolution could save itself and advance to a final victory was by overthrowing landlordism and capitalism.

The recent nationalisation of Venepal and decree on agrarian reform marked a clear turn of the revolution in the direction of a decisive confrontation with its enemies. These revolutionary measures will have been greeted enthusiastically by workers and peasants everywhere. However, they have aroused the fury of reactionaries from Washington to London. The enemies of the revolution are preparing a new counteroffensive against it. The only way to defeat them is by striking new and decisive blows against them.

But here a problem arises. It is well known that some in the leadership of the Bolivarian movement do not share the President's enthusiasm for the revolution and that some of his advisers are upset by his constant and outspoken criticisms of US imperialism. The President is clearly not impressed by this advice. In reference to the recommendations of some of his close advisors, he said that "some people say that we cannot say nor do anything that can irritate those in Washington." He repeated the words of Argentine independence hero José de San Martin *"let's be free without caring about what anyone else says."*

These words are absolutely characteristic of the man. Hugo Chávez is a man of great courage and integrity. He has shown himself to be implacable in his attitude to US imperialism. Chávez blamed the bad political relations between the USA and Venezuela on the "permanent aggressions from there". He criticized US Secretary of State Condoleezza Rice who recently asserted that Chávez was "a negative force in the region." He said those relations will stay unhealthy as long as the US continues its policies of aggression. "The most negative force in the world today is the government of the United States," he said.

The President criticized the US government for asking other countries to put pressure on Venezuela in the crisis with Colombia over the kidnapping of a Colombian guerrilla activist in Caracas last December. "Nobody answered their call... they are more lonely every day." Chávez added that US imperialism is not invincible. "Look at Vietnam, look at Iraq and Cuba resisting, and now look at Venezuela."

Arms in hand

The Bolivarian leader pointed out that Venezuela was prepared to defend itself arms in hand against any aggression, and added that his country's military forces are undergoing a period of modernisation of its weapon systems and resources, but asserted that it is aimed at defending the country's sovereignty. "Venezuela will not attack anybody, but don't attack Venezuela, because you will find us ready to defend our sovereignty, and the project we are carrying forward," he declared.

Like Simon Bolivar, that other great leader of the national democratic revolution in Latin America, Hugo Chávez has understood that the revolution cannot triumph if it is isolated in a single country. He has stated publicly that Trotsky was right against Stalin when he argued that the revolution cannot ultimately succeed in an isolated state. He has publicly stated that the aim of the Bolivarian revolution is to spread to every country in Latin America – and beyond.

In his speech Chávez highlighted the recent creation of Latin American satellite TV network *TeleSur*, "which will allow us to tell our people's reality in our own words." He added that *TeleSur* would be at the disposal of the people, not of governments. The Venezuelan President visited the Lagoa do Junco agrarian settlement in Tapes set up by Brazil's Landless Movement (MST), and later held a press conference with more than 120 media organisations, where he criticized the US government for claiming to lead a fight against terrorism while undermining democracy in Venezuela. These actions are not likely to earn him the plaudits of Washington!

Internationalist appeal

Despite the repeated provocations and aggressive conduct of US imperialism, the Venezuelan President always distinguishes carefully between the people of the USA and their rulers. Pointing out that all empires come to an end, he said: "One day the decay inside US imperialism will end up toppling it, and the great people of Martin Luther King will be set free. The great people of the United States are our brothers, my salute to them."

The President continued:

"We must start talking again about equality. The US government talks about freedom and liberty, but never about equality. They are not interested in equality. This is a distorted concept of liberty. The US people, with whom we share dreams and ideals, must free themselves... A country of heroes, dreamers, and fighters, the people of Martin Luther King, and Cesar Chávez."

He also said: "We can't wait for a sustained economic growth of 10 years in order to start reducing poverty through the trickledown effect, as the neo-liberal economic theories propose." The President lambasted the US-sponsored Free Trade of the Americas Agreement (FTAA). He told the closing meeting: "The FTAA is dead, what they wanted was mini-FTAAs because US imperialism did not have the strength to impose the neo-colonial model of FTAA."

He paid tribute to the cooperation with Cuba, which, along with several Central American countries, receives Venezuelan oil at below market prices, in exchange for assistance in healthcare, education, agriculture and other areas. He explained that about 20,000 Cuban doctors work in Venezuela at free medical clinics in poor neighbourhoods, and that Venezuela has used a Cuban literacy method approved by UNESCO that has allowed more than 1.3 million Venezuelans to learn how to read and write. He said Venezuela is using Cuban vaccines, which now allow poor children to be vaccinated against diseases such as hepatitis.

The President poured scorn on the stories spread by the western media about alleged plans by Fidel Castro and him to spread Communism in the Americas, overthrow governments and set up guerrillas, "after 10 years it seems like we haven't been very successful."

He said: "Cuba has its own profile and Venezuela has its own, but we have respect for each other, but we celebrate accords and advance together for the interest of our peoples." He said that any aggression against either country would have to confront the other, "because we are united in spirit from Mexico down to the Patagonia."

"When imperialism feels weak, it resorts to brute force. The attacks on Venezuela are a sign of weakness, ideological weakness. Nowadays almost nobody defends neo-liberalism. Up until three years ago, just Fidel [Castro] and I raised those criticisms at Presidential meetings. We felt lonely, as if we infiltrated those meetings."

He continued: "Just look at the internal repression inside the United States, the Patriot Act, which is a repressive law against US citizens. They have put in jail a group of journalists for not revealing their sources. They won't allow them to take pictures of the bodies of the dead soldiers, many of them Latinos, coming from Iraq. Those are signs of Goliath's weaknesses."

Neo-imperialism

"The south also exists... the future of the north depends on the south. If we don't make that better world possible, if we fail, and through the rifles of the US Marines, and through Mr. Bush's murderous bombs, if there is no coincidence and organisation necessary in the south to resist the offensive of neo-imperialism, and the Bush doctrine is imposed upon the world, the world will be destroyed," he said.

Chávez warned that global warming would bring catastrophic events if no action is taken soon, in reference to uncontrolled or little regulated industrial activity. Chávez added that perhaps before those drastic changes take place, there will be rebellions everywhere "because the peoples are not going to accept in peace impositions such as neo-liberalism or such as colonialism."

The most interesting part of his speech, however, was when he posed the need to pass from the national democratic tasks to the socialist transformation of society:

"*Everyday I become more convinced, there is no doubt in my mind, and as many intellectuals have said, that it is necessary to transcend capitalism. But capitalism can't be transcended from within capitalism itself, but through socialism, true socialism, with equality and justice. But I'm also convinced that it is possible to do it under democracy, but not in the type of democracy being imposed from Washington.*"

These words mark the first clear indication of a decisive shift in the Bolivarian Revolution. Until now, Chávez never suggested going beyond the bounds of capitalism. But the real march of events has posed the question with ever-greater clarity: it is impossible for the national democratic revolution to succeed unless it makes deep inroads on private property, unless it takes the decisive step of expropriating the landlords, bankers and capitalists.

The only hope for the Venezuelan Revolution is to transform itself into a socialist revolution. But the model of so-called real socialism that collapsed in the Soviet Union holds no appeal to the masses in Venezuela, imbued in the spirit of democracy. What is required is to return to the democratic traditions of the October Revolution, to the programme of Lenin and Trotsky. Only this can guarantee success! In this respect, Hugo Chávez said: "We have to re-invent socialism. It can't be the kind of socialism that we saw in the Soviet Union, but it will emerge as we develop new systems that are built on cooperation, not competition," he added.

The President stated that Venezuela is trying to implement a "social economy". He said, "It is impossible, within the framework of the capitalist system to solve the grave problems of poverty of the majority of the world's population. We must transcend capitalism. But we cannot resort to state capitalism, which would be the same perversion of the Soviet Union. We must reclaim socialism as a thesis, a project and a path, but a new type of socialism, a humanist one, which puts humans and not machines or the state ahead of everything. That's the debate we must promote around the world, and the WSF is a good place to do it."

Socialism is democratic or it is nothing. From the very beginning, the control and administration of industry, society and the state must be in the hands of the working class itself. That is the only way to prevent the formation of a bureaucracy – that abominable cancer on the body of the workers' state – and to ensure that the masses are actively identified with the Revolution from the start. The active participation of the masses is the first rule of socialism.

The President added that in spite of his admiration for Argentine revolutionary Che Guevara, he said Che's methods are not applicable. "That thesis of one, two, or three Vietnams, did not work, especially in Venezuela." That is quite correct. Che's aim of spreading the revolution to Latin America was correct and necessary. But unfortunately the tactic he adopted was mistaken. This led to his tragic death, which deprived the revolution of an outstanding leader.

It is necessary to draw a balance sheet and speak clearly: over a period of decades, the tactic of guerrilla war has led to one defeat after another in Latin America. The Cuban Revolution took the US imperialists by surprise. But they learned the lessons and applied them. As a result, every time a "foco" appeared, they immediately crushed it before it could develop further – as we saw with the tragic fate of Che Guevara in Bolivia.

Guerrilla war is a necessary auxiliary to the proletarian revolution in countries like tsarist Russia or China where there was a big peasantry. But it makes little sense in Latin America where the big majority of the population lives in towns and cities. So-called urban guerrillaism is only individual terrorism under another name. That tactic was always rejected by Marxists – particularly the Russian Marxists. It is a recipe for defeat, as the people of Venezuela, Argentina, Uruguay and Colombia know through bitter experience.

The great advantage of the Venezuelan Revolution is that it is a mainly urban revolution (though with important support in the peasantry) based on the active movement of the masses, in particular the working class and its natural allies, the urban poor, the unemployed, the revolutionary youth, the women and the progressive intelligentsia.

Hopeless sectarians

Hopeless sectarians think that parliamentary struggle can play no role in the Revolution. This shows they have no understanding of revolution – or anything else. The Russian Bolsheviks paid careful attention to the parliamentary struggle. They skilfully combined democratic slogans with the economic and social demands of the proletariat, linking them to the idea of taking power. That is the only way to build a mass base, to mobilise the masses and thus to create the objective conditions for a revolutionary overturn. There is no other way.

The Bolivarian Revolution began on the electoral plane and has dealt one blow after another against the counter-revolutionaries, culminating in the magnificent victory in the August 2004 recall referendum. By this means it has rallied the masses behind it. But the struggle is by no means over. It is a dialectical law that the struggle in parliament must eventually be resolved outside parliament. Reformists and parliamentary cretins do not understand this. That is why they always lead the movement to defeat – as in Chile. If the pro-bourgeois reformist wing of the Bolivarian movement wins, the same fate awaits the people of Venezuela.

However, the pro-bourgeois and reformist elements have not yet won. The masses are pressing from below. They want the revolution to advance, to strike blows against its enemies, to take power. The workers demand nationalisation of the factories, the peasants want to put an end to landlordism. This is a decisive fact! The revolution has not ended, as the reformists claim. It has scarcely begun!

Whatever the limitations of the Bolivarian movement, its vacillations and inconsistencies, its ambiguity and lack of a clear programme, it undoubtedly has the merit of having roused the masses to struggle, mobilising, inspiring and organising millions of oppressed people who were never organised before. That is a tremendous achievement! And the man who inspired this magnificent movement and provided it with a leadership and a banner is Hugo Chávez.

Those who try to denigrate Chávez, to belittle his role and also to attack the genuine Marxists for supporting him (while maintaining our organisational and political independence) show their complete inability to understand revolution or the role of Marxists in a revolution. What is necessary is not to criticize and grumble from the sidelines but to participate actively, shoulder to shoulder with the most advanced workers and revolutionary youth, explaining patiently what is needed, while at the same time pushing the movement forward. Anything else is just the sterile impotence of sectarianism.

Marx pointed out that for the masses one step forward of the real movement was worth a hundred correct programmes (and Marx knew very well the importance of a correct programme). Lenin said that for the masses an ounce of practice was worth a ton of theory (and Lenin never underestimated the importance of theory!). The masses in Venezuela have learned a lot from their experiences in the last few years. Their confidence has grown by leaps and bounds. Above all, they have developed a very keen sense of democracy. They will not tolerate bureaucracy and autocratic methods. This is the greatest guarantee against the danger of a future totalitarian state. It will be impossible (or at least very difficult) to impose a Stalinist dictatorship under such conditions. What is on the order of the day is a healthy, democratic workers' state – like the original Soviet state established by Lenin and Trotsky in October 1917.

For a Socialist Federation of Latin America!

In his speech, President Chávez cited Marx's phrase, quoted by the great Russian revolutionary Leon Trotsky, that "each revolution needs the whip of the counter-revolution to advance." He listed actions by the opposition and the US government to drive him out of power. "But we resisted, and now have gone onto the offensive. For instance, we recovered our oil industry... In 2004, from the oil industry budget we utilized $4 billion in social investments, education, health, micro-credits, scholarships, and housing, aimed at the poorest of the poor, what neo-liberals call waste of money. But that is not a waste of money because it is aimed at empowering the poor so that they can defeat poverty." He added "that money before stayed out of Venezuela or just benefited the rich."

He criticized privatisations by saying that "privatisation is a neo-liberal and imperialist plan. Health can't be privatised because it is a fundamental human right, nor can education, water, electricity and other public services. They can't be surrendered to private capital that denies the people from their rights." All this is very true. It is necessary to fight against privatisation. But the real solution is to establish a genuine socialist plan of production under the democratic control and administration of the working class.

There were, of course, some elements in Chávez's speech which Marxists would disagree with. He defended Brazilian President Luis "Lula" Da Silva, who has been sharply criticized by the Latin American left, and who was booed during his speech at the World Social Forum. Apart from the natural reluctance of a guest to criticize his host, Chávez naturally sees leaders like Lula in Brazil or Kirchner in Argentina, or the new leaders of Uruguay as potential allies in the fight against US imperialism. This also explains his favourable reference to President Putin of Russia.

There is nothing wrong in attempting to make use of every opening, no matter how small, on the diplomatic front that may help to break the wall of diplomatic isolation that Washington is attempting to construct around Venezuela. On the contrary, the Bolivarian Revolution is obliged to do so. It is compelled to seek diplomatic and trade relations with friendly states as long as the revolution remains isolated. But no firm reliance can be placed on these diplomatic points of support. To imagine (as some people do) that the Bolivarian Revolution can depend on this is to lean upon a broken reed. These supposed points of support can collapse – or even turn into their opposite – in 24 hours.

The only really reliable point of support for the Bolivarian Revolution is the millions of oppressed workers and peasants of Latin America and the labour movement of the whole world. The Bolivarian Revolution already counts on the sympathy of millions of people. If it shows that it is capable of taking the decisive step of breaking the stranglehold of Capital and ending capitalist slavery once and for all, that passive sympathy will be immediately transformed into militant action. US imperialism would be paralysed and unable to intervene because it would be faced with uprisings everywhere – and a mass movement inside its own borders.

The revolutionary idea of Simon Bolivar has been betrayed for 200 years by the Latin American bourgeoisie. It will become a reality only when the workers of Venezuela and the whole of Latin America take the power into their hands. What is needed is a bold lead. Armed with the correct policies and programme, Venezuela can give it.

Chapter Fourteen

The agrarian revolution:
Revolutionary realism
versus reformist utopia

London, 16th February, 2005

The Bolivarian movement is a mass movement that originated as a movement for the national democratic revolution – that is, a revolution that stood for a programme of advanced democracy, but which stopped short of challenging the foundations of capitalism. However, the progress of the Revolution has inevitably brought it into conflict with the vested interests of the oligarchy. At every step the demands of the masses in both town and village clash with the so-called sacred right of property. Upon the resolution of this contradiction the future of the Revolution depends.

The Marxists naturally supported the national democratic revolution and applauded Hugo Chávez's courageous fight against the Venezuelan oligarchy and imperialism. Even on a capitalist basis, this was tremendously progressive, and it was, and remains our duty to defend it. Not to do so would be a betrayal. But we have always pointed out the elementary truth that in order to succeed, the revolution sooner or later would have to go beyond the boundaries of capitalism and expropriate the Venezuelan landlords and capitalists.

Experience has proved we were correct. At every stage the Bolivarian revolution has come up against the most ferocious resistance of the landlords and capitalists, backed by imperialism. In order to overcome this resistance, it has had to base itself on the only genuinely revolutionary classes: the workers and urban poor in the towns and cities and the poor peasants in the countryside. A decisive stage in this conflict is now commencing in the countryside.

Land distribution is an age-old aspiration of the poor of the Venezuelan countryside. The peasants desire to work the land and improve their standard of living. But this justified aspiration comes up against the fierce resistance of the big landowners, who, together with the bankers and big capitalists, constitute the cornerstone of the Venezuelan oligarchy. *No real advance is possible in Venezuela unless and until the power of this oligarchy is broken. That is the real importance of the agrarian revolution.*

The attempt to move towards an agrarian reform has posed the central dilemma of the Bolivarian Revolution point-blank. It is not merely a question of modifying the existing set up. It must be swept away: the agrarian economic and social structure must be utterly transformed. As the Spanish socialist Largo Caballero once put it: you cannot cure cancer with an aspirin. For this reason the Venezuelan peasants, like their brothers and sisters in the towns and cities, are drawing the most revolutionary conclusions.

Modest reforms

In early January, President Chávez announced new measures to deepen and extend the agrarian reform, an essential component in the Bolivarian Revolution. The reforms themselves are quite modest in their scope, concentrating on the issue of under-exploited estates. Under a 2001 land law, the government can tax or seize unused farm sites. The Venezuelan authorities have identified more than 500 farms, including 56 large estates, as idle. A further 40,000 farms are yet to be inspected.

These measures are very modest and fall well short of what is required in order to fulfil the most elementary requirement of the national democratic revolution. Yet they were met with howls of rage from the enemies of the revolution. The opposition has accused the state of "invading private property" and introducing "communistic measures".

The protests of the Venezuelan opposition are mild, however, in comparison to the howls of rage in the international media. On 13th January the London-based *The Economist* magazine carried an article attacking Chávez's land reform. The occasion for its ire was the measures taken by the government to investigate the cattle ranch of El Charcote in Cojedes, a state in Venezuela's northern plains, which is run by Agroflora, a subsidiary of a big UK food monopoly.

The Vestey Group is the owner of this huge ranch comprising no less than 13,000 hectares (32,000 acres) of pastures and woodlands, as well as a dozen other ranches elsewhere in the country. It has investments in beef and sugar in Argentina and Brazil as well as in Venezuela. It is a typical example of the way in which big foreign companies have taken over the key sectors of the productive forces in the continent and drained them for profit.

The Economist admits that the family that owns the company are famous (or rather infamous) in Britain for its long history of tax avoidance as well as for meat. Nevertheless it defends their absolute right to hold onto their land, since their title to El Charcote "goes back a century and has been upheld by the courts." The article describes in colourful detail the spectacular way in which the inspection was carried out:

"On January 8th, the clatter of helicopters over the ranch heralded the arrival of Johnny [sic] Yánez, the *Chavista* governor of Cojedes, bearing the country's first 'intervention order' against rural property. He was accompanied by some 200 troops and heavily armed police commandos. Mr Yánez, a former army captain, announced that private property was 'a right, but not an absolute right'."

A state commission now has three months to decide whether the ranch is unproductive or not legally held and thus can be turned over to peasant co-operatives under the terms of the land-reform decree of 2001. Two days later, President Chávez set up a similar commission at national level. Its task is to speed up and bring order to the land-reform drive.

The case for land reform in Latin America is unanswerable. In Venezuela, over 75 percent of farmland is controlled by fewer than 5 percent of landowners. Rural poverty is a cancer that blights millions of lives. Even the right-wing *Economist* agrees that "Unequal land distribution is one of the historical causes of the wider inequality that scars Latin American societies." As President Chávez says, this is an injustice that must end. There can be no future for the Bolivarian Revolution without this. But an all-out assault on the property of the landlords will inevitably pose the question of the expropriation of the banks and industries as well. That is why the imperialists have raised such a hue-and-cry about the proposed measures.

Will agrarian reform damage production?

The bourgeois critics of land reform say that Chávez's policies will have a negative effect on agricultural production:

"By harrying the private sector," *The Economist* says, "the government has merely intensified Venezuela's dependence on oil – and all the economic distortions that go with that. The government says Venezuela imports 70 percent of what it eats. The opposition retorts that food imports have risen by a fifth since Mr Chávez came to power, while agricultural production has fallen."

The enemies of the revolution are running around screaming about the threat to investment and productivity, when in reality what worries them is something else. What really frightens *The Economist* is the fact that the president's promises have encouraged peasants to invade farms. It is arousing the rural masses from their slumber and bringing them into the revolutionary struggle. It is calling into question the "sacred principle of private property" and thereby is taking a big step in the direction of the socialist revolution. This is a prospect that fills the oligarchy and its imperialist masters with panic.

The Economist quotes with horror the words of Johnny Yánez: "Social justice cannot be sacrificed to legal technicalities," adding darkly: "This assault on property rights is likely to scare off investment." The article continues its tale of woe: "Back at El Charcote, herds of Brahma cattle still graze. The Vestey company normally supplies 4 percent of the beef consumed by Venezuelans. It has been a pioneer in genetic improvements to the national herd. But Diana dos Santos, the firm's local boss, says that at El Charcote all but one small pasture has been invaded; beef output has slumped. More than a thousand interlopers have put up rickety shacks and planted crops on the estate. They support the president—but despise Mr Yánez. So they may be evicted in favour of other, more reliable, political clients. And in a few years' time these in turn will probably end up back in urban slums, while Venezuela will have lost a source of wealth."

So there we have it! The big-hearted imperialists like the Vestey family have been so kind as to come to Venezuela with the best intentions in the world. Their only aim in life is to serve the people of Venezuela, feeding them with delicious beef, constantly improving the national herd with all manner of "genetic improvements" (we recall the kind of genetic improvements introduced by the British capitalist farmers in the United Kingdom, which gave us the blessings of mad cow disease). If incidentally they have earned a few bolivars by honest means, this was of course a secondary matter, in which neither the Bolivarian government nor the British taxman should take any interest.

Attitude of the petty bourgeois "democrats"

So crystal clear is the case for agrarian reform in Venezuela that even petty bourgeois groups, not noted for their love of Hugo Chávez and the Bolivarian Revolution, have had to grudgingly accept it. The Venezuelan human rights group PROVEA has welcomed the Venezuelan government's war on big landownership, calling the political will shown by government and opposition State Governors as "positive."

However, the revolutionaries should beware of praise coming from such quarters. The bourgeois "democrats" of PROVEA are no friends of the Bolivarian Revolution and their praise is a poisoned chalice that they offer to the Revolution, not to help it but to paralyse it and render it ineffective.

The government is being urged to be "inclusive" in its agrarian policy and to avoid rural violence. That is to say, it is being invited to represent the interests of all classes – the landlords as well as the peasants. It is being invited to make the lamb lie down next to the wolf. It is being invited to square the circle. *In short, it is being invited to do what cannot be done.* And those who advocate such nonsense actually consider themselves to be great "realists"! If the consequences were not so serious, it would be very funny.

When one is given a bill of support from such people, it is highly advisable to read the small print! And in the small print we read the following:

"The process should be undertaken within the rule of law and rejects the possibility that bodies other than those established in the Land & Agrarian

Development Law (ITDA) start processes of expropriating agrarian land."

These are priceless pearls of wisdom! The hypocrites of PROVEA read us pious lectures on "the rule of law" but conveniently forget that for years the Venezuelan landlords have been beating, torturing and murdering peasants who dare to question their authority and demand their rights. The landowners do not feel bound by the "rule of law" and will fight by any means at their disposal to prevent a meaningful agrarian programme to be carried out. Whoever denies this is either a fool or a rogue.

The peasants are not fools and will not allow themselves to be cheated by smart lawyers and "democratic" demagogues. They know that the land will never be theirs unless they fight for it, unless the ruthless resistance and sabotage of the landowners is defeated. They also know from bitter experience that their interests cannot be guaranteed by bureaucratic measures and nice sounding speeches by men in smart suits in Caracas. They know that unless the agrarian reform is backed by energetic movement from below, it will remain a dead letter – like all such laws in the past.

Therefore the peasants are organizing themselves. They are taking initiatives to seize the land of the big landowners. Genuine democrats will not oppose such initiatives but support them enthusiastically. Only a corrupt bureaucrat and an agent of the counter-revolution fears the revolutionary initiatives of the workers and peasants! It is only these initiatives that have saved the Bolivarian Revolution time and time again. Those who seek to stifle the initiatives of the masses are consciously or unconsciously striving to weaken the revolution, to deprive it of its main strength and motor force. The day these people succeed, the revolution will be doomed.

Legalistic sophistry

These unlikely "Friends of the People" continue: "State Governors can promote and facilitate processes that correspond to the National Institute of Lands (INTI) and provide technical support *but they cannot hand over land titles or touch land by expropriating.*

"Land owner's rights of property must be respected along with legal processes, just and transparent administrative measures, opportune payment and *just compensation.*

"In the case of idle lands, owners must be guaranteed expedition of improvable farm certificates, as established in ITDA Art. 52." (my emphasis)

These "clever" lawyers know the law back to front, inside out and upside down. Yes, they have studied their legal textbooks for many years, passed all their exams and made a lot of money out of using and abusing the law. They have turned the law into their private property – something that represents a very expensive cow that yields a lot of delicious milk for a privileged few. But the hungry masses, the poor peasant, the worker, the unemployed, have got very little out of it.

The Bolivarian Revolution has done a lot to rectify this position. It has torn up the old Constitution of the oligarchy and replaced it with a new and more democratic constitution. That is very welcome, but in and of itself it is by no means sufficient to change the position of the masses and to eliminate the injustices of the past, as so many Bolivarians so passionately desire.

The Bolivarian Constitution is only a weapon in the hands of the people. But a weapon is no use if it is not used to fight with. In the hands of the lawyers and bureaucrats the Bolivarian Constitution can be easily reduced to a scrap of paper – something that can be twisted and "interpreted" and turned into a dead letter. After all, even the most democratic constitution in the world has limited powers. It establishes certain limits within which the class struggle can be carried out. That is important because it can give a greater or lesser scope to the workers and peasants with which to carry out their struggle. What it can never do is to act as a substitute for the class struggle.

In order for the democratic Constitution to mean anything, it must be backed by mass action from below. Without that, it must remain only a dry husk, an empty shell devoid of all real content, the lifeless bones of a skeleton. Only the revolutionary movement of the workers and peasants can put flesh on these dry bones and fill democracy with a real content. To argue therefore that the Venezuelan peasants must confine themselves to what is acceptable to the lawyers, to accept "restraint", to moderate their demands to what the bureaucrats consider "reasonable" – in short to sit back and wait for the land to be handed to them on a plate – would be to give up any possibility of a genuine agrarian reform ever being carried out in Venezuela.

The line of argument of these legalistic ladies and gentlemen is the height of arrogance and insolence towards the masses. As mentioned above, they inform us that "state Governors can promote and facilitate processes that correspond to the National Institute of Lands (INTI) and provide technical support *but they cannot hand over land titles or touch land by expropriating*."

The first part of the sentence is surely redundant. It is to be supposed that *all* democratic state Governors are legally obligated to carry out the decisions of the legally elected government. Why need this be stated? *Unless of course, there are Governors who are working in collaboration with the big landowners and the Counter-revolution to sabotage the decisions of the Caracas government.*

Do such governors exist? Of course they do, and that is precisely why the peasants do not trust them to carry through a proper agrarian reform. That is precisely why the peasants have decided – quite rightly – to organize and to take their own initiatives. That is just what provokes the indignation of the "democrats" of PROVEA and other counter-revolutionaries, open and disguised.

The "sacred right of property"

Above all, the "Friends of the People" protest, the big estates must not be *expropriated*. Why not? Because that would be *a violation of the sacred right to private property!* But in a country where 75 percent of the productive land is in the hands of only about five percent of landowners, how is it possible to have a real agrarian reform without violating the so-called sacred right to private property? *To renounce this would be to renounce the whole idea of agrarian reform in Venezuela.* And that is just what our "democratic" men in suits would like, although politeness (and fear of the masses) prevents them from saying so openly.

These ladies and gentlemen prattle on about "just compensation". But if anyone is entitled to just compensation it is the millions of peasants who have been exploited, cheated and oppressed for centuries by the landlords who have enriched themselves at the cost of the people. Their ranches and mansions have been built out of the blood, sweat and tears squeezed out of generations of poor men, women and children. And where did they get their property from in the first place? The land was not theirs to start with. It was seized from the native population by violence and trickery. Where was the "just compensation" then?

These "clever" sophists try to blind us with legal niceties. But the whole history of Latin America shows that the parasitic class of landlords has never shown the slightest regard for such legal niceties when it was a question of their own selfish interests. They obtained the land through violence and have held it ever since by violence. What was stolen from the people must be restored to the people. The question of compensation does not enter into it. The landlords have made their fortunes on the back of the people. They do not deserve a single cent more.

PROVEA states that the government cannot deliver titles on private lands, if it has not undertaken expropriation procedures beforehand and followed Constitution Art. 115 regarding the expropriation of lands considered of social interest or public utility. The talk about legal niceties is only a smoke screen designed to confuse the issue, as in phrases like:

"In the case of idle lands, owners must be guaranteed expedition of improvable farm certificates, as established in ITDA Art. 52."

Our friends in PROVEA inform us that the revolution *must* do this and *must* do that, and that it *cannot* do this and *cannot* do that. Really? But the essence of a revolution is that it expresses the will of the people; that it stands for the interests of the majority over those of the minority. The laws that were made in the past were made by the rich minority to defend their own power and privileges. A revolution that allowed itself to be paralysed by such laws would not deserve the name of a revolution at all. It would be only a bureaucratic game, a fraud and an illusion.

When the masses voted by an overwhelming majority last August to endorse the Bolivarian Revolution, they did not intend their clearly declared intentions to be frustrated by their enemies who, having been ejected by the front door, are now seeking to re-enter by the back door. Having been defeated in open battle, they are resorting to manoeuvres and intrigues, hiding behind the law and using delaying tactics. If we accept this, it would mean subordinating the will of the majority to the machinations of a wealthy and privileged minority. Democracy would be reduced to a hollow phrase. The tail would wag the dog.

Fortunately, the masses have no intention of allowing this to happen.

The peasants mobilise for action

We recently received an interesting report of The Venezuelan Peasant Congress from *El Nuevo Topo*, signed by E. Gilman. This brief report clearly shows the real attitude that is developing at the base, not only among the workers but also among their natural allies, the poor peasants. In it we read the following: "Caracas: On February 5th and 6th took place in Tucari the 'Peasant Conference in Defense of National Sovereignty and for the Agrarian Revolution,' sponsored by the Frente Nacional Campesino Ezequiel Zamora.

"Nearly 100 delegates met at the Berbere Cooperative, which is a collective farm run by largely Black farmers.

"Though there was universal support for President Hugo Chávez, the Agrarian Reform Law was severely attacked as it allows only lands over 5000 hectares to be expropriated and these lands need to be uncultivated to be covered by the law. The peasants criticized the Agrarian Reform Institute, which they claimed was so slow and bureaucratic that owners of latifundios would cut down whole forests off the land while the Agrarian Reform Institute made up its mind. Also many had received defective seed from the Institute. Many peasants who have taken lands directly have complained local judges are on the side of the landowners and have had local police drive them off the land [...]

"The conference discussed the need for armed self-defence as well as the possibility of guerrilla warfare if there is a U.S. invasion. They defended the need to build collective farms rather than dividing up the land. There was discussion on the need for accounting and discipline with those who refuse to work. The Conference agreed to set up a school on the Berbere farm to teach collective agriculture.

"The peasants discussed blocking the Panamerican Highway to get their demands. The only discordant note was from the local Mayor who told the peasants to have more patience and that the law was like a 'father who makes rules for his child'. Her proposal for patience was solidly rejected. Many peasants stated they felt a 'revolution within the revolution' was necessary to have genuine People's Power (Poder Popular.)"

These few lines speak louder than all the books and articles that have appeared on the Bolivarian Revolution. Here we see the dialectical relationship between the masses and the leadership of Hugo Chávez at work. Reflecting the pressure of the masses, the government approves an agrarian reform. The peasants take heart from this measure and press their demands. They express "universal support for President Hugo Chávez", but at the same time they point out the limitations of the new law. It is welcome, but it does not go far enough. They therefore decide to help the government to go further by stepping up their actions from below.

The announcement of the new measures has prompted hundreds of land invasions and these have been met by the killing of dozens of peasant activists by the landlords and their agents. But as yet very little land has actually been awarded. This is admitted honestly by some officials. "That's a self-criticism the revolution has to make," says Rafael Alemán, the official in charge of the review at El Charcote. "We have not pushed this process forward."

This need not surprise us. The machinery of government is slow and cumbersome. The bureaucracy cannot be an adequate instrument for revolutionary change. It drags its feet, fulfilling its obligations without enthusiasm, or even sabotaging the laws passed by the Bolivarian government. In its ranks there are many *escualidos* and disguised counter-revolutionaries. The peasants do not trust it, and they are right not to trust it. They criticize the Agrarian Reform Institute for its slowness and bureaucratic methods that help the owners of lantifundios to sabotage the reforms. They know – and the whole people know – that only the mass revolutionary movement can carry through the revolution!

Displaying an unerring revolutionary instinct, they answer the critics of the agrarian reform in a way that shows a very high level of political maturity. The enemies of the agrarian reform say: the break-up of the big landed estate into individual peasant plots will damage productivity and cause chaos and hunger. The peasants reply: *we are for the expropriation of the big estates – but we do not insist on their division into a multitude of small peasant holdings. We advocate the establishment of collective farms on which the land can be cultivated in common, using all the advantages of modern machinery and technology and economies of scale.* To do this it is not necessary that the land should be owned by a handful of rich parasites!

The revolutionary peasants are not fools. They fully understand the need for

accounting and discipline on the collective farms. They will be run democratically by the producers themselves. Those who refuse to work will be disciplined by
the rest of the collective, which is interested in establishing a high level of productivity, and to this end proposes the establishment of schools on the farms to teach
the science of agriculture. What has this highly responsible attitude got to do with
the grotesque caricature of "ignorant peasants" sabotaging scientific agricultural
production that the western apologists of the landlords like to present us with?

Reformism or revolution?

Some sections of the leadership have tried to soothe the nerves of the opposition, reassuring them that the present measures do not threaten private property.
Vice President Jose Vicente Rangel has said farmers and ranchers with their titles
in order and their lands productive have "nothing to fear". But such assurances
will do nothing to calm the fears of the property-owning classes or reduce their
implacable hostility to the Bolivarian Revolution.

In a recent report on *Vheadline.com* we read the following:

"Carabobo State Governor Luis Felipe Acosta Carlez is gearing up to face an
embarrassing spate of land grabs and squatters that has divided the pro-govern-
ment Movimiento Quinta Republica (MVR).

"Sporting red T-shirts and using revolutionary lingo, people have been invading private property and allegedly idle lands throughout Carabobo.

"The State Public Security Secretary has been entrusted with organizing pre-
ventive controls in all zones and to establish dialogue with illegal squatters.

"The Governor has been accused of vacillating in tackling the problem and has
reacted preparing a decree of emergency to establish points of control to prevent
people from other States invading lands and properties.

"The National Guard (GN) and State Police will join the plan and the aim is to
secure a pacific eviction of lands ... part of the operation is to root out professional or political squatters and to prosecute them."

Of course, it is necessary to distinguish between land occupations carried out
by landless peasants and fraudulent activities carried out by so-called professional squatters, who in some places have invaded plots in order to sell them later.
Such activities are the work of parasites and counter-revolutionaries and must be
condemned. But in the first place it is wrong to use such incidents to try to condemn land occupations in general, and in the second place, the only way to prevent cases of fraudulent land occupations is to develop and extend genuinely revolutionary land occupations organized by democratically elected peasants committees.

Every genuine revolutionary democrat is duty bound to support the agrarian
revolution. But in order to succeed, the most energetic revolutionary measures

will be necessary. The peasants cannot depend upon the bureaucracy to give them the land. They know that they can depend only on their own strength. That is why they are getting organized, preparing to take direct action to get possession of the land.

The revolutionary mobilization of the peasants is the only guarantee that the agrarian reform of the Bolivarian Revolution will be carried into practice – that it will not remain a dead letter, a meaningless piece of paper lying in the drawer of some bureaucrat in Caracas. The peasants are realistic people. They understand that, whatever laws are passed in Caracas, the landowners will not give up their power, land and privileges without a fight. If they want the land they will have to fight for it!

PROVEA says more than it intends when it calls on the Public Ministry to speed up investigations into the *assassination of numerous social activists* in the countryside. What does this mean? Only this: that a bloody civil war is already raging in the countryside; that the landlords and their hired *pistoleros* are killing peasant leaders every day with complete impunity; that for the poor peasants the "rule of law" is just an empty phrase. And what solution do our learned friends propose for this problem? To ask the Ministry to "speed up its investigations". That is a praiseworthy suggestion, and we have nothing against it in principle. But the peasants know that the wheels of justice move slowly and the armed agents of the counter-revolution move swiftly. It is their lives that are at stake and they must do something to defend themselves.

Everybody knows that in the last few years many peasants have been killed by the landlords and their armed gangs. In the report of the peasant congress we read: "At the end of October 2003, in Barinas, 120 policemen helped the large landowners destroy a school on the occupied land as well as giving the landowner 240,000 pounds of corn produced by peasants." This is not an isolated case. The reactionary landlords are mobilizing to defeat the peasants and defend their power and privileges. They have no hesitation in resorting to violence. They have money, arms and influence. And, as this report shows, they are being aided by parts of the state apparatus.

Those who preach moderation and restraint to the peasants in order to avoid civil war in the countryside are missing the point. *The point is that there is already a civil war in the countryside.* This can only be cut short by the most determined revolutionary action by the peasants themselves, backed by their natural allies, their brothers and sisters in the towns and cities – the working class. The peasant will not remain with his arms folded while the reactionary gangs paid and armed by the landlords beat, intimidate and kill them.

"The conference discussed the need for armed self-defence as well as the possibility of guerrilla warfare if there is a U.S. invasion." Yes! But the enemy of the

Venezuelan peasants is not only U.S. imperialism. The enemy is at home! The Venezuelan oligarchy is nothing more than the local agency of U.S. imperialism. As long as it holds onto the land, the banks and key points of industry, the gains of the revolution will never be safe, and the agrarian revolution will remain a mirage.

Peasant committees

The peasantry must arm itself! That message has been given more than once by President Chávez. It is time to put it into practice. What is needed is not a guerrilla war, but organized self-defence, the establishment of democratically elected peasants committees in every village, armed with whatever weapons they can obtain to defend the people against the armed gangs of the counter-revolution. The committees should link up on a local, district and national basis, and in turn must link up with the committees of the workers in the urban centres.

This is the only way to bring about a peaceful and orderly transfer of power to the people in the countryside. The peasant committees can play a dual role: first, to mobilize and organize the peasant masses for the swift carrying out of an agrarian revolution, and then to establish democratic control over the management and administration of the collectivised estates. No other way is possible.

The agrarian revolution, if it is to succeed, must challenge the power of the oligarchy, and not only in the countryside. In order that agricultural production should not suffer irremediable damage, the expropriated farms must be run on collective lines. That can only succeed if they are guaranteed the necessary finance, cheap credits, cheap fertilizers, tractors and combine harvesters, lorries for transportation, and guaranteed markets for their products. That can only be achieved if they are integrated in an overall plan of production.

The first step in achieving this is the nationalization of the banks. Without control over finance and credit, it is impossible to control and plan the economy. It would be like trying to drive a car with no brakes, accelerator or gear-stick. The nationalization of the land and banks is an absolutely necessary measure – even as part of the national democratic revolution. But then the question would immediately be posed: why stop there? Why not expropriate the big firms that still remain in private hands? (We are not interested in the small ones.)

The reason why the oligarchy and the imperialists are panicking over the agrarian reform is precisely because they understand its underlying logic, which is to place a question mark over the so-called divine right to private property. That is absolutely correct! Instead of apologising and assuring the landlords and capitalists that they have nothing to fear, the Bolivarian Revolution should place at the top of its agenda the expropriation of the property of the corrupt and degenerate Venezuelan oligarchy.

President Chávez has stated correctly that capitalism is slavery. He has said that the future of the Bolivarian Revolution must be socialism. We agree with him one hundred and one percent. He has also publicly supported Trotsky's theory of Permanent Revolution. What does this say? *It says that under modern conditions the tasks of the national democratic ("bourgeois democratic") revolution cannot be carried out by the bourgeoisie, and that the national democratic revolution can only succeed if it transforms itself into a socialist revolution.*

The history of Venezuela – and the whole of Latin America – for the past 200 years is a graphic confirmation of this assertion. On the basis of capitalist slavery, no way forward is possible. It is necessary to break with landlordism and capitalism once and for all. *That is the real meaning of the slogan: "Revolution within the Revolution." It is the only way forward!*

Glossary

Altamira Square - Gathering point for the opposition in the rich east end of Caracas.

Aporrea - Online publication of the Popular Revolutionary Assembly.

Bay of Pigs - Beach used by the counter-revolutionary forces for the failed invassion of Cuba in 1961.

BCV - Venezuela's Central Bank.

Bolivarian Circles - Community based organisations that help the government to carry out social programmes. They have actively mobilised communities against counter-revolutionary attacks.

Bolivarian People's Congress - International gathering of supporters of the Bolivarian revolution.

bolivar - Venezuelan currency.

Carter Centre - Christian human rights organisation chaired by former US president Jimmy Carter. It is widely regarded as a front organisation for the CIA.

Clarin - Argentinian daily newspaper.

Class Struggle Democratic Trade Union Bloc - Anti-capitalist current organised in more than 50 unions. It played a key role in the organisation of factory occupations during the 2002/2003 lock-out.

Colombia Plan - US backed plan to end the 40-year long armed conflict and revitalise the economy through a draconian plan of privatisation. It is widely regarded as a legal cover to eradicate any kind of dissent in Colombia and throughout Latin America.

Comando Ayacucho - Political leadership of the Bolivarian movement replaced by the Comando Maisanta shortly before the recall referendum.

Coordinadora Democratica/Democratic Coordinator - Umbrella organisation that gathers all parties and organisations that oppose the Venezuelan Revolution.

COPEI - Christian Democratic party which is part of the Democratic Coordinator.

CTV - Venezuelan Workers' Confederation. Trade union confederation linked to Democratic Action. CTV leaders have been at the forefront of all counter-revolutionary attacks against Chávez.

Democratic Action - Social Democratic party which is part of the Democratic Coordinator.

Escualidos - Nickname for the Democratic Coordinator supporters.

Fedecamaras - Venezuelan bosses federation. It is one of the driving forces behind the Democratic Coordinator.

Frente Nacional Campesino Ezequiel Zamora - One of the biggest and most militant peasant organisations in Venezuela. It is named after military peasant leader from the 19th century.

Golpistas - Spanish word to name coup plotters.

Lake Maracaibo - Oil rich area in the north-western area of Venezuela.

Mercosur - Mercosur is an economic common market that began operating in the southern cone of South America in 1995. Venezuela is amongst the associate states, though it is not a full member.

Metropolitan Police - Local police body in Caracas. At the time of the coup d'etat and the lock-out the MP was under the control of a pro-opposition mayor and played the role of the opposition's army.

MVR - Movement for the Fifth Republic. Chávez's electoral party which has its origins in the military MBR-200.

OAS - Organisation of American States.

PAN - Mexican conservative party that currently rules that country.

PDVSA - Venezuelan state oil company. It was founded in 1976, the same year that the oil industry was nationalised. It is one of the major sources of cash to fund social programmes.

Pistoleros - Spanish word for hired assassins.

Popular Coordination - Umbrella group for 70 popular organisation based in Caracas.

Popular Revolutionary Assembly - Community based organisations created to link up with Bolivarian Circles and trade unions on the eve of the April 2002 coup d'etat.

Pronunciamiento - Spanish word for military coup d'etat.

Revolutionary Marxist Current - Revolutionary Marxist group born out of the merger of the Marxist currents around *El Militante* and *El Topo Obrero*.

Tancazo - Spanish word meaning a military coup employing the use of tanks. It was the name given to the first military coup against President Allende in Chile.

Tupamaros - Complete name Tupamaro Revolutionary Movement. Former guerrilla organisation that gave up guerrilla warfare and supports the Venezuelan Revolution.

UNT - Venezuelan trade union confederation created in April 2003 as a response of democratic trade unionists to the collaboration of the CTV leadership with the bosses and counter-revolutionary forces.

Bolivar, Simon - (1783-1830) Hero of the struggles in Latin America against the Spanish colonial rule. By 1825 he headed an army that liberated Colombia, Panama, Venezuela, Ecuador, Bolivia and Peru from colonial rule. The figure of Bolivar - also known as the Liberator - has inspired the revolutionary process.

Carmona Estanga, Pedro - Leader of Fedecamaras at the time of the coup d'etat of April 2002. He was appointed interim president on April 12th and resigned on April 13th.

Chavez, Cesar - Latino activist that fought for trade union rights for Californian farmers.

Marti, Jose - (1853-1895) Hero of Cuban independence. He devoted all his adult life to the struggle against the colonial rule. Marti spent time while deported in Spain and in the US linking up with Cuban emigree groups. He always believed that the national liberation struggle in Cuba had to be headed by the oppressed. He was killed in battle against Spanish forces.

Miquilena, Luis - Fomer leader of the bus driver's union and the Communist Party during the 1940s. Founding member of the MVR and political mentor of Hugo Chávez. When Hugo Chavez passed the 49 Enabling laws, Miquilena went over to the side of the opposition.

Ortega, Carlos - Former CTV leader who actively participated in the coup d'etat and the lock-out of 2002. He was one of the most outstanding opposition figures in Venezuela. After the defeat of the lock-out he fled to Costa Rica, until he was deported to Venezuela and arrested.

In Solidarity with the Venezuelan Revolution

The people of Venezuela need our urgent help. Sickened by decades of corrupt government and IMF-sponsored austerity, millions turned out in 1998 to elect Hugo Chávez as President, which began a popular social transformation.

The aims of Chávez's "revolution of the poor" were land reform, control over the country's oil, education and health care for all, and genuine democracy in the hands of ordinary people.

Thanks to the programmes initiated by the government -

● One million additional children have been brought into the educational system, 657 new schools were built and 36,000 additional teachers hired (the education budget has more than doubled in just two years). Four universities have been created since 1998 and three million people enrolled in literacy and education programs.

● 2.2 million hectares (5.5 million acres) of land have been distributed to 116,000 families organised in cooperatives.

● Health programmes have targeted 17 million Venezuelans. With over 13,000 Cuban doctors now in Venezuela, some 1.2 million people who had originally been denied health care have been treated in health centres.

●A new Bolivarian Constitution guarantees the public ownership of Venezuela's oil and the distribution of wealth to all citizens.
These and other popular measures have brought overwhelming support for Chávez, who has won popular elections on no less than nine occasions in the last six years.

At the same time, such policies have brought down the wrath of Venezuela's rich elite and the Bush administration. Venezuela's substantial oil reserves have not gone unnoticed in Washington. These interests have sought to destabilise and overthrow the government of Chavez.

Denouncing President Chávez as a "dictator", they supported and organised the far-right coup of April 2002. For them, it was to be a replica of the overthrow of the Allende government in Chile in 1973 by the CIA sponsored coup of General Pinochet.

This April coup saw the kidnapping of Chávez and the imposition of US-backed "President" Carmona – which was swiftly recognised by the United States and shamefully Britain. Carmona quickly dissolved the National Assembly "as a step towards restoring democracy"! However, the coup was foiled by the movement of the Venezuelan people.

Throughout his term, Chávez was faced with economic sabotage by the Venezuelan bosses, with a flight of capital, factory closures and cuts in production. Between December 2002 and February 2003, the government was faced with a serious bosses' lockout to destabilise the country and prepare another coup. The far-right Colombian government, supported by the US, were also being lined up against Venezuela.

However, when this failed due to the resistance of the workers, especially in the oil industry, the US-backed Opposition attempted to use a referendum campaign, and electoral fraud, to bring down Chávez. These plans were foiled as Chávez once again won an overwhelming mandate with 60% of the popular vote.

The re-election of George Bush has brought new dangers for Venezuela and Cuba – regarded as public enemy number one and two by Washington.

The Hands Off Venezuela Campaign, which is a broad-based campaign, was established to generate awareness about Venezuela within the labour and trade union movement and young people. Our main task is to promote the social gains of the Bolivarian Revolution and mobilise against US aggression towards Venezuela. HOV promotes solidarity and links between Venezuela and the labour movements of other countries.

Join Hands Off Venezuela!
Send your details to: britain@handsoffvenezuela.org

www.handsoffvenezuela.org

Other titles from Wellred

▶ **In the Cause of Labour - History of British Trade Unionism**
By Rob Sewell
Price: £ 14.99

Pub. Date: 2003
Format: Paperback
No. Pages: 480
ISBN: 1900007142

History of British Trotskyism ◀
By Ted Grant
Price: £ 9.99

Pub. Date: 2002
Format: Paperback
No. Pages: 310
ISBN: 190000710X

▶ **Lenin and Trotsky - What they really stood for**
By Alan Woods and Ted Grant
Price: £ 8.95

Pub. Date: 2000
Format: Paperback
No. Pages: 221
ISBN: 8492183268

Bolshevism - The Road to Revolution ◀
By Alan Woods
Price: £ 15.00
Pub. Date: 1999
Format: Paperback
No. Pages: 636
ISBN: 1900007053

▶ Russia - From Revolution to Counter-Revolution
By Ted Grant
Price: £ 15.00

Pub. Date: 1999
Format: Paperback
No. Pages: 636
ISBN: 1900007053

Reason in Revolt - Marxist Philosophy and Modern Science ◀
(Second Edition)
By Alan Woods and Ted Grant
Price: £ 14.95
Pub. Date: 1995
Format: Paperback
No. Pages: 443
ISBN: 1900007002

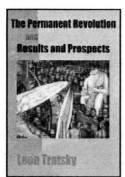

▶ The Permanent Revolution and Results and Prospects
By Leon Trotsky
Price: £ 9.99

Pub. Date: 2004
Format: Paperback
No. Pages: 277
ISBN: 8492183268

My Life ◀
By Leon Trotsky
Price: £ 14.99
Pub. Date: 2004
Format: Paperback
No. Pages: 512